THE BIDEN MALAISE

ALSO BY KIMBERLEY STRASSEL

Resistance (At All Costs): How Trump Haters Are Breaking America
The Intimidation Game: How the Left Is Silencing Free Speech

THE BIDEN MALAISE

HOW AMERICA BOUNCES BACK FROM JOE BIDEN'S DISMAL REPEAT OF THE JIMMY CARTER YEARS

KIMBERLEY STRASSEL

TWELVE

New York   Boston

Twelve
Hachette Book Group
1290 Avenue of the Americas, New York, NY 10104
twelvebooks.com
twitter.com/twelvebooks

First Edition: July 2023

Twelve is an imprint of Grand Central Publishing. The Twelve name and logo are trademarks of Hachette Book Group, Inc.

The publisher is not responsible for websites (or their content) that are not owned by the publisher.

The Hachette Speakers Bureau provides a wide range of authors for speaking events. To find out more, go to hachettespeakersbureau.com or email HachetteSpeakers@hbgusa.com.

Grand Central Publishing books may be purchased in bulk for business, educational, or promotional use. For information, please contact your local bookseller or the Hachette Book Group Special Markets Department at special.markets@hbgusa.com.

Library of Congress Cataloging-in-Publication Data
Names: Strassel, Kimberley A., author.
Title: The Biden malaise : how America bounces back from Joe Biden's dismal repeat of the
   Jimmy Carter years / by Kimberley Strassel.
Description: First edition. | New York : Twelve, 2023. | Includes index.
Identifiers: LCCN 2023003956 | ISBN 9781538756218 (hardcover) | ISBN
   9781538756225 (ebook)
Subjects: LCSH: United States—Politics and government—2021- | Biden, Joseph R., Jr.
Classification: LCC E916 .S73 2023 | DDC 973.934—dc23/eng/20230221
LC record available at https://lccn.loc.gov/2023003956

ISBNs: 978-1-5387-5621-8 (hardcover), 978-1-5387-5622-5 (ebook)

Printed in the United States of America

LSC-C

Printing 1, 2023

To Nick, the best man I know.
And to my mother, from whom I learned all the best words.

CONTENTS

INTRODUCTION

Most adults can remember a first moment of political aware-
ness. Not the moment when a person commits to an ideology or
a party—those moments come later (if at all). This, rather, is the
moment when a kid is surprised to realize that the world is not
solely governed by her parents, her teachers, her Girl Scout leader,
or the holiday vacation schedule. When she discovers that hanging
over it all—*running* it all—is this unknown thing called "government," made up of other things called presidents and senators and
OSHA and the IRS, all located in some place called Washington,
and all which have a surreal power to drive the grown-ups in her
life nuts.

My own moment came in the summer of my seventh birthday.
I was sitting with my younger sister in the back of my mother's
Buick Electra, a car so guzzly you could watch the gas gauge roll
backward when it climbed hills. We were waiting in a line. A very
long line. It was 1979, and not that I knew it then, but Iranian
political turmoil had produced an oil shock and U.S. gas lines.
Oregon was among several states that, in their wisdom, decided
to keep diverting gas to priority customers—thereby ensuring
the lines became longer. We'd been sitting in this particular line
forever, were barely moving, and my mother—like all mothers,
throughout history—was late for something.

Most of my childhood memories are of my mother as a smil-
ing, upbeat, rated-G parent. But sitting in the back of the Electra,

my sister and I noticed Mom was looking decidedly annoyed. As we crept along, she began muttering. The muttering grew louder. Soon, she was banging the steering wheel, then the dashboard, then the ceiling. We kids were just about to begin apologizing for whatever we hadn't done, when she rolled down the window and began shouting a stream of unfamiliar words, each one followed by the name "Jimmy Carter." Intriguingly, other drivers rolled down *their* windows and joined this angry shout-a-thon. I remember seeing a startled gas attendant abandon his post, run into the station, and close the door. This inspired everyone present to start laying on their horns. My sister and I were delighted, witnessing what it now turns out was a 1970s version of "Let's Go Brandon."

I learned three fascinating things that day. First, that my sweet mother could swear like a longshoreman. Second, that my grade-school dictionary was missing any number of useful four-letter words. And third, that some fella named Jimmy Carter, in addition to being something apparently awful called a "Democrat," was, according to my mother "the absolute worst thing that ever happened to America."

Perhaps until now.

When Jimmy Carter announced his presidential run, the first senator to endorse the Georgia governor was another fella, by the name of Joe Biden. Carter would later write in the White House diary that the first-termer from Delaware had been his "most effective supporter during the 1976 campaign." Biden remains a supporter still, in 2021 becoming the first president since Carter left office to sojourn to Plains, Georgia, to visit and smile for a photo op. As a former Biden aide told Maureen Dowd of the *New York Times*, "Those guys love each other."

And if imitation is the sincerest form of flattery, the Biden presidency is besotted. From how they came to office, to their hot messes of inflation, energy, and crime, to their foreign policy travails, to their public unpopularity—the two administrations are an eerie echo, separated by forty-four years. Biden's vice president,

Kamala Harris, even managed to channel Carter's infamous 1979 "crisis of confidence" speech when she in January 2022 bemoaned a nation with a new "level of malaise."

Yet as this book will show, the comparison is unfair—to Carter. The peanut farmer from Georgia in 1977 took the reins of a nation already beset by the Great Inflation, sky-high crime, and declining U.S. oil production. It's true that Carter managed to make every one of these situations worse with a slew of disastrous domestic and foreign policy decisions. Yet Carter presided over a Democratic Party that was far saner than today's version, and Carter himself pushed some half-decent policies. Historians often refer to the Carter administration as one that was "engulfed" by domestic and foreign crises—crises that simply outmatched an inexperienced and unliked president. This has an element of truth.

Biden has no such excuse. The forty-sixth president inherited a country that was just rounding the Covid corner. The economy's prior, strong economic fundamentals were poised to roar back as vaccines rolled out and lockdowns lifted. The United States just one year before Biden was elected president became a net total energy exporter for the first time since 1952—a milestone once unthinkable. Inflation on Biden's inauguration day sat at 1.4 percent, and the price for a gallon of regular was $2.39. Carter would've killed for such a start.

Biden certainly can't blame inexperience. Aside from a brief stint as a Delaware lawyer, he's never done anything *but* politics. In 1972 he was one of the youngest people ever elected to the U.S. Senate, and it's where he remained until he moved to the Naval Observatory as Barack Obama's vice president. As Biden likes to brag, he's seen it all.

And he took office with another big advantage: He had Carter's lessons of what *not* to do. The late 1970s are a textbook example of the perils of easy money, government micromanagement, and weak foreign policy—and Biden lived through them. He had all of Carter's painful history to warn him off his party's progressive

obsessions. As the coming chapters will lay out, he instead chose
to govern like the second coming of Bernie Sanders. His refusal to
heed history's lessons has exacted a devastating toll on the American economy, its foreign standing, and its national psyche. He had
to work *hard* to make things go so wrong. He had to deliberately
memory-hole decades of evidence of what works. As Sen. Tom
Cotton quipped in 2022: "Jimmy Carter has a defamation case
against anyone comparing him to Joe Biden."

Today's progressives make the mistake of ignoring one further
piece of the Carter saga: what came after. It's not unusual for the
American electorate to turn on a party in the White House, to
give the other guys a shot. Bill Clinton gave way to George W.
Bush, who gave way to Barack Obama, who gave way to Donald
Trump. What *is* rare is for a president and his policies to create
such a public backlash that he opens the way for a political sea
change, one that remakes the American electorate.

Jimmy Carter marked the crest of a half century of New Deal
and Democratic power in Washington. His agenda became synonymous in American minds with failed government, crippling
bureaucracy, antibusiness sentiment, cultural radicalism, and
U.S. humiliation abroad. That reputation was cemented in American minds by another fella, an articulate former governor of California named Ronald Reagan. He used a gospel of free markets
and strong foreign policy to win the White House, but also to
convert a generation of Americans to his cause. The Reagan revolution changed the nation's political demographics and redrew
its electoral map. In his 1984 reelection, Ronald Reagan carried
forty-nine out of fifty states—an electoral vote total (525) that no
other candidate in history has matched.

It was in no small part thanks to Jimmy Carter.

As painful as the Biden presidency has proven to so many average people, it's also provided an invaluable service. America came
out of the 1970s with a sharp appreciation for the vagaries of big
government and a new wisdom about the laws of economics.

That's been lost in more recent decades of steadily growing Washington. Biden's extreme policies are reminding the country of the danger of ignoring those hard-earned lessons of history.

This book will make the case that the Biden agenda is creating a similar backlash, and the early signs of a shift are already there. The Republican governors who won commanding 2022 reelection bids did so with support across the electorate, including among voters with whom the party often struggles. Florida governor Ron DeSantis beat his opponent by nearly twenty points, winning the woman vote, the Hispanic vote, and even the urban vote. Democrats are becoming the party of wealthy, coastal elites enamored with European-style welfare policies. This is providing Republicans the opportunity to form a broad and wide coalition of multiracial, working-, and middle-class Americans.

But this book will equally remind conservatives that they have to work for it. Just as Democrats would be wise to absorb the lessons of Carter, Republicans need to remember Reagan. The right remains fractured in the wake of Donald Trump's presidency, with Republicans taking potshots at one another's credibility and loyalty. Too many Republicans are abandoning sound principles, chasing populist sentiment, hoping to buy voters with Democrat-lite promises. Years of liberal norm-breaking—bogus FBI investigations, secret impeachment proceedings, stripped committee assignments, calls to end the filibuster—are tempting Republicans to focus on investigations and retribution rather than the business of governance.

Reagan didn't win with anger, accusations, purity tests, or probes. He was the ultimate happy warrior, who tempted the skeptical with the power of ideas, words, and humor, and who opened the tent to all comers. He demonstrated the principles of conservative governance by governing. He knew a divided Republican party—or an angry one—was a losing party.

Americans are deeply disillusioned. They live in what is supposed to be the most vibrant political system in the world, yet they are astonished by the daily failure of competence. Congress seems no longer capable of legislating. Democrats have abandoned federalism, the electoral system, and the concept of equality. The administrative state rules all. President Biden grandstands, even as he resolutely refuses to work with Republicans. He waves his magic scepter and decrees lawless eviction moratoriums, vaccine mandates, and student loan forgiveness. Judges—at both the federal and state levels—act as de facto policy makers. The country is yearning for change.

This book is meant to be a guide—to the enormous opportunity that suddenly exists for the party of free markets and free people. The conservative movement has another chance to recapture the imagination of a malaise-beset public. But it will require a refocus on innovative ideas. It needs a party willing to fully reembrace its constitutional duties, to legislate and to govern, and to stand accountable. One that recommits itself to proven policies that get government out of the way. One that will tackle the truly big problems that are slowly but inevitably dragging the United States toward European-style socialism.

Mostly it will take a leader. There was no Reagan Revolution without . . . Reagan. The GOP is living under the shadow of Trump. What his supporters love most about The Donald is his fight—his willingness to take on taboo issues, to punch back at critics. At the same time, nobody could mistake him as the next Great Communicator, capable of, or willing to, invest a new generation in a liberty philosophy. The Republican movement has a younger bench of accomplished leaders who've adopted the Trump fight—but who also have the vision and message. Conservative voters will have to decide if their loyalty to the former president is worth risking this unique political opening.

America can bounce back from the Biden malaise; it has the desire, the energy, and the formula. It just needs a guide.

THE BIDEN MALAISE

CHAPTER 1

WELCOME BACK, CARTER

Let's start with the obvious differences.

- James Earl Carter Jr. was a spry fifty-two-year-old when he took the presidential oath. Joseph Robinette Biden Jr., at seventy-eight, was the oldest human being to ever shuffle into the presidency.
- Carter was little known outside of Georgia, and only entered politics after a naval career and time running the family peanut farm. Biden since age thirty has haunted the halls of federal power.
- Jimmy was a bristly outsider. Ol' Joe is a backslapping insider.

It's about there the dissimilarities end.

In policy and politics, the parallels between the Carter and Biden presidencies—at least outwardly—are beyond striking. Starting with the strangely same way the two men obtained the highest office. Both triumphed in crowded Democratic primaries by presenting themselves as enlightened moderates—on board with their party's liberal wing, but not so crazy as to alienate average Americans.

Carter outmaneuvered a field of seventeen candidates, including liberals Jerry Brown (the lefty governor of California) and

Rep. Mo Udall, as well as the segregationist governor of Alabama, George Wallace. He played himself up as the outsider and touted—when useful—his conservative fiscal credentials. He didn't clinch the nomination until after June 1976.

Biden jumped into the largest Democratic field since that Carter race, featuring a scrum of twenty-nine candidates. Nearly all the contenders were vying for the votes of the ascendent, progressive wing of their party, chasing Bernie Sanders and Elizabeth Warren. Those senators set the primary tone by vowing to support the Green New Deal, bans on drilling, Medicare for All, and an end to the Senate filibuster. Biden split the policy differences, and, like Carter, presented himself—when useful—as the commonsense alternative. After a rocky primary start, his campaign was rescued only in the spring of 2020, when centrist Southern voters united to block a Sanders victory.

Both Carter and Biden ran in the general election as healing correctives to controversial predecessors. Carter made his bid to a nation exhausted by Vietnam and persistent inflation, and still reeling from Watergate. At times, you might not have known his opponent was named Gerald Ford. Carter mined the lingering disgust with Richard Nixon. His campaign slogan: "A Leader, For A Change." His trademark lines: "I'll never tell a lie," and "I want a government as good as its people." The promise of moral (and religious) leadership tapped into a public mood. Yet the nation remained deeply divided and Carter barely beat Ford—gathering fewer electoral votes than any president since Woodrow Wilson in 1916.

Biden's campaign was a near parallel. Donald Trump came into office a controversial figure, and Democrats added to the foment with a twenty-two-month special counsel probe into (false) claims of Russian collusion, an impeachment proceeding, investigations into Trump's family and businesses, and daily accusations that he was a dictator in waiting. Add to this an unexpected 2020 global pandemic that thrust much of the nation into lockdowns, school closures, mask mandates, and media-stoked anxiety. Biden, campaigning from his basement, hammered the controversial Republican on moral grounds, and highlighted two modest promises: to better handle Covid, and to be the anti-Trump, that is, to calm, unify, and heal a polarized nation. Yet again, the country was deeply divided, and Biden barely won, obtaining only narrow margins in a handful of states.

Despite these promises of healing and moderation, both men upon taking office governed in a far more liberal fashion than their divided electorates expected—and became lightning rods themselves. They both had the unfortunate knack for creating or exacerbating the types of messes that most infuriate average Americans.

Carter made his first priority high unemployment, and his disastrous solution was an ambitious spending program accompanied by pressure on the Federal Reserve to expand the money supply. Carter's Fed chief, G. William Miller, didn't move aggressively enough to raise rates and inflation soared from 5.8 percent when Carter took office to 13.5 percent by the end of his term. Carter's final Fed head, Paul Volcker, did manage to tame prices, but it came too late and the cost was recession.

Similarly, Biden chose a spending blowout as his first initiative— the $1.9 trillion American Rescue Plan. The administration larded out $1,400 checks to individuals; airdropped $350 billion on state and local governments; and dumped money on education. Yet it came after prior Covid relief bills in 2020 and was followed by further spending on infrastructure and a green agenda. Fed chairman Jerome Powell also waited too long to start taming an overheated economy. Inflation soared from 1.4 percent when Biden took office to 9.1 percent by June 2022.

Both men did damage to America's energy security. Carter inherited a nation trying to recover from a global oil shock. He made it worse with a windfall profits tax and a crazy environmental agenda on top of another oil crisis. Gas prices in 1976 averaged

61 cents a gallon ($2.93 today). By 1980 they were $1.25 a gallon ($4.14).

Biden was hit by energy problems stemming from Russia's 2022 invasion of Ukraine. But the president from his first day in office declared war on fossil fuels, and prices were climbing well before Vladimir Putin launched his aggressive attack. Biden inherited gas prices in 2020 of $2.39. By June of 2022, they'd topped $5 a gallon.

Both men reflexively turned to government as the answer to every problem, demagoguing the private sector and larding it down with new regulations that stifled economic growth. Carter saddled the country with two entirely new cabinet departments, fifteen major environmental bills, and price controls. Biden moved quickly to reimpose nearly every regulation the Trump administration had dismantled, and added plenty more to boot. He unleashed the most antibusiness cabinet in history.

Soaring inflation, rising interest rates, regulatory assault, and worrying economic indicators spooked markets in both eras, wiping out vast amounts of wealth and retirement funds. Two years into the Carter administration, the Dow Jones Industrial Average had lost 23 percent of its value, and the market when Carter left office was barely above where it had started. Biden? A Bank of America analysis for clients in October 2022 found that the first half of Biden's second year had been the worst for the S&P 500 since 1872.

The Carter and Biden years were similarly shaped by foreign policy fiascoes, the consequence of shared and naïve notions of sanctions, multilateralism and appeasement. Both men weakened America on the world stage and invited aggression—and, weirdly, from the same bad actors. Carter appeased a belligerent Russia that invaded Afghanistan; Biden appeased a belligerent Russia that invaded Ukraine. Carter contended with an Iranian revolution; Biden with the threat of a nuclear Iran. Carter in 1979 granted formal diplomatic recognition to the People's Republic of

China; Biden continues to coddle the regime, despite its hostility to human rights and Western interests. The Iranian hostage crisis effectively ended Carter's ambitions for reelection. Biden opened his presidency with a chaotic Afghanistan withdrawal—during which thirteen U.S. troops died at the hand of an airport suicide bomber.

The late 1970s and the Biden years even share oddly similar social upheaval, with public angst over race-conscious governance, gay rights, education, court decisions, and rising crime. Americans by the Carter years were growing angry over the rampant use of quotas and affirmative action. Carter chose activist judges who doubled down on the recently decided *Roe v. Wade*, setting off cries of judicial politicization. The thirty-ninth president was accused of rolling over to teachers' unions to aid his reelection bid. Despite Carter's campaign promise to slash rampant crime rates, America's cities grew more dangerous. Protests were everywhere.

Biden, Vice President Kamala Harris, and their fellow progressives are today preaching an "equity" agenda, critical race theory, and gender fluidity that has unleashed a new round of public backlash. The Supreme Court in June 2022 *reversed Roe v. Wade*, a decision the left gaslighted as a new era of judicial politicization. Biden's support of teachers' unions infuriated parents whose kids were left in lockdown. The left's embrace of the "defund the police" movement and progressive prosecutors helped fuel a surge in violent crime that is returning us to the malaise of the '70s. Protests are, again, everywhere.

In February 2021, *Cosmopolitan* magazine dropped this headline: "17 '70s Fashion Trends and Outfits Making a Comeback"—highlighting bell bottoms, bra tops, crochet, and clogs.

It really is déjà vu all over again.

Chiders-in-chief

Americans have a time-honored tradition of grousing about their leaders and their government. But not all grousing is equal. What's striking about the Carter and Biden periods are the unique hardships both presidents imposed on the nation, combined with their inability to course correct. Public dissatisfaction with Bill Clinton's sex scandal, or George W. Bush's Detroit bailout, or Barack Obama's messy health care rollout, simply do not rate next to the pocketbook miseries of the late 1970s and early 2020s. Inflation robs families of their spending power. Soaring gas prices and home energy bills put extraordinary stress on lower-income households, forcing millions to live paycheck to paycheck. Spiraling interest rates kill the American dream, making first homes unaffordable, or small-business loans impossible. Shootings, burglaries, and theft leave Americans anxious about their day-to-day safety. A tumbling stock market rewrites lives—requiring Americans to put off retirement or rip away their kids' dreams of college.

These types of "policy" fails infuriate Americans because they strike home. That's one reason all presidents since Carter have lived in fear of high inflation: There is no way for a leader to spin their way out of it, and few ways to quickly fix it. It's a political cul-de-sac.

It doesn't help that Biden and Carter share one more trait: singularly bad communication skills. Both confused lecturing with leadership.

Americans looked to Carter to solve the soaring energy prices of that time. They instead got a man in a cardigan sweater exhorting them to turn down their thermostats. Carter complained about the Organization of the Petroleum Exporting Countries (OPEC) and a "profiteering" petroleum industry—and the American people themselves. His infamous 1979 "malaise" speech never actually deployed that word. But it left the impression that the president was blaming his own country for a "crisis of confidence," suggesting the American public was contributing to the nation's problems by failing to adopt a better attitude. Americans wanted a moral president—not a moralizing one.

Biden spent his own first year hectoring Americans to wear masks, get vaccinated, and come on board with his plans for economic redistribution—attacking noncompliance as unpatriotic and selfish. His lifetime tendency toward verbal gaffes has become of late something far more concerning. He routinely makes meandering or disjointed statements that leave Americans nervous and his staff on perpetual clean-up duty. His response to inflation was to point fingers at his predecessor, Putin, oil companies, Saudi Arabia, the pandemic, refineries, even mom-and-pop gas stations. While yet to be seen in a cardigan, Biden had his own unappreciated suggestion for Americans frustrated by high gas prices: Buy an electric vehicle.

Biden in June 2022 even rolled out a version of the Carter "malaise" homily. An Associated Press reporter asked the president what he thought about a survey showing more Americans reporting "trouble with meeting their weekly expenses." The president responded that "people are really, really down. They're really down. Their need for mental health in America has skyrocketed because people have seen everything upset." Even Carter didn't go so far as to suggest concern over inflation equaled psychological illness.

The combination of domestic morass and bumbling leadership saddled both men with short honeymoons, toxic approval ratings, and midterm difficulties. Just a year into Carter's presidency, a January 1978 CBS News/*New York Times* poll found him with an economic net approval rating of −8. That was the lowest of any president at that point—until today's occupant of the Oval Office. The average of polls in December 2021 found Biden with −13 points. A CNN story in December 2021 noted that "the average president at this point in the last 44 years (since [CNN has] been polling on the topic) had a net economic approval rating of +5 points," putting Biden eighteen points down. Trump at that stage in his presidency beat Carter and Biden by a mile.

And the issues were largely spending and inflation. A November 1977 *Time* poll found that only 21 percent of Americans felt Carter was doing enough to combat inflation. A December 2021 Fox News poll found just 22 percent thought Biden policies were helping to get inflation under control (while 47 percent said they were hurting). Economist Arthur Okun long ago coined the "Misery Index"—the sum of inflation and unemployment—as a simple gauge of how the average American was faring economically. In 1978, as Carter confronted a midterm election, the index was 15 percent (6 percent unemployment plus 9 percent inflation) and in 1980 it would approach 20 percent. In July 2022, as Biden marched toward his own first midterm showdown, the index neared 13 percent.

Carter went into his 1978 midterms the usual underdog; parties that hold the White House almost always lose congressional seats. He had plenty to spare; Democrats held commanding majorities in both the House and Senate. He lost three in the Senate and fifteen in the House, a fairly modest beating for a midterm. But what mattered more were the ominous signs of the 1980 and 1984 Reagan electoral dominance to come. Among the more notable flips was Georgia's Sixth Congressional District, which had been held by Democrat Jack Flynt for twenty-four years. The Republican Party was largely an afterthought in Georgia (and much of the South) up until the 1970s. But the Carter presidency helped change that, and in 1978 a relatively unknown professor from the University of West Georgia won the seat in a surprising upset. The victor's name was Newt Gingrich.

Biden entered his own 2022 midterms with almost no cushion, because the 2020 presidential election threw up some surprising results. Biden narrowly edged out a controversial president, but the country made clear it was far from settled in its choice of a party. Even as Biden won, House Speaker Nancy Pelosi lost thirteen of her incumbent Democrats. New York senator Chuck Schumer finally realized his dream of becoming majority leader, but only because in the resulting fifty-fifty Senate, Vice President Kamala Harris served as the tie breaker.

After several months of polls suggesting Republicans would win in a red-wave rout, the GOP managed only modest gains. It won the House, elevating Kevin McCarthy to Speaker—but barely. And the GOP lost an additional seat in the Senate. Voters were angry with Democrats over inflation, rising crime, and an unchecked border. But they were uncertain about embracing Trump-picked primary winners with a lot of controversial baggage. Still, the GOP seizure of the House put a definitive end to Biden's legislative agenda.

Most presidents view midterm losses as a rebuke and a call to readjust. But Carter considered himself outside the usual political parameters and chose to view his midterm loss as more a judgment on his party than himself. He continued with his quixotic agenda, undaunted. Biden, in hock to his progressive wing, and spinning the GOP's modest gains as a Democratic "win," also ignored his unpopularity. Both men chose not to heed the political winds.

In Carter's case, the result was a Reagan trouncing of epic proportions. Biden may be setting himself up for a redux.

Lucky so and Joe

For as notable as all these comparisons are, they are also somewhat unjust: to Jimmy Carter.

It didn't take six months for Republicans to start making the Carter-Biden comparisons. "Joe Biden is the new Jimmy Carter," tweeted Ohio GOP representative Jim Jordan in May 2021, citing "stagflation," "higher taxes," and "rising gas prices." South Carolina senator Lindsey Graham in November of that year upped the insult, tweeting that Biden "has been the most incompetent president of my lifetime on foreign policy. Worse than Jimmy Carter." By 2022, even the Biden-favorable press was going there. "Morale inside 1600 Pennsylvania Ave. is plummeting amid growing fears that the parallels to Jimmy Carter, another first-term Democrat plagued by soaring prices and a foreign policy morass will stick," reported *Politico* in June 2022.

One dissenter was liberal writer Jonathan Alter, who in January 2022 wrote a *Washington Post* essay titled: "Joe Biden Is No Jimmy Carter. He Should Wish He Was." Alter in 2020 published a revisionist biography of Carter—*His Very Best*—meant to rehabilitate "a flawed but underrated president." The book writes off too many of Carter's mistakes to bad luck and is primarily a celebration of his liberalism. But Alter's *Post* headline got one thing right: As bad as Carter was, Biden makes him look stellar.

Carter was dealt a far harder hand. When Carter took over in 1977, inflation was already above 5 percent—a consequence of spending on Vietnam and Great Society programs. Unemployment was 7.4 percent, the result of misguided government policy and recessions. The nation was beset by disturbing levels of crime, public unrest, and Cold War aggression. Any president would have struggled to bring these forces under control, and the times demanded a decisive leader. Carter wasn't that guy, and his inexperience guaranteed the failure that became his presidency.

But Carter, for all his faults, was at least willing to go his own way in some areas. Postpresidency, Carter became one of the Democrats' most liberal voices. He famously voted in the 2016 Georgia primary for Bernie Sanders. But he wasn't always so. In office, he led a fractured party, one split between Great Society liberals, southern conservatives, and would-be progressives. Carter was a mix of all three, and could be liberal Jimmy or conservative Jimmy on any given day.

Carter's first big piece of legislation is a classic case in point. Prior to inauguration, Carter had proposed a quick economic "stimulus" package to aid the economy, ranging from $23 billion to $30 billion (as much as $150 billion today). Within days of taking office, the administration had upped the number to $31 billion, and laid out two main planks: an immediate and hefty $50 cash tax rebate for nearly every American, coupled with a public-sector jobs and public works program. The president's team talked up the cash payout, promising it would go to 206 million Americans. Treasury Secretary W. Michael Blumenthal insisted the rebates were vital, the "only way," as the *Washington Post* wrote, "to give the economy a quick stimulus that can boost consumer spending."

Carter's Democratic majorities got to work cutting deals, and by March both chambers had bills. The administration kept pushing for its tax rebate right up until mid-April, when it did an abrupt about-face and said it no longer wanted that very cornerstone of its package. Carter had looked at the recent uptick in prices and worried a further cash influx would prove inflationary. Democrats and Republicans alike were furious at the reversal, but Carter's decision to scale back his (overall inflationary) package may have spared the country worse.

And so it went, all through the Carter presidency. Carter spent too much—but also refused requests to spend more. He successfully managed in 1978 to free up some of the domestic energy sector—but also layered on energy-strangling green statutes in the name of "conservation." He deregulated crucial parts of the economy—even as he increased the heavy hand of government. Carter snubbed autocrats who were friendly to American interests, yet gave away the Panama Canal to one of Latin America's worst dictators. Carter's presidency was muddled, but not dogmatic. And he had at least some progrowth instincts and a respect for fiscal rectitude.

Biden's instincts seem to have deserted him long ago. The forty-sixth president came into office with everything going for him. The Trump administration, with its tax-cutting and deregulatory agenda, had produced strong economic growth. Prior to Covid, the unemployment rate hit 3.5 percent, the best number in fifty years. The jobless rates for African-Americans, Hispanics, Natives, and Asians all hit record lows. Wages grew in every segment of the economy, and jumped even faster for lower-income and blue-collar workers. The country produced new manufacturing and construction jobs; small-business optimism soared. Home owner-ship increased. Income inequality decreased. Inflation through the Trump years averaged 1.9 percent.

Thanks to a fracking revolution and pro-energy policies, the United States in 2018 became a net exporter of oil for the first time in seventy-five years. As the world's biggest generator of oil, America became a "swing producer," able to influence the quan-tity of world supplies, and diminish OPEC's longstanding position as price setter. Electricity, home heating oil, and natural gas prices stayed low and steady. Gas prices remained under $3 a gallon the entirety of the Trump years.

Covid lockdowns wreaked havoc in the first half of 2020, but even by the time of the election the economy was soaring back to life. During the third quarter of 2020, GDP jumped an astonish-ing 33.1 percent. And by the end of the year the economy had more than halved its pandemic job losses, adding 12 million back to the rolls.

With Operation Warp Speed, Vice President Mike Pence lever-aged the ingenuity of America's private sector, bringing through development and production a Covid vaccine in under a year—an unheard-of feat. Millions of vaccines hit the states a full month before Biden took office, the last step in getting the rest of Amer-ica back to work.

All Biden had to do was sit back and honor those two elec-tion promises—see through Covid, unite the nation—and watch the good approval ratings roll. And he might have been the man for that moment. He could have used his "nice guy" credentials and lifetime of Washington relationships to mediate policy dis-putes and temper the culture wars. He could have reached out to

Republicans and proved to a polarized nation that business can get done. At seventy-eight, Mr. Biden might have viewed his presidency as a one-term opportunity to reknit a fractured country. He didn't.

The Carter history book

Biden also had history to warn him off an aggressive agenda. He had the lesson of the 1970s, and what happens when administrations resort to easy money and government micromanagement in the midst of global turmoil. He had the lessons of the Reagan years, a road map to prosperity.

Carter wasn't so lucky. When he took office, economists were still wrapping their minds around the new concept of "stagflation"— the deadly combination of economic stagnation and high inflation. The term is generally attributed to a British Tory politician, Iain Macleod, who first used the word in a speech to Parliament in 1965, when Britain began to experience the phenomenon.

But it didn't mean anyone understood it. For decades governments had defaulted to Keynesian economic theory, which held that high inflation and high unemployment were mutually exclusive, as broadly described by the Phillips curve. Robert Bartley, my former *Wall Street Journal* boss, described the thinking at that time in his book *The Seven Fat Years*: "The cure for unemployment was a little more inflation, and the cure for inflation was a little more unemployment."

The brilliant American economist Milton Friedman was dismantling this thinking even in the 1960s. But most political leaders continued to blindly follow the Keynesian method. They didn't understand that stagflation is broadly the consequence of a supply-demand imbalance. The world in the 1970s was suffering too little supply (thanks in part to shocks in the oil market) and too much demand (thanks to easy money). Richard Nixon's wage and price controls only suppressed and masked the underlying problem, encouraging the U.S. government to continue feeding all the wrong fires.

As tactic after tactic failed to fix the underlying problems, politicians and economists started throwing every type of noodle at the wall. A *Wall Street Journal* editorial from 1974 excellently describes the economic confusion of the times: "If you don't look closely, all you will see is a Tower of Babel. Cut taxes, raise taxes, leave taxes alone, cut some taxes while raising other taxes. Allocate credit. Don't allocate credit. Ease money. Tighten money. Cut the budget hard, cut it a little, don't cut it at all. Impose controls, impose guidelines, leave wages and prices alone. Can all these people be talking about fighting inflation?"

Carter wandered into this maelstrom, and to the extent he worsened the U.S. economy, he can at least argue that other world leaders were making the same mistakes. Carter and Congress continued to spend on jobs and bigger welfare programs; they raised taxes; they grew government and regulation. In short they fueled demand and hampered supply, contributing to more economic turmoil and higher inflation.

Carter did take one important step that would prove fundamental to the economic enlightenment soon to come. In 1979 he nominated Paul Volcker to head the Federal Reserve. Volcker declared inflation enemy number one and started tightening. This necessary step came too late for the Carter administration to take credit, but it put the United States on the path to finally tackling the wage-price spiral.

Biden was warned of the risk of dumping more money on an economy that already had too much cash to spend, and too few things (thanks to Covid supply shocks) to buy with it. The *New York Times* in a July 2022 article recounted that "in the early days of the Biden administration," a gathering took place of "Treasury secretaries past and present." Larry Summers—who served in the Clinton administration—"expressed alarm to the group that inflation could worsen." He also expressed those worries publicly. Yet Biden Treasury secretary Janet Yellen blew off the warning and insisted prices were under control. Among those in attendance was W. Michael Blumenthal, Carter's Treasury secretary, who told the *Times* in 2022 that "the basic problem that [Biden] faces is really not too dissimilar from the one that confronted Carter." He urged Biden to abandon sweeping spending in favor of deficit reduction.

Biden instead used Covid as an excuse to attempt to completely restructure the U.S. economy, with a spending agenda more radical than anything ever proposed by any Democrat. *That's* what makes the Carter comparison so unfair. Biden knew better—and still doubled down.

Biden threw money at a hot economy—despite all the '70s taught us about inflation. He strangled an energy sector—despite the perilous warnings of the '70s oil shocks. He imposed tax hikes and regulations that are winnowing supply and feeding stagnation—despite the demonstrated success of the Reagan years. He hightailed out of Afghanistan and bent the knee to China. As the Carter years proved, U.S. weakness only invites more aggression.

While inflation began moderating in late 2022, the drop only came after punishing Federal Reserve rate hikes that continue to inflict their own pain. As of the writing of this book, house prices are soaring, companies continue to announce layoffs, banks are reeling, and the markets remain in a slump.

Who's in charge?

One bewildering question is: Why? Prior to the presidency Biden was never particularly dogmatic. As a senator he was best described as a moderate liberal, and his Senate tenure featured no sustained causes or campaigns. He might've used his presidential victory to define himself any way he wanted—to have stuck to those modest promises.

Progressive governance is clearly not working for the president, either in substance or politically. His approval ratings have been in the tank since his first year in office. His administration has seen more than its fair share of debacles and milestones—Afghanistan, inflation reports, the end of the president's first year, the 2022 midterms—moments it might have used as an excuse to pivot to a more palatable agenda. Biden knows well how this works. He was vice president when Obama in 2010—after a midterm thumping—chose to pivot (very slightly) to the issue of deficit reduction.

The answer is that Biden never has been, and never will be . . . a leader. If Biden's views were constantly shifting in the Senate, it was because he was constantly pulled by his party's center of gravity—which kept moving left. Biden's problem in his 2020 primary race was that he was old enough to have a record of more centrist positions—positions that were normal in Democratic circles in the past but that now offend progressive voters. His younger, liberal opponents battered him over his previous positions—his opposition to gay marriage, his support for the financial sector, his votes for tougher criminal penalties. This pummeling clearly left a mark. Biden continued to campaign as an inoffensive moderate, yet his first act upon sewing up the nomination was to announce his team would immediately start crafting a "unity" agenda with Sanders—the guy he'd just defeated. Whatever independence Biden promised his supporters went out the door. They might *as well have* elected Bernie—by the end of the unity task force process, Biden had essentially adopted his rival's platform.

This is the one area where Carter was luckier than Biden. The 1970s Democratic Party had more than its fair share of "liberals"— even radicals. Think George McGovern and Jerry Brown. But the party was at that time still diverse. Carter hailed from its more conservative wing, the head of a state that was growing more skeptical of taxes, unions, and government control. Jimmy during his presidency by necessity had to span his party's ideological spectrum, making deals to keep coalitions in place. But some of his more ingrained views—against wasteful spending or government control over core U.S. industries—at least had some backing within his party.

Biden's Democratic Party is today monolithically left, and his presidency has been one surrender after another to the progressives. He's advocated for the largest tax hikes since 1968. He's overseen the most kamikaze spending since the 1960s. He's adopted a Big Labor agenda unlike anything since the 1930s. He's promoted more new entitlement programs than any president since Frankin D. Roosevelt. He's advocated blowing up the Senate as an institution, all to get his legislative way.

Biden's governance also appears to have been driven by a near-manic reaction to the Trump years. Biden in his campaign primarily cast himself as the *moral* opposite of Trump, reverting again and again to the imagery of light "over" dark. Yet progressives over the years cleverly managed to conflate Trump policies with Trump the man. This allowed them to argue that ridding the nation of a "toxic" president also required purging every bit of his agenda. Biden upon taking the presidency enthusiastically embraced this view and set about systematically erasing every Trump action—whether that made logical sense or not. A perfect example of the illogical was Biden's decision in his first days in office to terminate Trump's Remain in Mexico policy, on the grounds it was "dangerous, inhumane and [went] against everything we stand for as a nation of immigrants." Migrants saw that high-profile reversal as an open invitation to pour north, and the United States has been struggling with a border crisis ever since.

All of this, of course, presumes Biden is actually in charge, something that's been in doubt since his earliest days in office. Biden took over Democratic majorities in both the House and the Senate, but he's never appeared to be in the driver's seat. Nancy Pelosi and Chuck Schumer during the first two years told the White House what would happen—not the other way around.

Whether because of age or lack of leadership, it isn't even clear that Biden is making the decisions within the Oval Office. The media has brimmed with stories about Biden's frustration at his team limiting his public exposure or walking back his impromptu statements. Are these Oval Office insiders protecting Biden or steering him? It amounts to the same thing. And it amounts to a purely progressive agenda—no matter the ongoing political failures or the clear lessons of the past.

The coming chapters will lay out in greater detail the striking similarities in how Carter and Biden mishandled everything from the economy to foreign policy to the border to the culture wars. Yet they will also demonstrate how much greater is Biden's culpability in creating the latest iteration of American malaise. The country deserved so much better.

CHAPTER 2

INFLATION NATION

Here's the thing you need to know about Jimmy Carter when it came to the 1970s economy overall: He tried.

Progressives today unrelentingly call for more spending, more entitlements, federal domination of states, a cradle-to-grave government experience. Carter in office didn't subscribe to most of that agenda. He made unforgivable mistakes, his policies his first few years a trainwreck of misguided Keynesian policy and scattershot proposals. But he at least believed in some fundamentals of the American project: prosperity, markets, and fiscal rectitude. Carter wanted things to get better.

Biden, by contrast, recklessly plowed ahead with a progressive agenda that history and his own experience foretold would prove disastrous. It's an important difference.

No one could envy Carter as he stepped up for his inauguration on January 20, 1977. The sun was shining (a rarity for Washington winter), but the weather was brutally cold. So was the mood of the country. Unemployment sat at a stubborn 7.4 percent. Inflation was more than 5 percent. The trade deficit was high. Productivity was declining. Carter was elected in part because he'd promised better government, one that would turn around the economic stagnation. "This Inaugural ceremony marks a new beginning, a new dedication within our government, and a new spirit among us all," he said in his address.

But when it came to the economy, Carter had no idea what he was doing—and he did a great deal wrong. He decided to focus his first big effort on the high unemployment number, and he defaulted to the demand-side spending policies that were (and sadly still are) Democratic orthodoxy. He flooded the economy with money.

Ford had wanted to sharply cut the rate of government spending to about 7 percent and lower business taxes—both of which would have helped with inflation. Carter rejected all that in favor of more money. His first major act, his $20 billion economic "stimulus," amounted to an ambitious spending program to create government jobs and spur infrastructure projects. And Carter's first budget to Congress proposed keeping the annual growth of federal spending at 10 percent. Carter exceeded even that while in office. Government spent 44 percent more in fiscal 1980 than it did in fiscal 1977.

Carter campaigned as an outsider, but he was quickly made to understand that getting things done meant playing political ball. Under pressure from Democratic constituencies, extra dollars continued to roll. In October of 1977, amid criticism from the Urban League and mayors, he signed an urban aid act that authorized $14.7 billion to help "revitalize" U.S. cities. In 1978, folding to the labor movement, he put his signature to the Humphrey-Hawkins Full Employment Act, which bestowed upon the government the power to spend to hire more public employees to deal with unemployment. Carter that year also got rolled by appropriations-hungry legislators into agreeing to what the New York Times described as a "record-breaking $51 billion four-year highway and mass transit bill"—significantly more than the administration had wanted to spend. Along the way there was a $1.6 billion bailout in federal loan guarantees for New York City, and a $5 billion extension of federal support for vocational rehabilitation programs, to name a few other liberal boondoggles.

Equally problematic was Carter's push for looser monetary policy. Captivated by modern Keynesian theory, the administration openly called on the Federal Reserve to expand the nation's money supply and took to complaining about Fed chief Arthur Burns. Burns had correctly worried that money supply was fueling inflation and started tightening credit. In an October 1977 speech he bluntly spelled out the real economic problem: sluggish business investment, brought on by uncertainty in the administration's agenda, which was further fueling unemployment and depressing the stock market. He publicly called on the administration to stop spending—and to stop jumping from issue to issue—and instead prioritize a clear, straightforward agenda focused on business growth. He wasn't alone in this view. A June 1977 *New York Times* story noted that "pure monetarist-disciples" of economist Milton Friedman of the University of Chicago argued that growing money to reduce unemployment was "unwise" and would only "worsen inflation." Even by this point, the smarter economists had figured it out. Carter, surrounded by his Keynesian elites, hadn't.

Carter's response to this healthy advice was to keep the business community guessing as to whether he'd reappoint Burns, whose term ended in early 1978. Only in the waning days of 1977 did Carter announce Burns was out. He chose as a replacement G. William Miller, the head of a Rhode Island manufacturing company. Miller believed the Fed itself could encourage business investment with expansive monetary policy—inflationary effects be damned.

It was the economy that was damned in the end. The combination of government spending and Miller monetary policy sent inflation soaring.

And yet, Carter's history isn't so simple. Yes, the president embraced more spending, in the misguided belief the economy would benefit from government dollars. But it went against his instincts. Carter was in his time (and certainly by today's Democratic Party measure) more fiscally conservative. Carter was notoriously frugal, and he despised government waste so much that he controversially sold off the USS *Sequoia*, the presidential yacht. Longtime friend Dot Padgett once described him as "tight as bark on a tree."

One of his first acts as president was to target for elimination a number of congressionally earmarked water projects, a fight that soured his relationship with Congress for the rest of his time in office. He infuriated his party by paring back many of their spending ambitions. Unlike today's Democrats, he was also willing to work with Republicans, who ended up voting for significant portions of his agenda.

And by the end of his time in office, he'd realized the disastrous consequences of the dollar money pump. A *Washington Post* opening paragraph from March 1980 put it this way: "President Carter unveiled yesterday a new anti-inflation program that he said would restore 'discipline' to both government and American consumers, partly by putting the federal budget in the black for the first time in 12 years." The plan was centered around a significant $13 billion in cuts to federal spending and restrictions on federal hiring.

By the end Carter had also found religion on monetary policy. In 1979 he reshuffled his own anointed Federal Reserve head, Miller, to the Treasury Department, clearing the way to name Volcker. The president of the New York federal reserve bank, Volcker had been outspoken on inflation. He immediately began aggressively raising the federal funds rate, ultimately to some 20 percent. His actions marked the beginning of the end of the Great Inflation. It just came too late to save Carter his presidency.

Where's Milton?

January 20, 2021, by contrast, might have been a good day for America.

It was an unusual inauguration, to be sure. With a global pandemic still in swing, the National Mall was planted with two hundred thousand flags to represent Americans who couldn't attend. Security was tight, after the unsettling attack on the Capitol two weeks prior. Notably absent was the outgoing president, the first to decline to attend his successor's swearing in since 1869.

Still, Joe and Jill Biden arrived at the Capitol to partly sunny skies and ovations. Biden delivered an inaugural address that echoed Lincoln, declaring: "Today, on this January day, my whole soul is in this: Bringing America together. Uniting our people. And uniting our nation."

CNN described the speech as a promise to "mobilize Americans against both the raging pandemic and the political divisions that have characterized the past few years." As the president and First Lady walked a brief stretch of Pennsylvania Avenue to the White House, capping the inaugural parade, reporter after reporter asked the same question: "Mr. President, can you unite the country?"

Biden had that opening, and it was thanks to extraordinary political good fortune. He'd struggled in the primaries, until the threat of a Sanders victory pushed the party to turn to the former vice president for rescue. The pandemic had highlighted Trump's leadership shortcomings and hobbled his economy, giving Democrats an opening against a sitting president. Biden lightly campaigned, largely from his basement. The media barely covered his agenda, instead fixating on his promises to fix the pandemic and calm the Trump storm. Biden took office with vaccines already rolling, the economy poised to rebound, the press in lockstep behind him. The voting public had also helpfully sent him a message with its split election decision: It rewarded Biden for his promises of unity with a White House job, though it simultaneously thinned the ranks of Democrats pushing a progressive agenda, leaving them bare congressional majorities. Both practicality and politics dictated restraint. Biden was a president with a rare opportunity: He was poised to benefit by simply letting the economy roar back to life, reaching across the aisle, calming the furies.

Instead, the administration decided to pretend the nation was gripped by—as Biden chief of staff Ron Klain put it—"overlapping and compounding crises," including Covid, the economy, and climate and racial justice. Under the guise of this fantasy fiction, the White House argued that the only answer was fundamental structural change to every aspect of the American system. Biden scraped clean the delicious platter of political fortune he'd been handed, in favor of presenting as the most radically liberal Democrat to ever take high office. The press pumped up Biden as the new FDR, and the mandate-less president chose to believe it.

The claims of crises were particularly galling given they were patently untrue. Vaccines were flooding out, and a return to normal life was on the imminent horizon. The prior economy had created one of the more inclusive in American history. Black and Hispanic poverty rates hit record lows in 2019. Women saw the lowest unemployment rate in seventy years. Wages were growing faster for the bottom 25 percent of workers than for the top 25 percent. The United States was leading the world in reducing carbon dioxide emissions, thanks to a steady transfer from coal to natural gas.

Every indicator also signaled the Covid economic crisis was over. Not long after Biden took office, the Commerce Department reported a healthy 4.1 percent GDP growth in the last quarter of 2020. This GDP of $21.49 trillion nearly matched the prior peak, hit in the last quarter of 2019. Private business investment and residential construction soared. Wages ticked up. The initial jobs reports in 2021 were lackluster, but by April the Department of Labor was reporting a vaccine jobs boom—the unemployment rate fell to 6 percent, down from 14.7 percent nearly a year earlier. The state economic engines of Florida and Texas had reopened in 2020, and by early 2021, most other states were following.

Consumers, free from lockdowns, started spending their accrued stimulus checks, and real GDP in the first quarter 2021 soared 6.4 percent. Jimmy Carter, eat your heart out.

The only flashing warning signs were those highlighting the risk of doing too much. The Congress in 2020 had poured extraordinary stimulus on the economy, passing five separate Covid relief bills. Washington spent $6.6 trillion in fiscal year 2020, 50 percent more than in 2019. The Congressional Budget Office in February 2021 reported that debt held by the public broke above 100 percent of the economy in fiscal 2020. The last time that had happened was 1946. In early March, as the Biden team pushed its first big spending plan, the *New York Times* reported that investors worried more dollars would spur a "resurgence of inflation." Liberal economist Larry Summers decried "the least responsible" U.S. macroeconomic policy in four decades (since Carter), foretelling a "pretty dramatic fiscal-monetary collision." And this wasn't some cloistered academic discussion within hallowed halls—it was a national discussion. Here's the *New York Times* headline from February 15, 2021: "Biden and the Fed Leave 1970s Inflation Fears Behind." Everyone understood the risk.

Biden brushed it all aside, instead taking marching orders from a progressive left that had decided it would use its rigged "crises" to steamroll through a dramatic agenda. The result would be the largest spending blowout in United States history, with Democrats spending another $6.8 trillion in fiscal 2021—even more than the year prior.

Carter advocated his stimulus in a (misguided) attempt to attack a real thing—a chronically bad unemployment rate. His spending was also aimed at job creation and public works. Biden by contrast showered money on a storming economy, and worse, poured it into Democratic social policies. It was the height of irresponsibility, and the direct (and avoidable) cause of the soaring inflation that followed.

Perhaps no one should have been surprised. While Candidate

Biden talked only sotto voce about most of his agenda, he did give a revealing interview to *Politico* in April 2020, just prior to locking up his nomination. The outlet noted that Biden was "fiery," and that he sounded "a bit like his angrier and less moderate primary rivals." Biden criticized the $2 trillion Covid relief bill that Trump signed in March 2020. The next round of stimulus, he said, needed to be "a hell of a lot bigger." He predicted, said *Politico*, that the virus would deal a blow to anti-government political thinking. "Milton Friedman isn't running the show anymore," Biden crowed.

And more's the pity.

First up was the American Rescue Plan, announced before Biden even took office. Democrats claimed the eye-goggling $1.9 trillion was necessary to "change the course of the pandemic" and "build a bridge toward economic recovery." Yet the bill had almost nothing to do with the pandemic, or with stimulus. Most of it was for income redistribution, and to reward longtime Democratic constituencies like Big Labor and teachers' unions. The bill contained a paltry $75 billion for vaccinations, testing and medical supplies, and another $20 billion for state health departments and community health centers. It also provided some needed additional funds to industries most hit by lockdowns, including a new infusion for the Paycheck Protection Program and support for restaurants, bars and airlines.

The rest of the bill was a slush fund of epic proportions. It included another $413 billion in stimulus checks to households, despite the fact that nearly every man, woman, and dependent had received two rounds of similar checks in 2020. It expanded the child tax credit, made it refundable, and put it on a monthly payout program—flooding homes with yet more cash. State and local governments landed $350 billion, even though state revenues were bouncing back to normal. The state payments were based on unemployment numbers, meaning blue states that had locked down the hardest received the biggest rewards. The legislation spent $86 billion to rescue multiemployer pension plans (a gift to trade unions), $130 billion in K–12 education (a gift to teachers' unions), and $40 billion to higher education (a gift to the ivory tower). The package grew ObamaCare ($35 billion) and grew Medicaid ($15 billion). It also contained billions for childcare, public transit agencies, rental assistance, mortgage help, energy costs, food stamps, Head Start, and, of course, Amtrak. Senator Chuck Schumer even managed to slip in $1.5 million for a pet bridge project in New York. Call it the No Democratic Constituency Left Behind Act.

Spending aside, the bill contained two particularly toxic labor provisions, included at the demand of progressives, yet practically tailor-made to hamstring the economic resurgence. In early 2021, even as jobs were coming back, employers were warning of growing trouble filling positions. Nobody wanted to work. This was because Congress in 2020 had greatly enhanced federal unemployment benefits, which, combined with state jobless checks and other federal and state transfers, allowed people to avoid the workforce. The bill nonetheless recklessly threw another $246 billion at keeping the enhanced federal unemployment dollars rolling through August. Then, to add injury to business insult, Democrats tacked a $15-an-hour minimum wage to the bill. The bizarre logic behind these two provisions: Make it harder for businesses to hire, while making it easier for workers to never return.

Even at this point Biden still had the opportunity to fulfill his campaign promises. A group of ten Republicans pilgrimaged to the White House to work with the president on the bill in a bipartisan fashion. They offered a $618 billion bill that committed to all the Covid money, as well as a smaller round of household checks, food stamp dollars, continued unemployment assistance, and more. They were barely out of the building before White House Press Secretary Jen Psaki declared that Biden "will not slow down work on this urgent crisis response and will not settle for a package that fails to meet the moment."

Biden stiff-armed the Republicans while Democrats chose to instead ram through the bill using the "reconciliation" process, a budget maneuver that required only fifty votes plus Vice President Kamala Harris. The Senate parliamentarian decreed the minimum-wage provision unallowable under reconciliation, but Biden signed the rest of the bill—passed on a pure party-line vote—on March 11, 2021.

It was official: Biden had no intention of uniting the country.

As was made crystal clear with the administration's next spending demand, unveiled just a few weeks later. Biden asked for $2.3 trillion for an "infrastructure" bill, with progressives defining "infrastructure" so broadly as to make a dictionary blush. The proposal contained only $115 billion for the types of projects most Americans define as infrastructure: roads, highways, bridges. It offered another $42 billion for other projects that might also fit a public-works definition—ports, waterways, airports. The bulk amounted to subsidies for the left's climate and union agendas—dressed up as urgently needed "investments" in America's future.

That included $175 billion for electric vehicles, in part to keep in place a tax credit for EV purchases that primarily benefits wealthy Americans. There was $100 billion to "decarbonize" the electric grid—code for shutting down coal and natural gas utility plants. Another $213 billion for "affordable housing," $100 billion to upgrade public schools, and $25 billion for childcare facilities. Also $165 billion for mass transit, including, again, Amtrak—much of which would serve as a bailout to the union and pension benefit plans that turn those enterprises into perpetual financial losers. But the piece of the bill that most highlighted the joke of the bill's title was its $400 billion to provide more . . . home health care.

Mary Kay Henry, the president of Service Employees International Union—one of Biden's most loyal labor supporters and the prime beneficiary of unionized home health care—said with a straight face: "We think that caregiving is an essential American infrastructure."

With that sort of flexibility, what isn't?

And the drunken sailors weren't yet done calling for rounds. A scant few weeks after "infrastructure," the Biden team released its call for $1.8 trillion for an "American Families Plan." The *Wall Street Journal* editorial board described it as "the plan to make the middle class dependent on government from cradle to grave." The plan envisioned no less than four huge new entitlement programs—to join the ranks of Social Security and Medicare.

They included: a new plan for national childcare, a universal pre-kindergarten program, free community college, and paid family and medical leave. The benefits would flow to pretty much every lower-income, middle-income, and even upper-income household in America.

Which is what made the proposed entitlements far different, and far more corrosive. They weren't in keeping with New Deal programs like Social Security or Medicare—programs that promised baseline government support after a lifetime of work. Nor were they social "safety net" programs like food stamps or welfare, created to provide temporary help to those in need. The Biden entitlements were instead handouts bestowed on everyone—working, nonworking, middle-class, poverty level—designed to hook the entire country on a European-style welfare state. They were designed to provide guaranteed income, with no tether to work or the social contract. As later analysis would show, the actual price of Biden's "families" agenda, once it included all provisions and was stripped of gimmicks, was more than $5 trillion.

Biden in 2021 also released his first budget, a $6 trillion document unprecedented in peacetime history. The administration's goal was to make permanent the 50 percent increase in government spending during the Covid crisis. This was made clear the next year with his second budget: $5.8 trillion.

And there was plenty else along the way. Biden in 2021 called for $37 billion to underwrite the U.S. semiconductor industry. The administration kept extending student loan forbearance—costing over $5 billion per month. In October 2022 (in a naked bid to buy midterm votes) Biden announced he was waving a magic executive wand and writing off student loans for millions of borrowers, to the tune of at least $420 billion. In that same year, the administration demanded a further $22.5 billion in "emergency funding" to buy yet more Covid boosters and treatments. And in both years, the White House continued to extend the federal Covid "emergency," providing enhanced food stamp benefits and federal matching funds for a 23-million-person increase in Medicaid enrollment during the pandemic.

In 2019, the last year before Covid, the U.S. government spent $4.4 trillion. All told, the Biden administration in its first two years proposed or enacted spending in excess of $22 trillion.

Like Padgett said, Carter was cheap.

Transitory dreams

Any economy would have struggled to absorb the amount of dollars the Biden Democrats were throwing at it, especially one still high on the 2020 Covid emergency fumes. But the economy had something else working against it, a force by the name of Jerome Powell. He will go down in history as the first Federal Reserve chief since the Carter days to blow the bank's mandate to keep inflation in relative check.

Powell took over a Fed in 2018 that was dominated by Keynesian economists (still is). The bank's economic models are today once again premised on the notion that demand is all that matters. This has led the bank to consistently overvalue the benefits of federal spending and undervalue the real growth that comes with tax cuts or regulatory modesty. The Fed's answer to the global financial crisis of 2008 was to engage in quantitative easing (buying assets to inject credit into the economy), and to keep interest rates low.

Powell turned to the same playbook when Covid hit: goose the money supply, keep rates low. Even in early 2021, Powell, like Miller, continued to focus on unemployment numbers, and used the jobless counts to justify the bank's huge monthly purchases of securities and bonds. But vaccines were already tackling the employment problem, and the bigger threat was government spending, still rolling amid supply crunches. Powell in 2020 had even publicly lobbied for Congress to keep throwing dollars out the door—a role that was decidedly not his job.

When Biden entered office, inflation was a healthy 1.4 percent. The report for April—one month after Biden signed his $1.9 trillion Covid "rescue" plan—showed the consumer price index had risen a startling 4.2 percent. (The Fed's target is 2 percent.) The monthly increase of 0.9 percent—stripped of food and energy prices—was the largest since 1982. It was eminently clear what was happening. U.S. consumers stockpiled an estimated $1 trillion during pandemic lockdowns, and Democrats had just provided them another huge infusion of cash and government benefits. Vaccines were now allowing them to burst back into the economy, spending like mad. But the economy simply didn't have enough goods to sate this hunger, pushing prices higher. The ongoing worker shortage—fueled, again, by continued government benefits—was also forcing businesses to pay more to hire, costs that were also pushing up prices.

Powell and other bank officials passed the April number off as "transitory," and promised life would soon be sweet again. As the inflation numbers kept rising, Powell kept repeating his "transitory" mantra. August: 5.3 percent. October: 6.2 percent. December: 7.0 percent. Powell ultimately wouldn't raise interest rates until March 2022, by which point inflation was raging at 8.5 percent—the largest twelve-month advance since May 1981, when Reagan first took over. Even then, Powell raised the rate by only a measly twenty-five basis points, the equivalent of throwing a cup of water at a forest fire.

The Fed soon after acknowledged that this wouldn't be enough, and embarked on a series of punishing hikes, month after month. It was brutal but, having waited so long, also necessary. One lesson from the 1970s is that inflation usually starts to fall only when interest rates exceed the inflation rate. Even after the Fed raised rates in February 2023—its eighth consecutive hike—the funds rate still sat below 5 percent (while inflation was running at more than 6 percent).

In July 2022, the United States announced a second consecutive quarter of negative growth—the technical definition of a recession. Democrats rejected the "recession" label, insisting that conditions this time were "unique" and that continued strong job growth meant the economy was fine. Yet as the summer and fall marched on, jobs growth slowed and tech and financial companies announced layoffs. Business investment sputtered. As inflation continued, and the economy faltered, economists began fretting over a new possibility: stagflation. Now, in what decade did we last hear that term?

See no evil

The White House employs an army of advisers and aides whose only job is to keep presidents informed. Which meant Joe Biden was hearing all the warnings, too. He was told the inflation numbers were ticking up, month by month, and that prices were rising across every service and every good and at the gas pump. He knew businesses were struggling to find workers, and that U.S. energy supply wasn't keeping up with demand. He had to have been told that energy and gas and food prices were swallowing up ever more of lower-income family budgets. And that inflation was eating away at paychecks and reversing any nominal wage increases.

But Biden, under ceaseless progressive clamoring, chose to ignore that public pain and go for broke. It's worth making the comparison here again to Carter. Carter also started out by spending, but refused to go for broke. Biden doubled down on the progressive dream of using a moment of "crisis" to create a permanent entitlement state.

Having passed his Covid "rescue" plan in March 2021, the Biden administration turned to its infrastructure and entitlement proposals. It hit on a particularly smart strategy with infrastructure: bribe Republicans with money. It was a tactic the administration used successfully on more than one occasion.

The GOP was too easily gulled into the deal. The party that loves to preach fiscal restraint lost a lot of it during the Trump years. The problem wasn't their 2017 tax reform—despite the mainstream press wails of "deficit spending." That reform proved the backbone of the good economic performance of the Trump years. Nor was the problem Republicans' decision in those years to begin rebuilding the military—which was long overdue. The problem was the party's refusal to offset those two efforts with spending discipline on the domestic front. The Covid blowout of 2020 was a big part of the problem. But even before then the GOP was spending too much, including Trump's signature on the Bipartisan Budget Act of 2018, which raised spending caps by $143 billion—a 13 percent hike from the previous year.

Republicans claimed in 2021 to have a good political reason for engaging in an infrastructure deal. Democrats initially broadcast their plan to pass infrastructure via another reconciliation bill that required only fifty Senate votes. But West Virginia senator Joe Manchin—more centrist than many of his Democratic brethren, and the fiftieth of those votes—disliked that approach. He told the White House it had an obligation to try bipartisanship first and set to work with a group of Republicans and Democrats to find an infrastructure compromise. Republicans hoped that by engaging with Manchin they would (a) prove to him the bipartisan approach was best and (b) keep him from agreeing to his party's bill for new entitlements.

The final product, released in summer 2021, was $1 trillion deal where both sides claimed victory. Republicans bragged that they'd stripped out proposed tax increases and a supersizing of the Internal Revenue Service. They claimed they'd kept the bill largely focused on roads, bridges, and ports. The Democrats crowed that they'd scored yet another $90 billion for mass transit (on top of the March bill), a huge new stream of green subsidies (including money for a new "national network" of electric-vehicle charging stations), and $65 billion to let the government interfere in the broadband-building market. The legislation was an embarrassment of hokey "pay-fors"—all of which were designed to allow negotiators to lower the advertised sticker price. It passed in August 2021, with sixty-nine Senate votes. Nineteen Republicans signed on, including Senate Minority Leader Mitch McConnell.

The keep-Manchin-close play worked for Republicans—at least for a time. The White House pocketed the bipartisan infrastructure bill and moved swiftly on to its plans to jam through its $3.5 trillion entitlement plan, via reconciliation. But progressives kept larding it up with ever-greater demands. Sanders in August 2021 unveiled a $3.5 trillion budget blueprint for the party's entitlement and climate ambitions. Included in it were not just all the prior Biden proposals—family leave, universal pre-K, free college, childcare—but Sanders's own demand for a dramatic increase in Medicare coverage for vision, dental, and hearing benefits. The climate portion included hundreds of billions more in subsidies, while the bill also provided money for permanently higher Obama-Care subsidies, home health care, and welfare programs. All of this was to be paid for with a combination of huge tax hikes and gimmicks.

Manchin's refusal to accept this price tag set off an intense pressure campaign against him. Democrats leveraged every interest group, friendly press outlet, and lobbyist to pummel Manchin into signing on. Interspersed were a chain of Democratic dramas—fights over the state and local tax deductions, energy, taxes, prescription drugs. It's unclear the party could have ever united all its warring factions around one giant bill.

Manchin put them out of their misery—for a time. Citing the threat of inflation and the size of the package, he stunned his Democratic colleagues in mid-December 2021 by walking away. He was particularly concerned by the way his party was hiding the true cost of the bill. Democrats had included all of their entitlement programs but funded them for only a few years. Their plan was to get them in law and operational, and then dare any future administration or Congress to roll them back. On paper, these time-limited programs met the parameters of what the party now claimed was a $2 trillion bill. But the independent Committee for a Responsible Federal Budget did an analysis of what the bill would cost assuming all the programs were covered over the standard ten-year period—which Biden Democrats were banking on.

The real taxpayer burden of the bill? It was $5 trillion.

Their entitlement bill seemingly dead, Democrats became more desperate for some sort of legislative win, and in the spring of 2022 refocused on a semiconductor bailout—termed a "compete with China" bill. It was a bad idea—modeled on China-like industrial policy, in which government directs the flow of capital. It was also unnecessary. The U.S. semiconductor industry already led in R&D budgets, and America is a leader in most areas of advanced technology.

But buoyed by Manchin's decision to kill the giant bill, Republicans decided it was safe to engage in more "bipartisan" spending. They told themselves this was yet another way to keep Manchin away from the entitlement bill (not to mention an excellent opportunity to throw money at their home-state industries).

What began as a $76 billion proposal to boost competition with China soon became the playground of big spenders and lobbyists. By the end, Republicans and Democrats had bloated the bill to $280 billion. The semiconductor industry snagged $76 billion in pork, but the federal government made out even better, its bureaucrats claiming twice that much. As Congress put its finishing touches on the bill, in July 2022, it got the news that inflation in June soared 9.1 percent. Nobody blinked an eye, and a bipartisan majority whooped yet another government infusion of cash out into the economy. Seventeen Senate Republicans voted for the bill.

Only this time, Republicans got played—and for fools. Even as they helped Democrats lard up the semiconductor bill, Manchin was secretly negotiating with Senate Majority Leader Chuck Schumer to revive some form of the bigger Biden plan. Hours after Manchin's Republican colleagues voted the chips bill through the senate, Manchin and Schumer announced their deal. It wasn't close to what progressives wanted, but it was $485 billion in new climate and health spending, and $468 billion in new taxes on an economy headed toward recession.

Democrats whipped the bill through in August of 2022—again on a straight party-line vote. They even had the audacity to name their latest bit of spending the Inflation Reduction Act. Biden marched into the midterms as the press swooned that his "legislative winning streak" would allow Democrats to defy midterm history and keep control of both the House and Senate. As the AP explained, the White House could now campaign on these "new laws designed to repair the economy and help consumers on a personal level."

Only the Inflation Reduction Act (surprise!) didn't reduce inflation. And as gas prices and grocery prices and electricity prices continued to increase that fall, people didn't feel very personally helped.

In a poll just a week prior to the 2022 midterms, surveys showed 71 percent of Americans felt the country was going in the wrong direction. That's nearly the number Carter faced as he went into the 1980 election.

Carter, of course, lost in a landslide. Biden Democrats for their part lost the House, which meant the Inflation Reduction Act was the last piece of legislative economic malpractice the Biden White House was able to commit.

But the damage was done, providing an unfortunate America with a vivid reminder of the perils of forgetting history and dismissing economic principles. Progressives pretended the laws of economics somehow didn't apply to their agenda. They embraced modern monetary theory, the idea that government can simply create more money without consequence. They coupled it with a vast expansion of government and insisted all this would produce security and record growth.

The result was that Democrats in a space of two short years produced soaring inflation, a shaky economy, and a falling standard of living. As my late colleague George Melloan and his wife, Joan, explained in their prescient 1978 book, *The Carter Economy*, Carter had managed to squander an opportunity to begin treating some of the country's underlying economic problems. But even Carter could never match this Biden record—nor would he have ever wanted to.

Milton Friedman might not have been running the show. But his rules of economics still applied.

CHAPTER 3

THE SUPERREGULATORS

And here's what you need to know about Carter when it comes to the other side of the economy—the supply side: He was . . . not terrible. Certainly not as terrible as Biden.

The 1970s was the decade the country witnessed the failure of Keynesian demand-side doctrine. Spend, spend, spend is no answer to anything. The 1980s was the decade the country learned just how centrally important was the supply side of the equation—policies that spur businesses to invest, grow, hire, and sate demand.

Carter in some ways helped the supply side—though not because he was some early Art Laffer. It was more straightforward. Carter ran his family's farm prior to going into politics; he respected entrepreneurialism. And Carter's generation of Democrats (including most liberals) looked nothing like today's anticorporate progressives. They weren't hostile to the *broad* concept of deregulation. Between the Interstate Commerce Act and New Deal politicians, government had grown its power over key sectors of the economy—energy, communications, and transportation. Bureaucrats controlled major business decisions as well as entrance to the market—which too often protected players from competition. The 1970s saw a backlash against this control and bipartisan efforts to break up what had become a government monopoly.

Democrats back then also still appreciated that businesses performed this vital little service known as . . . job creation. And they understood something that today's progressives don't—that when job creation goes well, headlines go well for politicians. The Carter Democrats were not on a mission to kill corporate America, or to replace major U.S. industries with government-run programs.

To the extent parts of the economy in the 1970s remained hobbled by rules, it was mostly because Washington had been too lazy to unpick the tangles. That's where Carter gets some credit, as the president willing to take on the broad deregulation of important sectors of the U.S. economy. His efforts were hardly perfect, but they made a difference.

Consider this: Carter's top priority upon taking office (in addition to stimulus) was boosting domestic energy production. Oil and gas at that time were the most heavily regulated sections of the economy outside transportation, and in response to continued fallout from the 1973 oil embargo, Ford made deregulation a driving mission of his time in office. Carter took up where Ford left off, and after intense congressional wrangling, signed a bill in 1978 that lifted some of the remaining constraints on oil and gas. (The bill contained a lot of other rules that undercut this effort, but more on that in the next chapter.)

Carter also gets credit for deregulating the airline, trucking, and railroad industries. He brought in Alfred Kahn—"the Father of Airline Deregulation"—to chair the intrusive Civil Aeronautics Board, where Kahn helped dismantle bureaucratic control over routes, fares, services, and market entry. The Airline Deregulation Act of 1978 officially phased out federal control, but also decreed that CAB would ultimately go away. It closed its doors in 1985, the first major regulatory agency to be abolished since the 1930s. Miracles never cease.

Carter in mid-1980 signed the Motor Carrier Act, letting trucking businesses set rates and throwing open the sector to more competition. The president's statement on signing the bill proved he understood that heavy government intrusion can hurt Americans: "This is historic legislation. It will remove 45 years of excessive and inflationary Government restrictions and red tape . . . reducing consumer costs by as much as $8 billion each year."

And one of Carter's last signatures in office was to the Staggers Rail Act. The business of rail deregulation began in earnest under Nixon and then Ford. But Carter continued the work with legislation that gave freight rail carriers and shippers more freedom over their rates and contracts. The Association of American Railroads estimates that since the Staggers Act passed, average rail rates have fallen 44 percent and railroads have plowed $760 billion of their own funds into their network.

My own favorite Carter deregulation is much smaller, though one that millions of Americans would surely consider his best. In 1978, Carter signed a relatively uninspiring bill about excise taxes, but it contained a provision legalizing beer brewed at home for personal or family use. The subsequent explosion in homebrewing—coupled with state authorization of brewpubs in the 1980s—opened the door to the craft beer industry. It certainly produced a better standard of drink than Billy Beer—the short-lived brew promoted in the late 1970s by Carter's redneck younger brother.

The tragedy of Carter's deregulation is that while it created freer markets in a few industries, it did little overall to help his economy. Carter jumped on the 1970s bandwagon of ending complete government control over a few industries. But Democrats, including Carter, still believed government was *awesome*, and best positioned to dictate health standards, safety standards, labor standards, environmental standards, and any other standard you can imagine. Jimmy was also the ultimate meddler—a technocrat who believed government could fix all, if it just had the right departments, rules, and regulations. For every major piece of deregulation Carter oversaw, he added dozens more pieces to the bureaucracy.

It was Carter who created two cabinet-level departments—the Department of Energy and the Department of Education. The necessity of both is still questionable today. His Environmental Protection Agency, his Food and Drug Administration, his Consumer Product Safety Commission, and his Occupational Safety and Health Administration were menaces, blanketing the nation with intrusive and costly regulations.

Then, as now, labor unions were the Democratic Party's most powerful constituency, and Carter for half a year threatened business with the prospect of crushing prolabor legislation designed to give unions a whip hand in collective bargaining. (It was barely defeated in the Senate in 1978.) But he did get across the finish line (at Big Labor's behest) a bill in 1977 that raised the national minimum wage by some 45 percent over four years—a huge new burden on private employers.

In 1978, Carter also unveiled his wage and price "guidelines," which were in theory voluntary, but which imposed sanctions on businesses that didn't comply. He flooded the sphere with a hodgepodge of proposals that ranged from overhauling energy policy, to reorganizing government, to the possibility of a new national health insurance program. As Burns (Carter's first Fed chief) noted, the uncertainty of the government's course paralyzed the corporate community. As did Carter's frequent demagoguing of corporations, including his claims the oil industry was "price gouging" and "hoarding."

Speaking of which, Carter's most economically consequential blind spot was his obsession with conservation—the 1970s version of today's climate fervor. Carter over his five years signed fifteen significant pieces of green legislation—a morass of new rules and mandates that misdirected capital and raised prices. As the next chapter will show, these misguided new laws undercut what progress Carter made in opening the way for more domestic energy production.

Carter's legacy on that other all-important supply issue—taxes—was also mixed. On the campaign trail, he'd called the complex U.S. tax code a "disgrace to the human race," and ran on a populist promise to close "loopholes" for fat-cat businessmen. But Congress and lobbyists balked, and the $18.7 billion tax bill Carter signed in 1978 was not a reform so much as a random mix of tax cuts and handouts. On the upside, some of the changes were progrowth, including income-tax reductions and a small reduction in small-business tax rates. On the downside, the bill erected a new alternative minimum tax, and made permanent a new experiment called the earned income tax credit. The idea was to increase the marginal incentive for lower-income Americans to engage in work. Instead, the credit has largely become another form of welfare, which politicians continue to expand to this day.

And what growth provisions there were in the 1978 Carter tax bill were likely nullified by other tax actions. Democrats wanted to pass the 1978 bill in part to make amends for 1977 legislation that imposed unpopular payroll-tax hikes on working Americans. And, of course, Carter would infamously impose a stinging windfall profits tax on the oil industry in 1980. Few tax ideas are as misguided as a windfall profits tax, since it serves primarily to reduce the production of its intended target. Sure enough, Carter's tax reduced domestic production by as much as 6 percent, and increased imports by as much as 16 percent. Congress repealed the colossal flop in 1988, both sides acknowledging it had raised a fraction of the expected revenue, and mostly served to increase the nation's dependence on foreign oil.

The only president since then who has given any serious thought to reimposing this measure is currently sitting in the White House: Joe Biden.

Meet the $65K "used" Tesla

Had Biden come to office and done absolutely nothing, the economy would have popped back to its former humming self. Yet if the Biden team felt the need to do *something* to hurry that process along, there was an obvious area to assist: the supply side. Covid lockdowns had produced some real supply chain constraints— from computer chips to lumber. The steady uptick in prices in early 2021 were telling an obvious story: The market was beginning to struggle to produce enough goods and services to keep up with the now-unleashed demand of consumers who'd been fueled by government pandemic "relief."

Consider used cars. Modern autos are basically semiconductor chips on wheels. Covid put the auto industry into temporary lockdown, and many automakers figured that the pandemic would result in a longer-term crash in auto sales. They canceled their chip orders. By the time they realized they had figured wrong— that consumers were raring to spend their pent-up Covid cash—it was too late. The pandemic had inspired a surging demand for personal electronics that sucked up the chip supply. Tens of thousands of cars sat marooned in lots, waiting for chips before they could go out to dealers.

Americans instead turned to used autos, sending prices spiraling to insane heights. By November 2021, used car prices were on average 50 percent higher than they were in February 2020, while some popular models saw even bigger spikes. According to analysis by the iSeeCars website, the Tesla Model Y by the end of 2021 was selling for 15 percent more used ($64,930) than it was new ($56,685)!

Businesses were meanwhile warning Washington about another kind of shortage—workers. The feds in 2020 expanded unemployment programs to cover more workers and provided thirteen additional weeks of benefits to those who exhausted state payments. In early 2021 they also passed a $300 weekly jobless bonus, and politicians kept extending it even as lockdowns eased and the economy started growing rapidly. Lower-income workers in particular discovered it was just as profitable to play Xbox as it was to show up for a job. Even in February and March, economic indicators were broadcasting a supply-side jobs problem, with jobs reports undershooting expectations and evidence of huge and growing job openings. Biden made this worse by imposing government and private-employer vaccine mandates, which many blue states and school districts copied. Unvaccinated workers quit or were fired rather than comply with the mandates, and government stats showed notable falloffs in employment for state and local education.

The solution was straightforward: End the disincentives for work, and double down on the message that government intended to get out of business's way. Biden needed to reassure industry that it would not face new tax hikes, regulatory burdens, or hostile bureaucrats. Better yet, Biden could have told the nation's employers that the federal government was ready to help unsnarl supply chains by temporarily lifting Washington barriers to production.

Biden did the opposite. As the last chapter described, he stuck to failed Keynesian canon, lathering the country in more cash, pushed the Fed to keep interest rates near zero, and pumped demand. But he did something equally destructive. He sent the message, at every turn, that he intended to bring the hammer down on business—catering to a progressive movement that hates free markets.

That policy started on inauguration day. Even as Biden smiled through the festivities, his administration unceremoniously fired National Labor Relations Board general counsel Peter Robb. It was an ugly break with tradition; Robb still had ten months in his tenure, and prior presidents had always allowed NLRB general counsels to serve out their terms. The president also fired Robb's deputy, Alice Stock. Biden had spent the past year complaining that Trump broke norms. Yet his first act was to destroy a bipartisan tradition so that he could claim to be the most pro-union president in history.

By the end of inauguration day, Biden had also signed seventeen executive orders, several designed to tell business that a new, antigrowth sheriff was in town. He put an immediate freeze on any Trump deregulatory actions in process and revoked a Trump order that required agencies to repeal two regulations for every new one they issued. Biden also took aim at specific industries. He directed agencies to extend their foreclosure and eviction moratoriums, despite vocal concerns from landlords that these were subjecting them to untenable levels of financial stress. In a sop to his environmental lobby, Biden revoked the presidential permit for the Keystone XL Pipeline—sticking it to Canada, U.S. workers, and international investors who had put $9 billion into that vital project. He simultaneously ordered federal agencies to begin locking up federal lands against energy exploration.

The next blow was the announcement of Biden's cabinet and agency heads—antibusiness officials unlike any ever seen in Washington. Every Democratic president brings with them an army of regulators, as Carter did. But this was something else. Many of Biden's nominees professed hostility to the very notion of private ownership, markets, and entrepreneurs.

Take Biden's first nominee for comptroller of the currency, tasked with regulating some 1,200 nationally chartered banks, representing some two-thirds of the banking system. Biden chose Saule Omarova, who'd graduated from Moscow State University on a Lenin Personal Academic Scholarship, and who wrote frequently of her belief that the Soviet system was superior to Western capitalism. She'd spent her academic career promoting wild ideas, including the belief that the federal government should dictate credit, capital, and asset prices. In one paper, she advocated the Federal Reserve commandeer consumer bank deposits and "effectively 'end banking' as we know it." Biden's nominee didn't want to regulate banks—she wanted to *get rid of them*. Former Pennsylvania senator Pat Toomey, one of the GOP's banking experts and not known for hyperbole, was flabbergasted by the nomination. Omarova "has been celebrated on the far left for promoting ideas she herself has described as 'radical.' That's a point we can agree on," he said in a Senate floor speech. "These are very, very radical ideas. In fact, I don't think I've ever seen a more radical choice for any regulatory spot in our federal government. I know that is a very sweeping statement to make. I think I can stand by it." When even several Senate Democrats proved wary of her nomination, Omarova withdrew. Yet what does it say that Biden nominated her in the first place?

Most of the rest of Biden's picks amounted to activists, academics, and ideologues—a lethal combination of market ignorance and business hostility. Carter had some aggressive regulators, but many at least had business experience or other prior interaction with the industries they oversaw. Many of Biden's people, by contrast, were picked because they checked an identity-politics box. In 2022, the Committee to Unleash Prosperity studied the experience of sixty-eight top Biden officials whose job it was to help oversee the economy. "Average business experience of Biden appointees is only 2.4 years," the study found. It also discovered that 62 percent had "virtually no business experience." The average Trump cabinet official, by contrast, had thirteen years in the private economy.

Biden's pick to head Health and Human Services: Xavier Becerra, California's attorney general, who'd made a name suing most businesses but who had no experience whatsoever in health care (and this with a pandemic ongoing). The pick for the Interior Department, which oversees oil and gas leases: Deb Haaland, a congresswoman from New Mexico who boasted sitting in on pipeline protests and who considered natural-gas development a "danger to the air we breathe and water we drink." The choice for secretary of Labor: Marty Walsh, a former Boston union chief with a lifetime record of disdain for employers. The Biden nominee for the Transportation Department, at a moment the country was experiencing supply chain breakdowns? Pete Buttigieg, a thirty-nine-year-old whose entire political career amounted to a stint as mayor of South Bend, Indiana (population: 100,000). If you were among the tens of thousands of passengers stranded in an airport in January 2023 as the Federal Aviation Administration's tech system melted down, thank Mayor Pete—and Biden.

Not every nominee was a bust. Biden's head of the Food and Drug Administration, Robert Califf, was a respected cardiologist with experience working with the pharmaceutical industry. Commerce Secretary Gina Raimondo had been a venture capitalist before jumping into politics. But these were the exceptions to the unqualified.

Nevertheless, if the mission of Biden's team was to completely disrupt, disadvantage, and demoralize the business community, they get gold stars. And in ways both small and large.

Every federal agency has the ability to target their specific industries. And every Biden cabinet and agency head did just that, whether it was Buttigieg's Department of Transportation lumbering the auto industry with crushing and costly new fuel-efficiency standards, or Tom Vilsack's Agriculture Department attempting to microregulate the meat and poultry industries, or Jennifer Granholm's Energy Department imposing costly new efficiency requirements on manufactured homes. This was the targeted stuff—and painful enough for the industries involved.

But the regulators with the power to do the most damage are those whose diktats apply economy wide. Think of them as the superregulators they are: bureaucrats who set the overall rules for business-labor relations, or those who lay down financial regulations that apply to most every corporate balance sheet. Those were topmost priorities for the Biden administration, and its picks for those regulators were the worst of the lot.

The union racket

Carter was a pro-union guy, but he didn't face the same pressure as Biden. While liberal unions like the United Auto Workers endorsed George McGovern in 1972, their rank and file remained more conservative, and polling found quite a few supported Nixon. Union leaders by 1976 worried they were out of step with their members, and when Carter stormed to primary victory in heavily unionized Pennsylvania, union heavyweights rallied around him. Big Labor's leadership retained qualms that Carter wasn't in tune with their priorities, and they were right to worry. Carter would disappoint them greatly with his failure in 1978 to get their labor-law reform through the Senate. Many progressive labor leaders still mark that defeat as the beginning of a long union decline—one that neither Bill Clinton nor Barack Obama was able to reverse.

Biden battled mightily for union endorsements in his crowded primary, and he did it by pledging to be the most pro-union president in history. In the 1960s, union members made up about one-third of the private workforce; today, that's closer to 6 percent. Growing numbers of young Americans prize flexibility and resent union hierarchy and union dues. Yet Big Labor keeps insisting the problem is that businesses have too much power. They made clear that they'd only get behind a Democratic candidate who placed union revival at the very top of a presidential agenda.

Biden's way of proving that commitment was to promise the PRO Act, the most radically pro-union labor change since the 1935 Wagner Act. The law is designed to give unions the whip hand in all scenarios, starting by killing off right-to-work laws in twenty-seven states, making union membership again compulsory. The PRO Act would also open new industries to union reach (think: independent contractors); give unions powerful new tools with which to organize; and deny corporations the ability to fight these campaigns, or to hire replacements during strikes. Biden plumped his union promises at every moment, and it won him a flood of endorsements at a crucial primary moment. But even as the president-elect headed to the White House, he knew he lacked anywhere near the sixty Senate votes necessary for PRO Act passage. His fallback was to go around Congress and enact the same agenda by regulatory fiat.

The tip of this antibusiness spear is the NLRB, and it explains Biden's Day One decision to break the rules and axe its general counsel, Robb. Biden immediately appointed an acting replacement, regional director Peter Sung Ohr, who rescinded more than a dozen Robb guidance documents that unions didn't like. Ohr was soon replaced with a permanent new prosecutor in chief, Jennifer Abruzzo, who had previously worked for a union powerhouse—Communications Workers of America. And Biden appointed two Democratic commissioners to the board—Gwynne Wilcox and David Prouty—who previously served another union titan, the Service Employees International Union. Any thought that the Biden NLRB would prove a neutral arbiter in business-labor disputes was out the window.

The Biden NLRB made clear its intent to turn Big Labor into the new power in any corporate environment. If larger companies proved hard to unionize, unions would now be free to attempt to organize smaller units of the company—bit by bit. Workers and employees of franchises—a business model that has boomed across U.S. industries in the past decade—would now be counted as employees of the parent company, making it easier to sue that parent for labor violations. And companies adjudged of violations would now be subject to far harsher penalties.

The NLRB also gave unions expansive new access to employers' property and employee records as part of their organizing campaigns. And when a union failed in an organizing drive, even with all these special privileges? In April 2021, a union election was held at an Amazon warehouse in Alabama. The Retail, Wholesale and Department Store Union poured enormous resources into the campaign, hoping it would be the first step toward organizing Amazon facilities nationwide. Instead, more than 70 percent of workers rejected the union. In November 2021, the NLRB shocked the business world by giving the union a do-over. The head of the union had whined about a "broken" system and complained that Amazon had installed a postal box outside the warehouse to make it easier for workers to post their mail-in ballots for the election. The NLRB used the box as its excuse to claim Amazon exerted undue influence in the election and to require a new vote. A second vote was held in April 2022, where it appeared workers rejected the union again (the NLRB is still deciding).

Abruzzo in 2022 meanwhile issued guidance overturning seventy-five years of legal practice, stripping companies of their rights to speak out against unionization. The memo is likely unconstitutional (she's facing lawsuits), but marks another example of the Biden team's casual dismissal of standards and norms when it suits. Abruzzo also put companies on notice that she—not they— was now the final word on the management of employees. In 2021 she sued Home Depot, Whole Foods, and Kroger for decisions to fire or discipline employees for sporting Black Lives Matter insignia—even though they clearly violated corporate policies against displaying political or religious slogans.

Unions saw their opportunity to unleash an assault on corporate America. The NLRB bragged in October 2022 (as part of a plea for more funding) that one year into a Biden-dominated NLRB board, union representation petitions were up a staggering 53 percent, and the number of unfair labor practice charges filed against companies in NLRB field offices had grown 19 percent. Did corporate America overnight become 19 percent meaner to its workers? Of course not. But the NLRB overnight did make the cost of maintaining a workforce spiral upward.

And it wasn't just the NLRB. The Biden administration in April 2021 set the ball rolling on a Labor Department rule to unilaterally raise the minimum wage that federal contractors must pay hundreds of thousands of workers, from \$10.95 to \$15 an hour. Only seven states (and DC) had adopted such a high minimum wage, given its negative economic consequences. The new federal rule puts contractors in the position of either swallowing the new financial burden (by dismissing lower-paid employees) or passing along the higher costs to the public. It also makes it far more difficult for small businesses to compete for contracts. The American Action Forum estimated the new rule will saddle federal taxpayers with an additional \$1.2 billion annually.

The very next month, the Labor Department brought the hammer down on millions of independent contractors, moving to rescind a Trump-era rule that ensured that workers who set their own hours aren't forced onto corporate payrolls (and union books). The ranks of independent contractors have soared this past decade with the growth of app-based companies like Uber and DoorDash, and amid younger workers who prize flexibility or use gig jobs for occasional supplemental income. But unions despise contractors, since they can't force them to become dues-paying members. The Biden administration was happy to take the side of union bosses over the freedom of hair stylists, freelance drivers, bookkeepers, photographers, and nonunion plumbers, electricians, and carpenters. Labor secretary Marty Walsh in a June 2022 House hearing patronizingly explained that the administration was doing all this for workers' own good, as it was "protecting" them. From what? The freedom to make their own choices?

While it's impossible to tally the economic effect of these labor changes on business writ large, the hit was substantial. At a time that companies should have been focused on unkinking supply chains and increasing production to satisfy the post-Covid buying boom, they were instead throwing valuable resources at fending off unionization campaigns; hiring teams of lawyers to sort through NLRB guidance; and taking on costs to comply with new federal diktats.

The financial gods

Elizabeth Warren isn't a government regulator. She just wishes she were, in addition to her Senate day job. Warren is the classic progressive hater of "greedy," "gouging," "corrupt," "unaccountable" corporate America—which she classifies as any entity with a business license. Warren spent time in academia studying financial regulation, and then more time with other academics and lefties building on each other's wild theories. She unfortunately managed to install many of these academics atop the Biden bureaucracy. They belong to another class of superregulators—those who govern America's financial and legal worlds.

Take Consumer Financial Protection Bureau director Rohit Chopra. The bureau was created with Warren's help in 2010 to regulate the world of consumer finance, and it oversees thousands of financial service providers—banks, lenders, mortgage servicers, debt collectors. By just four months on the job, Chopra had signaled his initial agenda: take over regulation of financial technology companies (Apple, Facebook, Amazon, etc.); redefine what counted as "fair lending"; harass credit-reporting agencies; pursue companies that engage in "buy now, pay later" products; terrorize the credit-card market; bird-dog for-profit colleges that provide student loans; and usurp state attorneys general when he feels they aren't being aggressive enough. And that was just the first four months.

Warren's Federal Trade Commission chair, Lina Khan, was equally ambitious. The FTC was long seen as less partisan than other federal agencies, with a tradition of bipartisan cooperation. At the FTC's very first meeting under Khan, in July 2021, she and her fellow Democratic commissioners voted to rip up decades of precedent and grant themselves sweeping new powers. The group eliminated the longtime role of the agency's chief administrative law judge to oversee rule makings and fact-findings. Khan took over the job herself. In the past, a majority vote of the commissioners was needed to launch an investigation; Khan made it so that one commissioner alone could greenlight a probe or subpoenas. And they ripped up an Obama-era policy statement that bound the agency to the doctrine that competition and antitrust must be viewed through the lens of "consumer welfare." Khan made clear she'd litigate for whatever reason she desired, since she saw her role as reshaping the "distribution of power" in the economy.

To that end, she went on a suing spree, sending the message that no company, and no behavior, was beyond her reach. She sued Meta to block it from buying a tiny virtual-reality fitness app (even though Meta did not own a fitness app already, so could hardly be accused of monopolizing). She sued Walmart for supposedly failing to do more to stop scammers (never mind Walmart's many antifraud programs). She sued Altria when it tried to take a minority stake in vaping company Juul, and she sued biotech firm Illumina when it tried to purchase a cancer-detection test maker named Grail. Judges ultimately struck down many of the FTC's novel theories behind these suits, but not before costing industry millions of dollars. In the past, companies would make deals and then approach regulators to work through what changes might be necessary to pass antitrust muster. Khan let it be known there would be no more talking. If companies didn't clear their proposals with her first, they'd get hit with a lawsuit after.

And then there was Gary Gensler, Biden's head of the Securities and Exchange Commission. Congress created the SEC to oversee public stock exchanges, and later gave it additional authority to require public companies to disclose "material" information. This means information that is directly material to a company's financial performance or risks. Gensler saw in the word "material" an opening to use disclosure to force every public company to succumb to the left's new "environmental, social and governance" demands. The agency vastly expanded the definition of "material" to include

information about a company's climate policies and political giving, since according to the agency these related to their "risks" and
to "racial justice." The final climate rule not only required public
companies to report their own greenhouse-gas emissions *but those
of their supply chains and customers.* All this was designed to soften
up companies for activist groups that pressure them to go more
woke. The SEC itself estimated the price tag for this reporting
would—in the first year alone—amount to about $640,000 for
each larger company, and $490,000 for each smaller one.

Another corrosive quality all these Biden superregulators
shared: They have largely chosen to rule by enforcement rather
than by rule making. Regulations are costly for business, but at
least they go through a formal process and lay out the rules of the
road. But the Genslers and Chopras don't want to take time to go
through that process, or give companies the opportunity to weigh
in with comments. Bringing ad hoc enforcement actions against
high-profile companies sent the quick message that the rules had
changed, though at the high cost of leaving businesses uncertain
as to what was or wasn't allowed. That kind of confusion leads to
business paralysis, as Carter discovered. The SEC announced that
in fiscal 2022 alone it had ratcheted up enforcement actions by
9 percent, and extracted a whopping $4.2 billion in fines—"the
highest on record."

These enforcement actions were in addition to a Biden Justice
Department that began spewing lawsuits against companies on
accusations of fraud, false claims, or antitrust. DOJ bragged in
2022 that it had collected $5.6 billion in settlements and judg-
ments the prior year under the False Claims Act—the "second
largest amount recorded" in history. Yay team.

An American Action Forum analysis estimated the regulatory
costs of Biden's first year were three times that of Obama's first
year and forty times that of Trump's. Companies by the end of
2021 were looking at an additional $201 billion and 131 million
hours of paperwork to comply with this tsunami of new rules. Yet

there is no evidence any of them made the country cleaner, safer, or healthier.

Just how terrible was Biden compared to Carter on regulation? Biden in July 2021 issued (another) executive order, this one directing his administration to "promote competition." It was the opposite—a call for his team to bring sectors back under the thumb screws of the government. Among the industries he called to reregulate? Railroads.

Department of International Tax Control

Democrats of old came to office willing to cut taxes if it helped the economy (Kennedy, Carter). Modern Democrats have come to office focused solely on raising taxes on as many people as politically possible. Then there's Biden. The forty-sixth president isn't just obsessed with taking more from taxpayers. He's intent on making sure that nobody else—*in the world*—can give his victims a tax reprieve.

Taxes are another vital piece of the supply side. Layer companies with costly and complex regulations, and they have less money to invest in innovation, expansion, or employees. Worse, slap them with higher taxes—or even the threat of higher taxes—and they might just cut back in fear of how bad it might become. Either way, it's a supply killer.

Biden didn't bother to float a tax hike with his first piece of legislation—his Covid "rescue" plan. Why bother raising public anxiety over tax hikes when you can use a global pandemic as an excuse to deficit spend? The Democrats passed the entirety of that $1.9 trillion blowout straight on to the national tab.

But the bill did contain one provision that offered a glimpse of Biden's more sweeping strategy when it came to taxation. Democrats used their Covid "rescue" plan to funnel hundreds of billions of dollars to the states—though with an important restriction.

At the last minute they tucked into the bill a prohibition on states using the funds for tax relief. States would receive this federal gift and be allowed to use the money for pretty much anything they wanted—just not to provide relief to Americans crushed under federal tax burdens. It was aimed at red states, which had successfully been using lower taxes to lure businesses away from high-tax blue states. A federal judge within months had struck down the provision as a blatant "federal invasion of State sovereignty." A full year later, the Biden administration was still arguing for a federal appeals court to restore the provision.

Biden instead dropped the tax hammer in late March, as part of his American Families Plan agenda to increase entitlements and green spending. His corporate tax increase proposal amounted to a giant $1.5 trillion hike over ten years—with an additional $1.5 trillion in higher investment taxes and on individual income. The $3 trillion in taxes was equal to 1.36 percent of GDP each year, the largest tax increase on that measurement since 1968's hike to pay for the Great Society and Vietnam.

The Biden plan would have reversed the 2017 tax reform that helped simplify the United States' complex and anticompetitive corporate tax code. That reform was a foundation of the Trump economic success, in part because it reversed "inversions"—corporations that fled the United States to headquarter in lower-tax countries. Companies brought back home more than $1.5 trillion from overseas from 2018 to 2020, which they used to grow U.S. businesses and the U.S. economy.

Biden proposed to erase most of 2017's corporate tax cut, raising the corporate level from 21 percent to 28 percent. He unveiled plans to tax dividends, capital gains, and other forms of investment income. The president's overall proposal would have pushed the U.S. corporate tax burden to one of the highest in the developed world—potentially topping 60 percent. And those taxes would have rippled through the economy. Anyone with a brain knows that corporations don't pay taxes—they pass them through to employees, suppliers, and consumers. Shareholders—including 401(k) holders—would have also footed the bill in terms of lower return on investment. Biden kept claiming that all he was asking was for wealthier people and corporations to pay their "fair" share—a very old Democratic line, one that even Carter used. But his plan would have hit everyone—not just the wealthy or businesses.

The administration meanwhile moved to ensure that no company would be able to evade his tax regime by again fleeing U.S. shores. High-spending countries like France and Germany had for years lobbied for developed economies to adopt a global minimum corporate tax rate—the better to deny European competitors like low-tax Ireland the chance of stealing their companies. The United States had always refused to go along on the bipartisan grounds that such a deal would be rotten for U.S. companies and U.S. competitiveness. Yet as Biden announced his domestic tax-hike plans, Treasury Secretary Janet Yellen informed the world's largest economies that the U.S. was now willing to join the high-tax suicide pact. And she wanted the group to go bigger. The Organization of Economic Co-operation and Development was discussing a global minimum of 12 percent, but Yellen talked G-7 leaders up to 15 percent. The plan was to lock in the world economy at that rate, then slowly pressure other countries to keep hiking the minimum to match Biden's 28 percent corporate rate. Biden planned to fund his spending blowout with corporate spoils and wanted to make sure no other countries upset his plans.

The problem is that all other 130 countries in the OECD—to the last—need to agree. And many rightly worry that China and other developing nations will refuse to take part in the tax self-harm, instead using their own tax freedom to lure corporations running from the OECD tax regime. It was another classic Biden bad move. Even as the president claims China is our greatest economic and military threat, he's taking steps to give China the economic advantage.

The good news for the U.S. economy is that herding 130 countries makes herding cats look easy, and while Yellen achieved an agreement in principle, nobody has yet settled on final details. The new global tax cartel was supposed to be operational by the middle of 2022, yet by that date they were still swimming in disagreement. And since the deal must be ratified by the U.S. Congress, the Democrats' loss of the House in the 2022 midterms put to short-term rest the prospect of a global accord.

But don't think the left has given up on the idea.

Biden's "fair share"

Biden's domestic tax plan looked even worse as the fiscal 2021 year brought a tax-revenue flood, and proof that existing rates were doing a fine job of capturing profit and incomes. The Congressional Budget Office in October 2021 estimated that federal receipts for the first time in history topped $4 trillion. Corporate income taxes grew by 75 percent for the year—totaling $370 billion—thanks to the 2017 reform's lower rates. Individual income taxes rose 27.5 percent to hit more than $2 trillion. This revenue stream would have easily put the United States in the black, had it not been for Congress's excessive Covid spending, in particular Biden's final $1.9 trillion Covid "rescue." There was no reason whatsoever to raise taxes, and given supply-side shortages, every reason not to. But the Biden progressives wanted their entitlement blowout.

Democrats spent the summer of 2021 squabbling over the size and contours of their Build Back Better bill. One of the fights was over taxes. Arizona's Kyrsten Sinema—crucial to getting the bill through the Senate—declared that she would not tolerate any hikes to corporate or income-tax rates, on the totally sensible grounds that it would hurt "economic competitiveness."

Sinema's refusal to go along with traditional tax hikes forced

Democrats to take a different route and highlighted just how insane liberal thinking on taxes had become since Carter's day. Progressives rushed to dream up alternate ways to generate revenue. First up was a proposal to create a wealth tax on billionaires. The United States had never seriously contemplated a wealth tax for about, well, a billion reasons. For starters, it's likely unconstitutional. Wealth taxes are also insanely complex (try calculating unrealized capital gains). Americans meanwhile view taxes levied on a lifetime of work, and on only select individuals, as inherently unfair. And European countries' experiments with wealth taxes phenomenally backfired, as their wealthy fled to better tax domiciles. Another problem: According to *Forbes*'s 2021 billionaires list, there were only 724 in the U.S., with a total net worth of $4.4 trillion—not anywhere near the base necessary to finance the left's spending dreams. Oregon senator Ron Wyden nonetheless conjured up a 107-page proposal, explaining that it was needed to raise "revenue for sorely needed investments in our infrastructure and economy"—because the trillions Democrats had already spent was apparently still not enough. The proposal died the day it was introduced, as Democratic senators beyond just Sinema worried over its potential political and economic fallout.

In the weeks following the death of the wealth tax, Democrats randomly threw out crazier and crazier proposals with no heed for the economic fallout. There was the plan to impose a 5 percent surcharge on taxpayers earning more than $5 million, and another 3 percent on income above $25 million. Expand the ObamaCare surtax to small businesses, said some. Impose corporate minimum taxes, said others. One chunk of the Democratic caucus wanted to go all in on a carbon tax. This was opposed by another chunk, which rightly feared industries would pass on the costs to consumers (that's how it works), allowing critics to say the party was raising taxes on the middle class.

In the end, the debate was for naught. In mid-December,

Manchin pulled the plug. He told his party he would not sign on to a bill, given "geopolitical uncertainty," "staggering debt," and "inflation taxes that are real and harmful to every hard-working American at the gasoline pumps, grocery stores and utility bills with no end in sight." Too bad he later changed his mind.

Taxes are bad. But even the *threat* of taxes is bad—at least when it comes to the business environment, and one also coping with post-Covid supply stress. For the entire first year of Biden's presidency, the real possibility of enormous taxes weighed over every large, medium, and small business in the country. Biden's first tax plan made clear his intention to target companies of every size, and the willy nilly replacement proposals created even more uncertainty.

Companies, like households, have budgets. And like households, they don't throw a bunch of money into a project when the real threat exists that their capital will be taken by the government. The Biden tax threats left a big mark on the economy. And the real tax pain was yet to come.

IRS: Beast mode

Biden got his taxes in the end—at least some of them. As the 2022 midterms approached, Democratic leaders decided to take one more run at getting the president's Build Back Better agenda over the finish line. Manchin shocked Washington when he walked away in December 2021; he shocked the town all over again when he announced at the end of July that he was back on board.

Democrats dialed down their expectations and reluctantly accepted that Manchin (and Sinema) were in charge. The deal Manchin and Schumer announced was nowhere near the $5 trillion in new spending the left wanted and contained none of Biden's original entitlement provisions—a bitter blow to progressives. It's $485 billion in new spending was instead aimed at new energy and climate provisions, and an expansion of ObamaCare. The bill paid for these new provisions with tax hikes on . . . everyone.

All public companies were hit with a 1 percent tax on share buybacks—a penalty on shareholders and a new obstacle to the efficient allocation of capital. Companies with more than $1 billion in profits were slammed with a 15 percent minimum tax on book income, siphoning $200 billion out of the private economy. Small businesses were targeted with new loss limits, raising their taxes by $50 billion.

Biden promised on the campaign trail not to raise taxes on households earning less than $400,000. But the administration's bill came up with a clever way to evade that promise. It threw $80 billion at the Internal Revenue Service, aimed at supersizing the agency's enforcement division. This was more than six times the IRS's annual budget, all of it aimed at squeezing more out of taxpayers. Democrats claimed this "investment" would earn back the government $200 billion in revenue.

The White House tried to claim this was aimed at wealthy tax cheats, but the Joint Committee on Taxation noted that only 4 percent to 9 percent of money raised from underreported income would come from those earning more than $500,000. That's because the superrich have an army of accountants and lawyers who make IRS enforcement costly, and who often win. JCT explained that 78 percent to 90 percent of revenue would come from those making less than $200,000 a year. Particularly hard hit would be small businesses that file under the individual tax code. House Budget Committee Republican leader Jason Smith got it right, explaining that the real purpose of the money was to unleash an army of IRS agents "to search under the couch cushions of every living room in America for more money, to audit and harass families just trying to get by."

Yellen, whose Treasury Department oversees the IRS, tried to change the narrative by sending a letter to IRS Commissioner Charles Rettig that insisted the new enforcement money "shall not be used to *increase the share* of small business or households below the $400,000 threshold that are audited." (Italics added.) All Yellen was really promising was that audits wouldn't be disproportionately aimed at those households—not that they wouldn't increase. Democrats gave away the game when during debate on the bill Republican senator Mike Crapo offered an amendment barring the IRS from using *any* of the new enforcement money for audits on those earning less than $400,000. Every Democrat voted it down. The left wasn't able to raise the top individual tax rate; putting the IRS in beast mode was its fallback plan.

Biden signed the bill in August 2022, even as new government statistics showed that tax receipts—both individual and corporate—continued to soar, providing the government with plenty enough money for current operations. And he threw nearly half a trillion dollars more into an economy that reported an eye-watering 8.5 percent inflation in July 2022. Hilariously, Biden promised his latest spending bill "tackles inflation" by "lowering costs for regular families."

On the brink

American companies faced other threats during those first two Biden years. Warren in May 2022 showed her 1970s stripes by introducing a bill to punish companies engaging in what she called "price gouging." The proposal amounted to the resurrection of price controls, just by another name. It would have allowed the Federal Trade Commission to impose huge penalties on larger companies that sold goods or services at an "unconscionably excessive price" during periods of "market shock." The kicker was that the bureaucrats got to define what counted as "excessive." Nixon-era price controls had phenomenally backfired. When governments tell producers that they can't sell beyond a certain price, their response is to withhold supply, causing shortages and an explosion of prices when the controls come off. The proposal mercifully went nowhere.

Businesses were meanwhile spared at least a few of the Biden supply slaps, after courts stepped in to halt obviously illegal actions. That included overturning the Centers for Disease Control's moratorium on evictions (which was crushing landlords) and the administration's sweeping vaccine mandate for private employers.

But overall, Biden managed to create a business environment far worse than the Carter years. In the first quarter of 2021—as Biden was stepping into office—the Conference Board survey of CEO confidence hit 73, the highest mark recorded in seventeen years. By the beginning of the fourth quarter of 2022—after Biden's triple whammy of spending, tax hikes, and new regulation—it had fallen to 32. The Conference Board noted these were "lows not seen since the depths of the Great Recession"—the 2008–09 housing bust. The survey found that 98 percent of CEOs were preparing for a U.S. recession, and 34 percent (the largest category by far) said the biggest challenge facing their company was "political and governmental instability." Even as that survey was released, U.S. businesses had started new rounds of layoffs.

Washington Democrats ratcheted up demand to enormous levels, but simultaneously ratcheted down the supply of labor, goods, and services with mandates, regulations, and new taxes. It was a textbook case of supply-demand mismatch. And most depressing was that it was purposeful.

When Biden unveiled his first budget in May 2021, his economists estimated that U.S. growth would average below 1.9 percent for much of the rest of the decade. Such a low number is what economists call secular stagnation—something that usually worries presidents. The Biden team by contrast embraced it. If low growth was the price to be paid for higher taxes to create handouts and more regulations to punish business—so be it.

The administration may well get its wish—or worse. By the first quarter of 2023, you couldn't find an economist who wasn't predicting recession. Bloomberg News in an early January article put it this way: "Barclays Capital Inc. says 2023 will go down as one of the worst for the world economy in four decades. Ned Davis Research Inc. puts the odds of a severe global downturn at 65 percent. Fidelity International reckons a hard landing looks unavoidable." But it *was* avoidable. Biden made the choice to pursue a rabidly anti-business agenda, drowning the market in new regulations and taxes. He took a hammer to the supply side just when the economy needed growth the most. The United States is the linchpin of that global economy, and Biden's war on his own business community is playing a big part in the brewing economic storm.

CHAPTER 4

THE UNJOLLY GREEN GIANT

"Are interest rates higher than Carter's IQ?"
"Keep the Canal, give Carter to Panama!"
"Don't blame me, I voted for Ford!"
"President Carter, KISS MY GAS!"

These were just a few of the bumper stickers of the late 1970s, though it's the last one that proved most popular on fenders. Americans had differing views on many Carter policies. But pretty much *everyone* hated Carter's energy agenda.

And justifiably. Home heating oil prices more than doubled from the beginning to the end of Carter's term. Electricity prices marched up, and up. Gas prices when Carter took office were $2.46 a gallon, according to ABC News. They'd climbed nearly 50 percent by the time he ran for reelection, and that was in addition to gas rationing, gas lines, and gas shortages. Stuart Eizenstat, Carter's top domestic policy adviser, once joked to *Time* magazine that even the Oval Office staff felt the pain. "I had to wait 30 minutes in line [for gas] to get to the White House to deal with the problem of the gas lines." A stagnant economy made it hard for even the employed to make their inflation-whipped paychecks cover the energy bills.

Energy policy is the one area where Carter and Biden are near awful doppelgangers. Carter beats today's president on one crucial score: He embraced domestic energy production. He understood the need to make the United States less dependent on OPEC oil and was an advocate for more U.S.-produced oil, gas, and coal. Carter, remember, helped deregulate the oil and gas industry.

But Carter was also in thrall to the country's earliest version of the environmental lobby, and their pitch struck a personal chord. The skin-flinty farmer looked down his nose at anything he saw as waste, and he complained frequently about what he viewed as an overindulgent American lifestyle. He was at heart a Malthusian and saw conservation as necessary and patriotic—the only thing that would prepare the country for coming resource depletion. Carter's deeply held religious convictions also played a part; he viewed it as his God-given duty to shepherd God-given natural resources. He actually called his energy challenge "the moral equivalent of war." Whatever small progress Carter made toward unshackling energy supply was crushed by the mountain of green laws and regulations he enacted.

In a much scarier way, Biden is in thrall to the modern incarnation of that environmental movement: the quasi religion known as climate activism. Carter might have failed to fix fissures in the energy sector. But Biden took the strongest energy market America had ever known—and broke it.

An "unpleasant talk"

Carter didn't intend to instantly jump into the energy arena, but the weather had other ideas. January 1977 produced an unusual cold wave across the country. Acute shortages of natural gas, home heating oil, and electricity forced blackouts; factories and schools closed. A fierce end-of-the-month blizzard pushed the wind chill factor in parts of Minnesota to a hundred degrees below zero, destroyed Florida's citrus crops, and cut off Buffalo from civilization for days. (NB: extreme weather was around 50 years ago, long before environmentalists started linking it to climate change.)

Carter's first response—made within a day of being in office—was to ask Americans to turn their thermostats down to fifty-five degrees at night. The nation—already shivering in the cold snap—collectively groaned. His second response was to demand Congress give him emergency authority to redirect natural gas supplies between the states. It did—and this accomplished precisely nothing.

The problem was that the United States was operating with no room for energy error. Washington's impossible web of oil, gas, and coal regulations hampered domestic production. American oil production peaked in 1970, after which it began steadily growing its oil imports—primarily from OPEC countries. Nixon made the situation worse with his 1971 wage-and-price controls, which he also applied to oil and gas. Seeing no chance for profit, domestic energy companies scaled back production more. Then, in 1973, OPEC countries cut oil shipments to the U.S., in protest of U.S. support for Israel. The embargo lasted only a few months, but the combination of all these factors kept supplies tight, and even minor disruptions caused price spikes or shortages.

Carter in April 1977 presented Congress with what he called the nation's first comprehensive energy policy. Congress wouldn't pass it for another eighteen months as they bickered over details. But the issue wasn't so much the timing as the contents. Carter gave a national address to explain his plan and made it clear he subscribed to the liberal, apocalyptic view of that time: The world was running out of resources. "I want to have an unpleasant talk with you," he opened, going on to explain that at current rates, humanity was on track to use up all its proven oil reserves in little more than a decade. Put another way, Carter believed the globe would be out of oil by 1990. Conservative economists had vigorously refuted professor Paul Ehrlich and his doom-and-gloom crowd, which predicted population bombs, global famine, and energy depletion. But Carter bought in to it all. "Ours is the most wasteful nation on earth," he chided, and said the answer was "conservation," which would solve both the nation's energy and environmental problems.

Carter, to his credit, didn't give up on production. Even as he heaped abuse on the oil-and-gas industry, baselessly accusing them of gouging and playing a role in high prices, he prodded Congress to pass the National Energy Act of 1978. The law contained some incentives for more oil and gas drilling, and set the framework for ongoing decontrol of the natural-gas market. He also pushed through initiatives to increase the use of coal. The country's later oil-and-gas renaissance traces some of its origins to this period.

But the rest of the bill—and Carter's additional actions—were all focused on forcing frugality, by raising prices, pushing transitions to "renewables," and generally having government manage energy use.

Carter instituted a sweeping new addition to the national bureaucracy: the Department of Energy. It helped cement the idea that the federal government needs to set and direct national energy policy, a position that continues to undermine energy markets today. The only thing worse than 535 members of Congress coming together to spend money is 535 members of Congress using energy legislation to prop up their pet industries (wood chips, ethanol, solar-panel makers, algae, palm biodiesel) at the expense of the American consumer.

The law also contained the first considered effort to use generous tax incentives to change energy production and use. The bill rewarded utilities that transitioned to wind and solar. It simultaneously made it harder for power plants to use natural gas or oil as their primary energy source, keeping demand for those products artificially low and further decreasing investment in those industries. Add in efficiency standards for new construction and for appliances, and federal dollars for weatherization grants and other boondoggles.

And that was just the 1978 legislation. Carter in office also passed major new amendments to the Clean Air Act, ratcheting up auto emissions standards. He changed the Clean Water Act in 1977 to give government more intrusive control over areas of the United States like wetlands. He turbocharged the relatively young Environmental Protection Agency; it bombarded industry with costly new disclosure rules and bans on entire categories of products. One of his last acts was to sign a bill putting EPA in charge of a new Superfund program—a toxic waste cleanup program that has to date cost hundreds of billions of dollars yet remains mired in bureaucratic inertia and legal disputes. His other brilliant plan was to create the Synthetic Fuels Corporation, which over its short and embarrassing life blew nearly $1 billion on cockamamie ideas to replace crude oil. And let's never forget his decision to put solar panels on the White House.

Carter's administration was so busy hectoring people about the efficiency of their washing machines that it failed to take the most obvious step to help domestic production. Nixon lifted most of his wage and price controls in 1973 but left them in place for oil and gas. Carter didn't begin to phase them out until 1979, a delay that even his advisers later admitted took a terrible toll on production. C. Fred Bergsten, a Carter Treasury official, told the *New York Times* in 2022 that the price controls were an "abysmal failure" that "discourage[d] production and held down the supply side over time."

Even as Carter got rid of that boneheaded idea, he replaced it with another. Fearing the lifting of controls would cause prices to skyrocket, Carter asked for and received from Congress legislation allowing him to impose that windfall profits tax in 1980. All it did was stifle production.

The 1979 Iranian revolution tightened global production yet again, and prices soared. Carter's failure through his tenure to truly get serious about production—to stop obsessing on conservation—meant the United States once again faced shortages, long gas lines, and (if you were me) angry mothers. It left a sour mood just as the country geared up for another presidential election and played a huge role in Reagan's victory.

Reagan would remove the remaining price controls on petroleum products, build on Carter's deregulation, and unleash a domestic energy industry that would in the 1980s embark on what became America's "shale revolution." By 2019, the U.S. had hit a milestone Carter never would have thought possible: It became a net energy exporter. All it took was a little economic freedom.

Then came Biden.

Twelve years to doomsday

The 1970s taught the country the hard way the cost of backward energy policy. Inhibiting fossil-fuel production puts a nation at risk. Conservation and alternative energy will not save the day. Energy independence is key. A happy, prosperous U.S. is predicated on cheap and reliable energy (and politicians want happy, prosperous voters).

Every president since Carter understood these takeaways—including Democrats. Clinton wasn't hostile to federal drilling, and even signed a bill in 1996—supported by industry—to simplify the royalty process. Obama banged on about climate and made federal resource extraction much harder. But he also cynically knew he could get away with it. He made a point to not get in the way of a fracking revolution that was happening on private land and keeping prices low.

Biden inherited one of the strongest energy markets in the country's history. We were the largest oil and gas producer on the globe. Gas prices were low. Electricity prices were low. Heating costs were low. Importantly, Biden also inherited a country that was the leader in carbon reductions. The United States' rapid transition to natural gas had resulted in the largest decreases of carbon emissions of any developed nation on the planet. Biden could have followed in Obama's footsteps: Put a few symbolic drilling sites off-limits, cut back on leases, throw more money at renewables; kumbaya with the global community at the next United Nations climate change conference.

But something big had changed since Obama. Democrats began to understand the degree to which they could leverage climate hysteria. The logic goes like this: If—as progressive Alexandria Ocasio-Cortez insists—we will "destroy the planet" in twelve years without rapid carbon elimination, it becomes imperative for government to quickly restructure every aspect of American life. Not just energy markets and consumption—everything. That's convenient if you are in the business of government control.

AOC showed the sweep of her ambitions in early 2019 with her introduction of the Green New Deal—a plan to rapidly get rid of all carbon emissions. The text of her resolution was near hysterical—it explained that climate change was causing "sea levels to rise, and an increase in wildfires, severe storms, droughts, and other extreme weather events that threaten human life." (None of this has been proven by science.) The resolution claimed climate change would cause "mass migration" and $500 billion in lost U.S. economic output annually, and the death of most coral on the planet and an end to Christmas (kidding, but it could have been in there). It laid out progressive plans to take over pretty much every aspect of American life—in a period of ten years.

The deal called to eliminate most fossil fuels. It would get rid of every "combustion-engine" in existence—cars, boats, planes, trucks, but also lawn mowers, weed eaters, generators, all-terrain vehicles, you name it. Like cooking with gas? Too bad. Like your historic home? Again, too bad. The bill called to retrofit every building in the country. The initial talking points also laid out a plan to make American vegan, getting rid of meat production, since cow farts increase emissions.

Most notable, because this transition would cause upheaval, the talking points explained that government also needed to guarantee every American a job that included a "family-sustaining wage, family and medical leave, vacations and a pension," while also providing "economic security" to those "unable or unwilling" to work. Think about that statement. It also called for free college and trade school for all. Senator Ed Markey, who cosponsored the Green New Deal resolution with AOC, put out a press release that underlined how Democrats were hijacking the environment as an excuse for the rest of their agenda. The Green New Deal would "enforce labor standards, guarantee rights to retirement security and health care, and conduct inclusive decisionmaking." Oh, and the release added—almost as an afterthought—it would also address "the existential challenge of climate change." Good to know.

This is how Democrats take a discreet environmental problem and turn it into a mandate to dictate how we live, where we live, what we eat, what we earn, and what we own. My middle child, only eight at the time AOC released her plan, watched the TV news report from our home in Alaska and snarfed part of her dinner. "Tell you what," she said, "when nutso lady shows me how to swim from Anchorage to Seattle, I'll sign up for her plan to get rid of airplanes."

My eight-year-old got it, but Biden didn't. He cynically chose to embrace the climate "existential threat" as the central rationale for his agenda. On the campaign trail he'd quietly spelled it out. "No more drilling on federal lands, no more drilling including offshore—no ability for the oil industry to continue to drill—period." No one believed such a crazy declaration, but they should have.

Calling climate the "No. 1 issue facing humanity," Biden oriented his entire government around this priority. He grandly signed the United States back up for the Paris climate accords. He chose former senator John Kerry as his new climate envoy and turned the position into a cabinet-level post. He brought back former EPA administrator Gina McCarthy and made her domestic climate czar. Every cabinet head—from Commerce to Interior to Veterans Affairs—was told to structure their agenda around the climate threat. How on earth, you ask, does the Department of Veterans Affairs prioritize climate? See the department's August 2021 "Climate action plan," which contemplates, among other things, changing the terms of its home loan program for veterans who choose to live on a coast or in a forest—given the greater risk from supposedly climate-caused hurricanes or wildfires.

Biden, in direct contrast to Carter, made no bones about his ambition to kill off domestic supply of fossil fuels. His first-day actions took a wrecking ball to every part of the domestic energy industry, erasing with the stroke of his pen tens of billions in investment and years of dealmaking, from the Keystone XL Pipeline to exploration activities on federal lands, including Alaska's Arctic National Wildlife Refuge. He put some one hundred energy and environmental policies on pause, pending review, hamstringing thousands of planned industry actions.

The president wasn't interested in just stopping *current* projects. Equally damaging was the administration's work to block fossil-fuel companies from pursuing *future* development. Drilling is a costly and long-term planning exercise that involves years of exploration and permitting. This is why Congress mandates the U.S. government produce five-year offshore leasing plans and why the Interior Department holds rolling auctions—to provide industry with necessary lead times.

Yet in early January 2021, the administration announced it was imposing a pause on all oil and gas leasing on public lands while it conducted an environmental review. This was code for no more drilling. A federal judge a few months later ruled the pause a violation of congressional statute and ordered Interior to resume sales. Yet the administration used every opportunity to delay. In

November 2021 it finally held one auction in the Gulf of Mexico, though the sale was conveniently struck down by a liberal judge.

By the spring of 2022, with no planned auction in sight, the industry was facing a potential three-year gap in the sale of new leases. Manchin grew so frustrated by the delay that he insisted on a provision in the Inflation Reduction Act to require the administration to engage in further lease sales by specific dates. The *Wall Street Journal* reported in September 2022 that the administration had leased fewer acres offshore and on federal lands than any presidency in its early stages dating to the end of World War II—back when Harry S. Truman was in charge and offshore drilling was only beginning. Leasing was down a shocking 97 percent from the first nineteen months of Trump.

The administration also dragged its feet in releasing a new five-year offshore plan, and what it did release in the summer of 2022 further shocked the industry. Its draft envisioned holding up to eleven sales off the coast of Alaska and the Gulf of Mexico. But it also put forward the equal possibility of holding *zero* lease sales in the 2023–28 period. Interior Secretary Deb Haaland didn't leave anyone guessing which option she preferred: "From Day One, President Biden and I have made clear our commitment to transition to a clean energy economy," she said. To put this in perspective, the Trump proposal for the same time period envisioned forty-seven sales.

Meanwhile, the administration began to slow-walk permitting for companies that had already won leases. *Politico* in March 2022 noted that the number of gas and oil permits issued by the Bureau of Land Management for federal lands had "plunged" to just 95 in January 2022—compared to more than six hundred a month that were happening in the period as Biden took office.

But killing off fossil fuels requires much more than just locking up federal lands—and green radicals know it. Oil production from federal lands and waters amounts to about 24 percent of total U.S. oil production. Natural gas from these lands is about 11 percent of overall natural gas production. The rest is conducted on state or private lands. Obama turned a blind eye to state and private fracking, since it benefited him politically to have cheap oil and gas. But the environmental lobby grew wise to this political maneuver and was determined not to let it happen under another Democratic president. It began lobbying candidate Biden early in the game to be more sweeping, and he agreed.

So how do you run carbon fuels into an early grave? Use broader federal regulations to make it harder and more costly for producers to drill anywhere. And also make it harder and costlier for consumers (in particular businesses) to continue their use of fossil fuels.

Enter that SEC rule mentioned in the last chapter. Gensler's emissions disclosure regime would require every public company to confess to its fossil-fuel use, and to make that confession annual, expensive, and risky (regulators don't like it when companies get disclosure wrong). The forced "transparency" is particularly targeted at fossil-fuel producers—including those operating exclusively on state and private lands. Environmentalists are eager to use each new disclosure as an opportunity to berate companies for production, to blame them for continued climate disasters, and to bully them into pulling back.

But the goal is to do the same to *users* of fossil fuels, which are also required under the rule to disclose their carbon emissions, and those of their customers and supply chains. The next time a Disney or a General Electric admits to an expansion of their carbon footprint (rather than a reduction), environmentalists will mobilize protests and push activist shareholders to demand year-on-year reductions. This won't stop until companies commit to net-zero emissions, which in turn will put new pressure on utilities to switch to renewables, which in turn will push more companies to go green—and on and on the circle goes.

The left already knows how well this weaponized disclosure can work. Years ago it backed a new "environmental, social and governance" (ESG) movement, to hound and push public companies into woke agendas. The ESG machine has grown so large that many companies are reluctant to become its targets and preemptively surrender. Just one example: Banking giant Goldman Sachs decided in 2019 that it would no longer finance new oil exploration, prompting other Wall Street banks to follow suit.

The feds have plenty of other tools they can use to block state or private drilling. Consider the Biden administration's aggressive new embrace of the Endangered Species Act. Despite all the attention it receives, the species act has a dismal record of actually aiding any plant or animal and is in desperate need of overhaul. But climate activists prefer it in its current blunt and sweeping form. Any species listed as endangered or threatened is given special protections, and those protections apply no matter the geography—federal land, private land, state land, tribal land.

Here's an example of its power. The Obama administration in 2014 sought to list as threatened the lesser prairie chicken, a type of grouse. Some 95 percent of the bird's range falls on private property across Texas, New Mexico, Kansas, Oklahoma, and Colorado. This just happens to overlap the Permian basin, one of the most productive shale fields in the United States. A federal judge in 2015 blocked the listing, saying the administration hadn't done enough to consider alternatives. That spurred the oil and gas industry, states, conservationists, and private landholders to come together on a wide-ranging plan to help the bird. Oil and gas companies alone contributed some $60 million to the effort. And a study in 2020 for the Western Association of Fish and Wildlife Agencies found the bird's population had nearly doubled since 2014.

But environmentalists sued, and the Biden administration used that as an excuse five months into office to relist the bird as endangered—a move that will potentially undermine years of innovative public-private partnership. Climate activists see the listing as a twofer——it not only strikes a dagger at Permian Basin drilling but will also wreak havoc in those states' agricultural sectors, including meat production. Republicans were quick to call out the administration's power grab and its motives. Kansas senator Roger Marshall railed that "private property in [the lesser prairie chicken] range might as well be federal lands if this egregious policy goes into effect," and noted that the real targets were "Kansans who raise cattle for your hamburgers and drill oil for your gasoline."

He's right. The saddest part of the relisting is that the administration could care less about the bird itself. Recent history has shown that deals that ensure cooperation between business, landowners, and state entities are far more successful at aiding flora and fauna than the rigid, outdated species act. The administration is reembracing the statute for one reason alone: to kill fossil fuels.

Here's another administration trick: Going after what ends up in the air, rather than what comes out of the ground. The Clean Air Act, passed in the 1970s, allows government to police air pollution. The U.S. Supreme Court in a misguided decision in 2007 ruled that the government was allowed to decide whether carbon dioxide counted as said pollution. The Obama administration rapidly moved to do so, and today the EPA asserts authority over any number of greenhouse gases.

That includes methane, a gas that environmentalists say contributes more dramatically to global warming than even carbon dioxide. Methane is emitted at natural gas well sites, and the EPA had already asserted its right to police emissions at newly drilled wells. The Biden administration in late 2021 announced its intention to dramatically expand that control, to now monitor every oil and gas wellhead in existence——*old or new.* It later expanded the scope to include even the smallest wells from private developers, which the EPA can more easily hound out of existence. You might think an administration would be embarrassed to attack small businesses. Not this one. White House national climate adviser Ali Zaidi explained the team's "relentless focus to root out emissions wherever we can find them."

And let's not forget vehicles. Climate activists consider gas-consuming engines public enemy number one, even as the public adores them. The Biden administration turned to an old standby—the fuel efficiency standards first implemented in the 1970s. Trump had asked automakers to hit a fleetwide average of forty miles per gallon by 2025—no easy task given the vast majority of Americans continue to prefer bigger vehicles (in the first four months of 2022, 73 percent of total passenger car sales were SUVs or pickup trucks). By the end of his first year Biden had set a mind-numbing new mandate of 55 mpg by 2026. Up to now, automakers had managed to sell just enough tiny or electric cars to pull down fleet averages enough to hit the targets. Now, the only way for automakers to meet these aggressive goals will be to phase out popular, bigger models.

Which is the point—forced transition. The federal government has for years tried to lure Americans into electric vehicles. It has shoveled hundreds of billions of dollars to automakers to aid them in producing EVs that most Americans don't want to buy. And it has offered hundreds of billions more to Americans in the form of subsidies as a reward if they buy a costly EV they don't want. Yet 99 percent of the passenger fleet remains gas or diesel driven. So now the administration intends to take away any choice.

And as a back-up enforcer, they have "Mayor Pete," Biden's Transportation secretary. In July 2022, Buttigieg's Federal Highway Administration announced a huge expansion of its remit. It claims that since federal law allows it to set performance goals for the national highway system, it now has authority to regulate CO_2 emissions on those roads. It will require states to submit to the federal government plans for "declining targets for reductions for tailpipe CO_2 emissions" on the highways that run through their states. It isn't clear how states are supposed to measure any of this. Random checks of tailpipe emissions at weigh stations? Don't ask Mayor Pete. He rolled out the rule, explaining "we don't have a moment to waste," but left the pesky details to the states. He explained he was giving them "flexibility."

The Putin oil shock

Carter governed through the nightmare of a country that wasn't prepared for another global oil shock. Biden lived through that time, too. Biden sat in a Senate that in 1979 approved a Carter standby rationing plan for gasoline. You'd have thought the memory of the nation's gas lines would stick with him as a warning.

If the '70s didn't leave a lasting imprint, Biden could have turned to the more recent warning from Europe—an early adopter of climate hysteria. Only a decade ago, the global oil and gas industry was looking to replicate America's shale revolution in Europe, which has plenty of its own shale fields. But mass protests against fracking cowed Europe's politicians, and the continent's gas production has plunged by half over the past ten years.

At the same time, lefty European leaders began aggressively subsidizing renewable energy and shutting down their coal plants to satisfy their commitments under the UN climate accords. Yet it is a well-known fact (except, apparently, among European leaders) that the wind does not always blow and the sun does not always shine. Funny that. Countries still need fossil fuels to fill in the gap. This came home hard in the summer and fall of 2021 as Europeans suddenly found themselves short on wind, even more short on fossil fuels, and facing a full-blown energy crisis.

A proximate cause was Vladimir Putin. Even as Europe had shut down its own fossil production, it dramatically increased its imports from Russia. In what was in retrospect preparation for war, Putin in 2021 began slowing his exports to the continent, draining gas-storage facilities and making countries like Germany even more reliant on his day-to-day supplies. Europe offered itself up for extortion, and Putin was happy to oblige.

On February 24, Russia launched a large-scale invasion of Ukraine—Europe's largest ground war since World War II. Prices had already been rising in the United States, thanks to Biden's climate policies. Inflation was also taking a toll. Post-Covid consumers were demanding more energy, pushing up prices. In the first thirteen months Biden was in office, gasoline went from $2.39 a gallon to $3.53 a gallon—a 48 percent increase. Home heating oil went from $2.57 a gallon to $3.96—a 54 percent increase. And this was before Putin's invasion.

In a way, things were going entirely to plan. Climate alarmists want to get rid of fossil fuels, and economics tells us the quickest way to strangle a product is to make it cost more. That's why the left remains in favor of carbon taxes. Biden went about it by stifling production, and successfully. At the time of Putin's invasion, U.S. production was a hefty 1.5 million barrels a day below pre-pandemic levels and 15 percent below a 2019 government forecast of where industry would be at that time.

Yet Democrats have never reconciled their goal of pricing out fossil fuels with the reality of the political fallout. And Russia's invasion made the politics increasingly ugly. Russia continued slowing exports to Europe, tightening supplies across the globe, while a diminished U.S. industry was unable to add any slack. As Louisiana Republican senator John Kennedy likes to quip, Biden's energy policy comes down to "wind, solar and wishful thinking." None of which offered any resilience in the wake of Putin's invasion.

Biden found himself in a situation much like Carter's in 1979—only this one was largely self-engineered. Prices for gas, heating fuel, propane, diesel, and electricity soared. And it came just as the Biden spending blowouts were triggering inflation in other areas. The inflation rate in January 2022 was already at 7.5 percent. By June it had hit 9.1 percent. And the midterms were coming.

The obvious solution—from both policy and politics perspectives—

was for Biden to make a simple speech declaring an end to his war on U.S. production. He didn't have to abandon his climate goals. He could have simply explained that the outbreak of war was a wake-up call, reminding America that energy is crucial to national security and economic growth, and that the globe cannot afford to abandon the field to tyrants. Transition to cleaner energy is possible, just along more realistic timelines.

Biden instead resorted to blame shifting and gimmicks. He began referring to the run-up in energy prices as "Putin's price hike." Only that didn't explain why prices had been soaring in the United States well before February 2022. Taking a leaf from Carter, he also tried dumping blame on various sectors of the oil and gas industry. He accused drillers of "war profiteering" and threatened to resurrect the windfall profits tax. He blasted oil refineries, falsely accusing them of cutting back on production to pad profits. He even tried blaming mom-and-pop gas station owners, tweeting a warning over the July 4 weekend in 2022. "Bring down the price you are charging at the pump to reflect the cost you're paying for the product. And do it now." The president got roasted for that one, as it suggested he lacked the most basic understanding of market dynamics.

As for gimmicks, the administration started releasing oil from the Strategic Petroleum Reserve, and insisting this action was reducing prices. By September 2022, Biden had released more oil from the reserve than all other presidents combined. The releases might have affected prices by pennies at the margin, but at a far greater national security cost. The SPR sat at its lowest level since the 1980s, unable to provide much of a cushion if the United States were confronted with a true emergency.

Biden also took to begging. He traveled to Saudi Arabia in July 2022 to ask the kingdom, and other OPEC nations, to produce more. And the administration in the fall secretly pleaded with Saudi Arabia to convince OPEC to delay a planned cut in production—until after the midterm election. No agenda there!

Yet Biden's high-handed approach to the Saudis (see chapter 5) in the opening year of his presidency had won him few friends, and on both occasions his pleas were ignored.

It was nonetheless stunning to see the president beg OPEC to save the United States from its own misguided decisions. Carter knew OPEC posed a direct threat to the U.S., and he took steps to make America more resilient. Biden put his climate agenda ahead of U.S. security, safety, and economic well-being.

The worst part of Biden's climate agenda is that it's undermining the U.S. economy and global standing—*for absolutely no purpose.* Even the most radical U.S. reductions won't make a whit of difference to global temperatures. India, Africa, and China continue to ramp up emissions in their quest to become developed regions. Under the nonbinding Paris accords, China plans to continue emitting freely. The nonprofit Global Energy Monitor notes that as of July 2022, China had 258 coal-fired power stations in planning or under construction.

Scientist Bjørn Lomborg ran the numbers on what would happen to global temperatures if every signatory to the Paris climate accords fulfilled every one of their commitments by 2030. Total temperature reduction would be 0.048 degrees Celsius by 2100. And if they fulfilled all promises for a further seventy years? They would reduce temperature rises by 0.17 degrees Celsius. For this, Biden is willing to take away your diesel pickup truck, your lawn mower, and your ability to cook with gas.

Democrats insist their climate agenda is popular, but not one piece of evidence supports that claim. Polls routinely show climate at the bottom of the list of most things Americans care about—especially when they vote. By contrast, the climate agenda is contributing to soaring costs and economic malaise, things American voters put at the top of their list of concerns. And it isn't just prices anymore that are worrying them. The rapid switch to renewables is making areas of the country vulnerable to surprise weather, leading to increasing blackouts.

Biden's climate agenda has been brutal for average households. Energy inflation takes its hugest toll on lower-income households, since they devote a greater share of their income to energy needs. The higher the prices, the less there is for anything else. In exit polls conducted for CNN during the 2022 midterms, three-quarters of voters said the economy was "poor" or "not good," and two-thirds said gas prices had caused them hardship.

Biden might have only narrowly lost the House in those midterms, but he still lost it—and his climate agenda bears part of the blame. Those same exit polls found that for the nearly third of voters who said inflation (which includes energy inflation) was their top issue in deciding who to vote for in the House, 70 percent of them voted for Republicans.

And yet as the midterm dust settled, Biden still refused to course-correct. In remarks on the Wednesday after the election, the president crowed that the drubbing had not been as bad as expected and so "I don't have to change any of the policies that have already passed."

Carter clung to his environmental religion to the bitter end, and Biden looks set to do the same.

CHAPTER 5

OPERATION DISASTER

Carter officially lost reelection on November 4, 1980. But his presidency unofficially died on April 24 of that year.

In November 1979, militant Iranian students, in thrall to their revolution and furious over America's support for the deposed shah, overran the U.S. embassy in Tehran and took fifty-two American citizens hostage. Carter engaged in fruitless negotiations for more than five months before deciding to launch a military rescue.

Operation Eagle Claw was an unmitigated disaster. Deltas, Rangers, special forces, and CIA agents were tasked with assaulting the embassy and Ministry of Foreign Affairs, as well as seizing an airbase to aid in escape. But the operation fell apart before the assault even began; equipment was damaged on the way in, and two aircraft collided in the desert, causing an explosion. Eight servicemen died and two more were badly wounded. Helicopters and classified mission documents were abandoned for the Iranians to seize. Carter ultimately agreed to free to Iran some $8 billion in frozen assets to secure the hostages' release. Even then, Iran waited until after Carter left office to finally free the Americans.

Joe Biden didn't even make it seven months before engineering his own overseas debacle. After twenty years of U.S. support for Afghanistan, Trump in his final months set a timeline for troop withdrawal. Biden's advisers—both military and civilian—warned the new president that this plan was too rapid. They advised Biden to maintain a residual force in the country, to aid the Afghani government in holding off the Taliban.

Biden, convinced of his own genius, ignored them all and publicly announced in April that every troop would be out by the symbolic but arbitrary date of September 11, 2021. The Taliban took that as an invitation to go on the march, and they captured Kabul on August 15—forcing a chaotic, humiliating U.S. evacuation, during which a suicide bomber killed thirteen U.S. service members. The United States meanwhile abandoned in country thousands of Afghanis who had aided it during the conflict and now had targets on their backs.

These twin foreign policy calamities have provoked plenty of Carter-Biden comparisons. And there are certainly similarities in their foreign policy. Both preferred a noninterventionist approach. Both preferred diplomacy over shows of American strength. Both neglected defense budgets. Both sat idle as American adversaries grew in power and belligerence.

But once again, the connection is somewhat unfair to Carter. Carter believed in U.S. leadership. His problem was a foreign policy that was overly idealistic and a mess of conflicting priorities. He knew what he *didn't* want his foreign policy to look like—that of Henry Kissinger's realpolitik. He just never managed to formulate anything that was coherent as a replacement. Add to this inexperience and naïveté. The result was a medley of contradictory human rights initiatives and diplomatic forays that left America more vulnerable and that emboldened our enemies.

Biden's foreign policy is equally incoherent—but with this notable difference: He doesn't *want* the burden of global leadership. Like Obama, he prefers to "lead from behind" the skirts of multilateral institutions. He bragged in Europe in June 2021 that "America is back" as the leader of global democracies. But the boastful speeches have produced little of substance. His interest is in grandstanding on vogue issues like climate change, and his real priority (as every rogue across the globe can see) is radical, structural transformation of his own country. There is also his terrible judgment, of the sort that produced the chaos of Afghanistan. Like Carter he's leaving America far weaker, and it's a reason why Putin felt free to invade Ukraine, why Iran is stepping up its plans for nuclear weapons, and why China aggressively chose to send a spy balloon over the U.S. homeland and is increasingly hostile toward Taiwan.

Biden's lack of leadership couldn't come at a worse time. Carter was president as a long chapter in foreign policy was ending—the Cold War was giving way to a remarkable rise of democracy around the world. Biden now presides over another shift—a growing global disorder in which tyrants from Moscow to Beijing to Tehran seek to dominate bigger pieces of the globe. The world desperately needs a strong and unwavering United States.

Human rights or righteousness?

Carter certainly had his goals. He felt the country had become overly preoccupied with Soviet containment, and that it would benefit more from a U.S. that engaged in *moral* leadership.

But translating hifalutin ambitions into a realistic foreign policy is hard—as Carter quickly discovered. Just a day after inauguration, Andrei Sakharov, the Russian physicist and activist, wrote a letter asking the new president to aid those fighting for democracy in the Soviet Union and Eastern Europe. Carter vowed to do just that, in a letter that Sakharov made public in February—to huge headlines. Carter met with exiled and outspoken Soviet dissident Vladimir Bukovsky in March, and also delivered a human rights speech to the United Nations. One particular passage infuriated the Kremlin: "All signatories of the UN Charter have pledged themselves to observe and respect basic human rights. Thus, no member of the United Nations can claim that mistreatment of its citizens is solely its own business."

So far so noble. Yet also at the top of Carter's foreign policy agenda was arms control with the Soviets, particularly his ambition to cement a second round of the Strategic Arms Limitation Talks (SALT). Carter seemed to think he could simply delink his objectives—that he could both berate the Soviets for their treatment of dissidents and also get them to kumbaya on an arms deal.

The Soviets gave him plenty of warnings that this was not to be the case. A Soviet press attack on Bukovsky in the lead-up to his White House meeting was essentially a demand by Moscow for Carter to call it off. And Soviet premier Leonid Brezhnev responded to Carter's UN address with his own speech: "We will not tolerate interference in our internal affairs by anyone and under any pretext. A normal development of relations on such a basis is, of course, unthinkable." Unsurprisingly, when Secretary of State Cyrus Vance showed up in Moscow at the end of March to push deep cuts in arms, the Soviets sent him packing. Carter wouldn't get his SALT II agreement until June 1979. And the imminent Soviet invasion of Afghanistan would doom Senate ratification.

These contradictions and tensions defined Carter's foreign policy. Who was a human rights abuser? Who wasn't? Just how bad of a bad guy did you have to be to get the American cold shoulder? The Carter administration was never able to say, and hard reality often forced it back to realpolitik principles.

The administration cut aid to Nicaragua—once regarded as Washington's strongest Central American ally—over President Anastasio Samoza's treatment of guerrilla Sandinistas. Carter's decision to stake out the moral high ground—to retreat from the country and to undermine the credibility of the government— helped give radical Sandinistas the upper hand, and Samoza fled in 1979. As Jeane Kirkpatrick explained in her brilliant 1979 essay "Dictatorships & Double Standards," the Carter administration

managed to replace in Nicaragua (and in Iran) "moderate autocrats friendly to American interests with less friendly autocrats of
extremist persuasion."

But even as the administration snubbed Samoza, Carter made
it his personal mission to work with a noxious autocrat—Omar
Torrijos—to give away the Panama Canal. Torrijos had come to
power in a 1968 coup that overthrew Panama's elected president.
He reigned supreme until his death in 1981. Going by the low-key
title "Maximum Leader of the Panamanian Revolution," Torrijos
shut down political activity, took over the media, and tortured
and killed opponents.

But Carter viewed U.S. control of the Panama Canal as immoral,
a "symbol of subjugation." He negotiated two treaties that ceded
control of a strategic asset that the United States had maintained
since 1903, and even shook Torrijos's hand at the signing. Amus-
ingly, Torrijos (briefly) lifted his restrictions on political parties
and the press for several weeks prior to Panama's public vote on
the treaties, to give the veneer of democratic ratification. Torrijos
was meanwhile replaced by an even bigger thug, Manuel Noriega,
who cracked down even harder on the Panamanian people.

On and on the contradictions went. The administration viciously
criticized the Pol Pot regime in Cambodia yet supported it keeping
its United Nations seat in the face of Vietnam's invasion. Carter
normalized relations with China despite that country's own brutal
human rights regime and its own invasion of Vietnam. He started
out hostile to Pakistan over its nuclear program and military
coup but switched support after the Soviets invaded Afghanistan.
Among the many human rights abusers Carter continued to support were Zaire's notorious Joseph Mobutu.

Meanwhile, how to balance human rights with self-determination?
Carter didn't know. As with Nicaragua, Iran proved that trying to
balance those contradictory goals was an exercise in self-defeat.
The shah of Iran, Mohammad Reza Pahlavi, was also an unelected
ruler—albeit one who had introduced economic reforms, and one

who remained a U.S. ally. Carter, in this case, maintained support for the autocrat, right up until the point when it really mattered. When the shah began to face public unrest and the rise of religious fanatics, Carter put Iranian self-determination ahead of strategic considerations or human rights, declaring that any decision was for "the Iranian people to make." Yet after the shah fled, Carter welcomed him to America to undergo cancer treatments, infuriating the new Iranian regime. Not long after, students stormed the embassy and demanded the shah's return to face trial as a condition for releasing U.S. hostages. Cue the effective end of Carter's presidency.

Carter's broad policy of nonintervention meanwhile sent a clear message of U.S. weakness to opponents. As his own national security adviser, Zbigniew Brzezinski would later write, Carter "did not fire enthusiasm in the public or inspire fear in his adversaries." The Soviet Union in particular used Carter's studious avoidance of conflict—and interest in an arms deal—to its benefit, ramping up its influence around the globe. It strengthened its control and proxies in the Caribbean, Southern Africa, and Eastern Africa. And in 1979 it invaded Afghanistan, seeking to cement its dominance over the chaotic country. Carter was caught flat-footed by an invasion that ended a long détente and threatened further Soviet advances in southwest Asia.

It did however give Carter a belated wake-up call. He asked the Senate to delay work on the SALT II ratification, strengthened ties with Cold War allies, and increased aid to mujahadeen fighters against the Soviets. He also finally started paying attention to defense budgets. Carter spent his first years attempting to cut defense—sending a terrible signal to adversaries. His final budget called for a real increase in military spending. Better late than never.

There were moments when Carter's personal diplomacy made a difference. In 1978 he oversaw an extraordinary thirteen-day summit between Israel's Menachem Begin and Egypt's Anwar Sadat that ended with the Camp David Accords. The subsequent peace agreement was the first between Israel and any of its Arab neighbors, and a model for the Oslo Accords, the Israel-Jordan peace treaty in 1994, and the Abraham Accords the Trump administration negotiated between Israel and the United Arab Emirates and Bahrain. Carter gets real credit for this groundbreaking moment.

He also gets credit for emphasizing democracy and rights. Reagan did the exact same thing: "Mr. Gorbachev, tear down this wall!" But Regan's emphasis on rights was rooted in reality, and in an understanding that American calls for democracy would count more when backed by military strength and resolve. Carter's mistake was thinking anyone would listen to a weak America.

Motormouth

Robert Gates served as George W. Bush's defense secretary, and Obama kept him on for several years. That gave Gates a close view of Vice President Joe Biden's foreign policy chops. In a later book, Gates offered this brutal assessment of the man who is now commander in chief: He "has been wrong on nearly every major foreign policy and national security issue over the past four decades." He's right, and he's not alone in that assessment. The late, great Charles Krauthammer in 2012 called Biden "the Herbert Hoover of American foreign policy." Biden was against Reagan's expansion of defense budgets, which ultimately bankrupted the Soviet Union. Biden opposed the 1991 Gulf War. He supported the invasion of Afghanistan but not the later surge that made the operation successful. He was even against the mission to get Osama bin Laden. Gates in general found Biden to be a "motormouth" who constantly presumed to know more about counterterrorism than four-star generals, and who frequently undermined and attacked the integrity of senior military officials.

It would appear time has done little to improve the situation.

Biden has instinct working against him. But he was also influenced heavily by his time in the Obama administration. Obama campaigned against the interventionism of George W. Bush, and replaced it with an all-in embrace of "multilateralism." In office, he pushed Congress to enact cuts to the military, promising to defend the United States with fewer resources.

When in 2011 America teamed up with the French and British to oust Moammar Gaddafi, Obama left the decision-making to the Europeans, a move that one of his advisers described as "leading from behind." It became a hallmark of the Obama presidency. He deferred to the Europeans in the handling of Putin. He let the Iraqis and Kurds take on ISIS in Iraq. He tapped the Saudis to deal with an insurgency in Yemen.

Yet at least Obama (especially when Gates was defense secretary) made clear he was willing to give fight on issues of particular strategic importance to the U.S. He approved troop increases in Afghanistan (even as he began withdrawing forces from Iraq). He significantly increased the number of drone strikes against terrorists. He took out bin Laden. And importantly, Obama used trade deals in an attempt to increase U.S. influence, in particular in Asia with his Trans-Pacific Partnership.

Biden by contrast has readopted the "lead from behind" strategy while sending repeated signals that the United States is more focused on domestic concerns than it is global stability. These signals have emboldened America's enemies and frustrated America's allies.

Signaling weak

Those signals started on day one, when Biden put climate symbolism ahead of the United States' relationship with one of its strongest allies and closest neighbors—Canada. Biden canceled the Keystone XL Pipeline for cynically political reasons. The pipeline was a central component of Canada's plan to develop its crude oil fields in Alberta. Even the Obama State Department found—no less than five times—that the pipeline would make no appreciable difference to greenhouse gas emissions, since Canada's crude will still come out of the ground and be transported via rail or tankers (which will actually *increase* emissions). The project also meant ten thousand American union jobs.

But green activists made Keystone a test of Biden's commitment to climate, and he answered the call. Canadian officials were furious at this U.S. double-cross. Jason Kenney, the then head of Alberta's provincial government, which had invested more than $1 billion in the pipeline, didn't mince words: "This is a gut punch for the Canadian and Alberta economies. Sadly, it is an insult directed at the United States' most important ally and trading partner."

Next the administration humiliated the U.S.—on the global stage. Just a few months after Keystone, Biden's new ambassador to the United Nations, Linda Thomas-Greenfield, told a group of American activists that the U.S. would seek to reclaim a seat on the United Nations Human Rights Council. Trump had abandoned that seat in 2018—given the council is stacked with human rights abusers and mostly serves as a forum to pile on Israel. Thomas-Greenfield explained to the activists that the only way the U.S. would regain its seat was if it acted with "humility" and "acknowledge[d]" that we were an "imperfect union" from the start, a country where "white supremacy is weaved into our founding documents and principles."

Republicans were appalled. Texas senator Ted Cruz weighed in with a modest suggestion: "Perhaps our ambassadors should defend America. And not kiss up to the brutal tyrants (including Cuba, Venezuela, Russia & China) on the UN Human Rights Council." But Secretary of State Anthony Blinken took it a step further in July, when he formally asked the UN's human rights officials to investigate U.S. "racism."

The HRC had already decided to do just that—forming a panel to investigate "systemic racism against Africans and people of African descent" by law enforcement everywhere (although really just in the U.S.). The Blinken request was a formal invitation for the world's rogues to falsely claim the United States has a human rights record worse than their own. It was yet another dangerous projection of American weakness, another sign Biden was willing to put his pet political posturing ahead of U.S. power.

Biden's Senate progressives were also eager to set back American foreign policy. One embarrassing example was their hostage taking of Rahm Emanuel. By the time Biden announced his intention to nominate Emanuel to the post of ambassador to Japan, in August 2021, America's most important ally in the Asia-Pacific region had been without an official envoy for two years. Trump's ambassador had resigned in the summer of 2019 to run for elected office, and Trump's replacement pick never got a Senate vote.

Emanuel's confirmation was urgent. China had stepped up its saber rattling toward Taiwan, and Japan had declared that any attack on that island would undermine its own security. Its new prime minister had called for a surge in new military spending, and the U.S. needed to send a message of support with an ambassadorial presence. His confirmation also should have been a breeze. A longtime Democratic insider, Emanuel had served in the Clinton administration, in Congress, and as Obama's chief of staff, before becoming mayor of Chicago.

Senate Democrats instead chose to turn Emanuel's nomination into a referendum on . . . *policing reform*. George Floyd's death put a new spotlight on Emanuel's eight years as Chicago mayor, resurrecting anger over the 2014 police shooting of a seventeen-year-old black man. Activists responded with fury at early Biden administration talk of nominating Emanuel as secretary of transportation. Rep. Jamaal Bowman, a fellow Democrat, declared: "We can't restore the soul of the nation with Rahm Emanuel in public office." Progressive senators then piled on Emanuel's proposed ambassadorship, hounding him with questions in his nomination hearing. Their opposition helped delay a full vote in the Senate, and he wasn't formally confirmed until December 2021—and only then because eight Republicans came to his rescue. Progressives Elizabeth Warren, Ed Markey, and Jeff Merkley voted against Biden's choice, pandering to racial politics.

Like Carter before him, Biden also broadcast his disinterest in U.S. military and defense spending. His first budget, unveiled in April 2021, said it all—and you can bet Putin and China's Xi Jinping noticed. Biden called for a stunning 16 percent increase in domestic discretionary spending, including a whopping 41 percent increase in the Education Department budget; 21 percent more for the EPA; and 23 percent more for health spending.

The Pentagon? He asked for $715 billion, a 1.6 percent increase. Even this overstates the ask. The first rumblings of inflation would have turned that amount into a *defense-budget cut*. And it gets worse. The administration explained in its budget that it also wanted a chunk of that paltry sum to go not to upgraded hardware, but to "mitigate impacts of climate change."

It was a return to the Obama years of defense cuts. Biden's former boss had shrunk defense spending as a share of GDP to 3.1 percent, from 4.7 percent when he took office. Trump modestly reversed this, pushing defense outlays back to 3.3 percent of GDP just prior to the pandemic.

Biden's proposed cuts showed a stunning lack of concern for growing global threats. The United States faces a resurgence of military competition globally, even as its own forces are deteriorating from years of financial neglect. Russia, Iran, and North Korea are threatening the U.S. homeland and allies with missiles, hacking, and land grabs. China is moving rapidly to become a naval power, and now boasts more modern ships (360) in the water than does the U.S. (296)—a stunning statistic.

Yet Biden's initial budgets proposed decommissioning more ships than building new ones, potentially paring the overall U.S.

fleet down to 280. The U.S. Air Force had approximately 4,000 aircraft in its inventory in 1991; today it has about 2,000, and the average age is nearly thirty years old. U.S. stockpiles of munitions continue to fall, and some experts warn that a wide-scale conflict could deplete them entirely in the space of weeks. The Air Force has too few squadrons, the Marines too few battalions. The Navy doesn't even have enough maintenance yards to keep up with needed repairs. And this urgent need to upgrade existing equipment and build capacity comes as the United States also needs greater investment in cutting-edge technology like hypersonics and artificial intelligence.

Not even a *new European land war* could move Biden to change his military-spending tune. Russia's invasion of Ukraine showed the risk of projecting military weakness. As Russia invaded Ukraine, the president submitted his second budget. He did ask for a slightly bigger increase in defense spending than in his first year—4 percent. But with inflation now rampaging, the actual increase would have again been about 1.5 percent. Putin's invasion had provoked even European countries to rethink defense; many for the first time in years began planning for defense budget increases. But Biden remained more interested in pouring money into progressive projects. As Putin rampaged in Ukraine, Biden was calling for $10 billion for a Civilian Climate Corps.

His cuts ultimately proved too dangerous for even Senate Democrats to contemplate, and in both of Biden's first two years a bipartisan Congress voted to overrule him. In 2021, they added $25 billion to the Biden defense budget, pushing it back up to a 5 percent increase. In 2022, they voted for an additional $45 billion, including more money for ships and for sea-launched nuclear cruise missiles that Biden had sought to kill. Yet even with these increases, U.S. military spending is still around 3 percent of GDP. And it's only there because a few pro-military Democrats were willing to face down progressives who continue to demand even deeper defense cuts.

"Extraordinary" Afghanistan "success"

Then there was Afghanistan. Trump in February 2020 signed a peace deal with the Taliban, then fighting an insurgency against the Afghani government. Biden to this day continues to falsely claim that Trump's deal tied his hands—that he had no choice but to withdraw U.S. forces completely by August 31, 2021. In truth, the Trump deal was contingent upon the Taliban honoring certain commitments, including dialogue that would lead to a permanent cease-fire and to agree to a political road map for Afghanistan. The Taliban reneged on all that, and Biden at any point could have declared the agreement null or have renegotiated it.

But he wanted out. Biden had long opposed troops in Afghanistan, even as vice president. And he wanted to be the president who grandly announced the end of America's involvement twenty years after the events of 9/11. He wanted out so badly, he ignored the counsel of his senior-most advisers, who warned that withdrawing U.S. forces completely risked reversing two decades of U.S. effort. When Biden made his April 2021 announcement of total withdrawal, the press reported that he'd been advised against that course by no less than the chairman of the Joint Chiefs, Gen. Mark Milley; U.S. Central Command leader, Gen. Frank McKenzie; and numerous State Department officials. Many told Biden that the best course was to leave a residual force of 2,500 troops to aid the Afghani army, protect U.S. personnel, and guard against the country again becoming a terrorist haven. They noted that the U.S. hadn't had a single casualty in Afghanistan in the year prior.

But President Motormouth rashly carried on, ignoring the military officials who knew the situation on the ground. He even demeaned those who argued for keeping a small force as leverage. "We gave that argument a decade," he groused in an April speech announcing full withdrawal. "It's never proved effective, not when we had 98,000 troops in Afghanistan, and not when we were down to a few thousand. Our diplomacy does not hinge on having boots in harm's way, U.S. boots on the ground. We have to change that thinking."

The world then saw what comes of Biden's thinking. Biden removed a significant portion of U.S. troops in the spring, inspiring the Taliban to go on the offense. As it scooped up territory, advisers warned Biden that the Afghani government and military were at risk of collapse. Biden could have readjusted the military plan; he instead pressed on. The pace of drawdown was so rapid the U.S. was forced to abandon its stronghold of Bagram Air Force Base in July. This left the U.S. unprepared for the sudden collapse of Kabul on August 15, 2021. The events that followed were an American humiliation on par with the fall of Saigon or the Bay of Pigs.

Americans watched as U.S. forces were hemmed in at Kabul's airport, desperately attempting to airlift Americans and Afghani allies to safety. It was a scene of chaos and death—desperate locals running alongside U.S. aircraft, holding on to undercarriages even as planes took off, falling to their deaths. U.S. troops came under fire, and amid the operation a suicide bomber killed thirteen U.S. service members and 170 Afghan civilians. The U.S. military acted throughout it all with extraordinary bravery and skill, in fifteen days evacuating more than 120,000 people. But their irresponsible commander in chief should never have put them in that position.

The president shamefully absolved himself of all responsibility. He blamed the mess on Trump's deal. His dishonestly claimed that his only choices were full withdrawal or an "escalation" of troops. He described the evacuation as a moment of triumph—an "extraordinary success"—rather than an embarrassment. He took a cheap shot at Afghanis, for not fighting harder. And he falsely claimed this meant that "the war in Afghanistan is now over."

Hardly. The Taliban won a major victory and the country is already again becoming a recruitment area for terrorists that the

United States will face in the future—only now from a position of weakness. Afghanistan was meanwhile left to rot, and since withdrawal has faced famine, starvation, economic collapse, and the return of a brutal, medieval theocracy.

Resetting the reset

Americans weren't the only ones watching this shameful episode. Putin was, too. His takeaways: The U.S. was in retreat; the new president lacked the will for a fight; and Biden would be loathe to ever commit U.S. ground troops to combat aggression. The same April that Biden announced the U.S. would abandon Afghanistan, Putin began major military exercises on Ukraine's southern border.

Putin already had a measure of Biden's mettle. It was Biden who in 2009 went to Munich and said it was time to "press the reset button" in relations with Russia. The Obama administration went on to help Russia join the World Trade Organization. In 2014, the Russian autocrat seized the Crimea from Ukraine. It was the biggest land grab in Europe since World War II and violated the UN Charter and several other international agreements. Yet the Obama-Biden administration barely blinked in response. It was more interested in teaming up with Russia to negotiate a nuclear deal with Iran. The administration also refused to sell key military equipment to Ukraine, which it wanted to help deter Russia against further aggression.

Biden returned to these policies of appeasement upon taking up residence in the Oval Office. Blinken explained that Biden wanted a "more stable, more predictable relationship" with Russia—not that Putin had shown one iota of interest in reciprocating. He'd been broadcasting for years his intention to reassemble the old Soviet Union, clawing back what he insisted was the Russian "motherland."

Biden's response to Putin's April 2021 troop buildup on the Ukraine border was to give Putin *a win*. The administration in May 2021 waived sanctions against the company and CEO developing Russia's Nord Stream 2 pipeline—slated to provide cheap natural gas from Russia to Europe. Putin couldn't have believed his luck.

Biden officials spun the move as a way to improve relations with Germany, which strongly supported the project. But it simultaneously angered the rest of Europe, which was opposed to giving Putin more energy leverage over the continent. Biden even got slapped by members of his own party for giving Putin an economic reward for his unchecked behavior. "I urge the administration to rip off the Band-Aid, lift these waivers and move forward with the congressionally mandated sanctions," said Democratic senator Bob Menendez, the head of the Foreign Relations Committee. Biden instead held a summit with Putin in Geneva in June 2021—still trying to reset the reset. And he choked off the supply of weapons Trump had been sending Ukraine to discourage Russian aggression.

Putin tested Biden again in the spring and summer of 2021, when media reports suggested Russian entities were behind a number of cyberattacks on American interests. Biden's response was to give Putin a list of sixteen critical infrastructure areas that he was declaring off-limits to Russia cyberhacking—thereby suggesting *everything else* was fair game. The president said he'd respond if Russia cyberattacked again but was unclear as to what consequences, if any, there would be. And just weeks later, the Biden administration officially blessed the completion of Nord Stream 2, even though it meant Ukraine would lose millions in transit fees as Russia rerouted its gas through the new pipeline.

After the spectacle of Afghanistan, Putin clearly felt he had nothing to lose. Within a few months of the scenes of disorder in Kabul, Putin had built up more than ninety thousand troops along the Ukrainian border. Biden responded with a not-so-scary warning that the United States would impose "strong economic and other measures" if Putin invaded. Putin snorted and launched a full-scale invasion on February 24, 2022.

Biden to his credit responded by sending Ukraine billions in economic aid and military equipment for its fight. Yet the administration also had to be pushed by Congress into every major action. It was slow to deliver true missile-defense systems. It was slow to deliver drones. It was slow to resupply munitions. It was slow to agree to give tanks. It refused outright to provide certain equipment, including aircraft, on the grounds that it would take too long to train Ukrainians to use them. This rationale proved a bigger and bigger loser as the war dragged on and it became clear that earlier delivery might have allowed the Ukrainians to drive Russia out faster and saved lives.

Biden also made the mistake of broadcasting his desire to do anything to avoid "escalation." He drew his red line around defending "every inch" of NATO territory, leading Putin to assume that anything up to that line was allowable—potentially even a chemical attack in Ukraine or the use of a strategic nuke. And while the administration publicly claimed it would be up to the courageous Ukrainians to decide how long to wage this conflict, it at times quietly broadcast to the media its openness to at some point exerting pressure on Ukraine to cut its losses and give Putin a partial victory.

As for Russia itself, Biden imposed a raft of sanctions. But the U.S. wasn't able to truly strike at Russia's economic power, since Europe remained so dependent on its energy and demanded delays in oil sanctions.

By the fall of 2022, the extraordinary and unflagging efforts by the Ukrainian military and people had pushed Putin's army out of huge swaths of the country. But not before Putin had bombed cities and civilian infrastructure and caused the largest refugee crisis in Europe in nearly eighty years. The U.S. estimates Putin's war has already resulted in tens of thousands of dead Ukrainian civilians and troops. It happened on Biden's watch.

In January 2022, *Foreign Affairs* magazine asked thirty experts to grade Biden on his first year in office. How went "the president's 'America is back' agenda"? The grades were unremarkable, and the comments had a common refrain: "high-flown rhetoric but little substance"; a lack of "clearly articulated" goals; "not evident"; "yet to put forward a positive vision"; "no clear and coherent articulation of policies." And these might even be called easy graders. Biden had promised an end to Trump's somewhat chaotic and mercurial foreign policy, and had broadly sketched out promises to patch up relations with Europe, and pivot his focus to China. Yet years into his administration he's produced no strategic vision for dealing with any one part of the globe.

Across Europe, allies were furious at the Biden administration abandonment of Afghanistan. Numerous NATO allies had also spent blood and treasure on rebuilding that nation. Britain and Germany were particularly irate. Allies most at risk to continued Putin aggression, like Poland, were appalled by his decision to sign off on Nord Stream 2. Eastern European allies remain unhappy over the administration's efforts to hamstring their economic flexibility with his global minimum-tax plans. Biden in September 2021 signed a smart deal to joint-develop submarines with Australia to counter China. But the administration somehow forgot to tell France, which was blindsided by a pact that lost it a big defense contract. The diplomatic fumble smacked of amateur hour and produced unnecessary tension with a key ally.

The Middle East? Biden threw away the potential for progress there while still a candidate. He climbed on his own high horse about human rights, taking aim at longtime partner Saudi Arabia. Saudi journalist Jamal Khashoggi was murdered in an Istanbul consulate in 2018. A U.S. government report laid the murder at the feet of Saudi Crown Prince Mohammed bin Salman (MBS). The killing was unconscionable, but the Saudis had also proven a key partner in recent years, and MBS as de facto ruler of the country promised reform.

Trump largely ignored the Khashoggi killing, but Biden made it a talking point in his presidential run. He promised to make the Saudis "pay the price, and make them in fact the pariah that they are." The administration paused arms sales to the country and withdrew support for the Saudi-led coalition fighting Iran-backed rebels in Yemen. It imposed a travel ban on Saudi officials.

And how did all that work out? Saudi Arabia had in recent years become a partner in reining in Iran, which continues to use proxies to wage insurrections and promote instability throughout the region. The Saudis are also central to potentially expanding peace deals between Israel and other Arab nations. America needs to keep Saudi Arabia close, to dissuade the kingdom from turning instead to Russia or China. As Putin's invasion highlighted, it's also good to have an OPEC ally at times of unexpected global oil emergencies.

Biden in July 2022 went on what was ostensibly a fence-mending trip to Riyadh, though the meeting proved an even bigger fiasco than the events that led to it. Someone (who should have been fired) suggested to the president that the best way to greet the man he'd accused of murder was to give him a fist bump rather than a handshake. As Saudi expert Karen Elliott House would later describe in the *WSJ*: "Things went downhill from there . . . The United Arab Emirates promptly announced its effort to return an ambassador to Tehran and resolve differences diplomatically. Saudi Foreign Minister Faisal bin Farhan Al-Saud contradicted Mr. Biden's claims of enhancing Saudi-Israel relations, and reiterated that any increased oil production won't be a Saudi decision but one by the Organization of the Petroleum Exporting Countries Plus, which includes Russia. That's a not-so-subtle way of saying Saudi will maintain its warming relations with Vladimir Putin regardless of what the U.S. thinks." The Saudis in October 2022 would go on to snub Biden's request to delay production cuts until after the election.

Biden also frustrated Middle East allies by resurrecting the Obama playbook and restarting negotiations with Iran for a nuclear deal. The smarter approach would have been to build on the Abraham Accords, cementing the relationships and using a more united region to put maximum pressure on Tehran. Especially because most everyone on the planet other than Team Biden seems to understand that Iran isn't going to stop seeking a bomb even if it does do a deal.

In Latin America, Biden's domestic politics have eroded ties. The president's reactionary stance to Trump's presidency led him to immediately reverse a number of border policies, exacerbating a migratory and humanitarian crisis. The president snubbed two key allies in the region—Brazil and Guatemala—mostly because of their center-right political leaders. And he's been unwilling to take a strong stance against left-leaning strongmen, for fear of upsetting America's left-leaning progressive base. China has significantly increased its own trade and diplomatic presence in the region in recent years.

The run-up to the much-vaunted Summit of the Americas in June 2022 summed up the administration's foreign policy disarray. The summit was meant to be the first on U.S. soil in nearly thirty years, and expectations for the Los Angeles event were high. It should have been a moment for Biden to speak with moral clarity on the U.S. values of freedom and prosperity. Instead, his administration dithered over who to invite, and allowed threats of boycotts to pile up. Mexico's and Honduras's left-leaning presidents said they wouldn't attend unless Biden invited the dictators of Cuba, Venezuela, and Nicaragua. The administration ultimately chose to exclude the troika, but not before highlighting to the world its waning influence in the southern hemisphere.

Africa? The Biden administration seems to have no policy whatsoever. It infuriated the entire continent at the end of 2021, when it imposed a travel ban on several African countries, after South African scientists reported the discovery of the new Omicron variant of Covid. Global health officials slammed the bans as ineffective and a "punishment" for countries that were transparent with their science, but Biden cared more about the optics. Beyond that, the administration has largely focused efforts on protesting attempts by African nations to develop their own energy resources.

Most perplexing is Biden's inaction on China and the growing threat in the Asia-Pacific sphere. Biden claimed this would be his top priority, and when in July 2021 he gave an update on the withdrawal from Afghanistan he justified it in part on the grounds that America needed to "focus on shoring up America's core strengths to meet the strategic competition with China."

Biden gets credit for the Aussie submarine deal, and for strengthening coalitions like the Quadrilateral Dialogue, a group that includes the United States, Japan, Australia, and India. Yet this is now the replacement for a plan for handling China. The U.S. has failed to press China for more answers about its role in the origins of Covid-19. The Biden State Department also sat back and allowed China to treat American diplomats with impunity as part of its "zero Covid" strategy. Whistleblowers reported to Congress that dozens of American diplomats had been confined for weeks or even months at a time in China's "fever" facilities—locked in barred rooms where they were given little food or water and subjected to intrusive Chinese testing.

To the extent the administration has signaled a foreign policy, it seems to rest on the idea of competition with China, and slowing Beijing's ability to overshadow the U.S. Yet beyond the sub deal, the Biden administration has showed little interest in challenging China's growing military dominance in the Pacific. And it has been completely AWOL on renewing Obama's trade agenda with allies in the region, as a way of countering China's influence. The administration hasn't even attempted to gin up new economic or tech initiatives with Europe to compete with Chinese. Critics worry the administration is almost obsessively focused on coaxing the Asian giant into agreeing to carbon emissions reductions.

At the same time, Biden's diplomatic gaffes have exacerbated tensions—especially with his random comments about Taiwan.

On several occasions the president has suggested he'd unilaterally changed America's longtime position of "strategic ambiguity" as to the official status of that island. Biden more than once suggested the U.S. would move to defend the island in the event of a Chinese attack.

The United States may need to adopt that position. But the Biden staff's scramble to walk back his comments on each occasion showed there had been no formal change in position, and this was the president wandering off teleprompter. China meanwhile is escalating its belligerence toward Taiwan, ramping up military drills around the island. And China has all but abandoned any efforts to help the U.S. rein in North Korea's Kim Jong-un. It's instead launching spy balloons over the U.S.

Biden has taken a few small actions to show American force. He approved airstrikes against Iran-backed militias in Syria following attacks and threats on U.S. personnel. And in May 2022 he sent a small force of five hundred troops to Somalia, where a powerful Al Qaeda affiliate has continued to amass territory.

But overall, the president seems unwilling to acknowledge the U.S. is facing a new global disorder, one in which illiberalism is spreading, and old nemeses—Russia, Iran, and China—are seeking to reestablish regional dominance. Putin doesn't just want Ukraine; he wants to reassemble the former Soviet Union and he wants NATO out of Central and Eastern Europe. China doesn't want to just dominate the Asia Pacific region; it wants to be *the* global superpower. Iran wants a bomb, which would give it frightening new power to dictate the contours of the Middle East. Growing cyberthreats, proliferation, and regional bad actors are not just distant problems. They are a threat to American freedom and prosperity.

Putin's invasion of Ukraine was Biden's opportunity to acknowledge this changing environment and to shift his presidency. The American public was shocked by Putin's aggression and would have backed a new Biden agenda that turned to rebuilding the military, to empowering the American energy sector, and to working with national-security Republicans. Biden did none of that. In his State of the Union address, just weeks after Russia's invasion, he laid out a rehash of his year one agenda. He extolled the "powerful economic sanctions" he'd levied on Russia and his new "dedicated" Department of Justice task force that would "go after the crimes of the Russian oligarchs." He bragged that Putin "has no idea what's coming." At the same time, Biden laid out what *wasn't* coming: "Let me be clear: Our forces are not engaged and will not engage in the conflict with Russian forces in Ukraine." Biden didn't warn off Putin from launching missiles into civilian neighborhoods or from starving cities. He instead signaled to Putin that he could take any action in Ukraine, no matter how atrocious.

The president has one thing right: He describes today's world as a fight between autocracy and democracy. That's all fine and good, but America needs a president willing to make sure the right side wins.

CHAPTER 6

WELCOME TO FEAR CITY

It's a mystery why any presidential contender makes big promises on crime—it's *always* self-defeating. Both Carter and Biden learned the mistake of leaning in on public safety, and to their political peril.

The federal government can only exercise the limited law enforcement powers enumerated to it by the Constitution. These are things like laws related to the postal service, or to revenue and tax statutes, or to protecting the federal government. Over the years the feds have taken an expansive view of those powers and given themselves a bigger role. They've outlawed certain classes of drugs; set minimum sentencing laws; expanded the reach of the Federal Bureau of Investigation. And let's not forget the federal government's infamous, fruitless fight against the demon liquor, courtesy of America's experiment with the Eighteenth Amendment.

But the federal government does not exercise *general* police powers. That is the exclusive remit of state and local governments, and nearly all the crime Americans care about falls into that category. The feds can take down the occasional mob boss, or bust up Medicare frauds, and that's for the good. But its local cops that handle the crimes that are the true scourge of American cities—burglaries, auto thefts, assaults, murders, pickpocketing, and disturbances of the peace.

Yet presidential candidates never seem able to help themselves—they jump into debates on law enforcement and leave the impression that they have some ability to clean up crime. They don't. Meditating on law enforcement policy is an invitation to get blamed for crime rates that a president has no real ability to control.

Both Carter and Biden did just that. Carter became president at a time when crime rates were already high. He felt knowledgeable on the issue, as he'd been engaged in law enforcement reforms as governor of Georgia. And so he weighed in—excoriating his Republican opponents for failing to follow through on crime-reduction vows, and promising his leadership would result in a more "orderly society." It didn't happen. Crime continued to increase, and Americans had a new person to blame—Carter.

Crime rates were generally low when Biden ran for president. But he managed to help create a crime problem. Candidate Biden in May 2020 seized on the tragic killing of George Floyd and turned a pledge to "root out systemic racism" into a central plank of his campaign. While never fully joining the "defund the police" movement, as both candidate and president he promoted policies that gave its promoters aid and comfort. He promised to unleash his Department of Justice on local police departments, and he sided with progressive prosecutors who worked to weaken the bail system. As these policies kicked in and weakened police departments, crime rates began to increase across the country. Americans blamed Democrats, and notably the guy at the top—Biden.

Carter proved helpless to change the crime spree that became synonymous with the 1970s. But Biden, once again, beats him in the ranks of political mistakes. Biden used his bully pulpit to undermine decades of smarter state and local law enforcement policies. And when the murder and assault rates began to rise, he could do nothing but own it.

The political mean streets

President Lyndon Johnson declared a War on Crime in March 1965. America in the mid-1960s didn't *actually* have a terrible crime problem, but social discontent and the 1964 Harlem riot (which spread to other cities that summer) had unsettled the country. Johnson was rattled by how effectively Barry Goldwater had used crime as an issue in his 1964 campaign. Johnson stood up a Commission on Law Enforcement and the Administration of Justice, which linked crime to poverty, racial antagonism, family breakdown, and restless young people. This fit neatly with Johnson's Great Society plans to expand the reach of the federal government. Congress passed legislation giving the feds power to push large sums of money and policy initiatives to local law enforcement, via what became the Law Enforcement Assistance Administration (LEAA).

Throwing more money at the problem was no answer—it rarely is—and Johnson's fears of crime instead became reality. Riots flared in large cities, and protests broke out on college campuses. The murder rate per 100,000 people in 1965 was 5.1, not too much higher than it had been the prior fifteen years. By 1970 it was 7.9. And by 1976—as Carter's campaign moved into full swing—it had hit nearly 9.

Carter was a technocrat and policy geek, famous for reading reams of paper and for believing any problem could be fixed with the right government tinkering. He took that exact approach on law enforcement while leading Georgia. A memo prepared for Gerald Ford's team noted that Carter's crime approach as governor had been "generally praised"; it was broadly conservative, with a few liberal flourishes. Carter had favored a statute to expand law enforcement's use of surveillance equipment in serious crimes; had supported reintroducing the death penalty in the state; he favored giving judges more ability to deny bail. At the same time, he'd devoted significant attention to reforming Georgia's outdated prison system, which was, according to one newspaper description, "mired in the old chain-gang mentality."

Carter brought the same mix to his 1976 presidential campaign. He laid out his belief in "swift, firm and predictable punishment" for lawbreakers and called to revise federal sentencing laws to give judges less discretion. He advocated the death penalty for certain crimes. He promised to crack down on drug trafficking. At the same time, he emphasized the need for better rehabilitation programs; favored a handgun registration program; and came out in support of decriminalizing (not legalizing) simple marijuana possession. But it was his overarching crime message that set him apart and made sense to voters. The most substantive way to reduce crime, he said, was to reduce unemployment.

It was on October 15, 1976, just weeks before the election, that Carter made his mistake. He came out swinging as the law-and-order candidate, making a lot of big promises. In remarks to the Economic Club of Detroit, he excoriated "eight years of Republican rule," in which "serious crimes have gone up by 58 percent, and 27 percent in the last two years alone." He lamented the burglary rate, the rape rate, the murder rate, and "gangs of teenaged criminals" that are now "a major threat in many of our cities."

Interestingly, Carter sought to tie continued public disgust over Watergate to crime rates, claiming that Republicans "set an example" of "violation of the law," noting that "two Republican Attorneys General in the last eight years have been convicted of serious criminal acts." Forty-six years later, Biden would in his first midterms claim that Republican lawbreakers and the January 6 riot meant that "democracy" was on the ballot. Turns out ole Joe did learn a few things from Carter.

Carter said restoring order was a question of "leadership," and that he'd reform the LEAA, clean up a scandal-tarred Drug Enforcement Agency, streamline an overcrowded court system, and push local authorities to focus on violent crime. In a populist touch, he also promised to crack down on "white collar" criminals, who he said too often "get off with a slap on the wrist." In classic Carter style, he laid out a sixteen-point plan. In doing so, he delivered a very clear message: Elect him, and he'd "turn the tide against the scourge of crime."

Carter would quickly discover just how limited was his ability to turn around anything. Nixon had officially declared a "war on drugs" and Carter in his own August 1977 address laid out his plans to put a greater emphasis on international narcotics control and to crack down on domestic drug traffickers. Decades later America is as mired in its war on drugs as it ever was, while federal and state governments have started rethinking policies like mandatory sentencing laws that filled prisons with far more drug users than traffickers. Americans have only added to the old '70s and '80s roster of drugs, and the country is today awash in meth, fentanyl, and opioids.

Alongside greater narcotics enforcement, Carter's attorney general, Griffin Bell, put a new emphasis on white-collar and organized crime, ramping up "strike forces" of experts from across agencies to tackle complex scams. But while they certainly nailed some wealthy fraudsters, it made little difference to the growing numbers of serious crimes plaguing American neighborhoods. Bell in a 1978 speech in Atlanta recounted that Carter had straight off the bat asked him for a "new approach" to the "control of crime." The AG said he'd "thought about it a good bit" but the conclusion was that any DOJ role would be "narrow," since "95 percent of all law enforcement is in the hands of State and local forces." Something Carter would have known—and should have thought about—before promising to clean up America's streets.

The administration also took a run at revamping the LEAA, the agency that was pushing as much as $1 billion annually to local police forces. Carter had criticized LEAA for its waste, and Bell for a time wanted to get rid of the agency entirely, or at least cut its budget. But this set off howls among members of Congress and criminal justice groups who'd come to rely on its dollars. Congress instead took a stab at reforming the program, but it remained a shambolic mess of erratic grants and policy proposals. The agency was abolished in 1982.

The murder rate continued to climb over Carter's time in office, hitting 9.7 per 100,000 in 1979, and 10.2 in 1980— what remains the highest annual number on record. To be fair to Carter, the murder rate remained relatively high for the next fifteen years, even as economic prosperity expanded. What did change was policing techniques. In 1982, George L. Kelling and James Q. Wilson published a transformative article titled "Broken Windows." Its theory: When law enforcement abides too much local disorder, criminals assume a public and police tolerance and engage in more crime, including more serious offenses. The answer, argued the paper, was for the police to crack down on low-level crime. This not only reinvigorated neighborhoods, but low-level arrests often led to the apprehension of more serious felons—a virtuous circle. By the 1990s, major cities across the country were introducing Broken Windows reforms, and the result was a dramatic reduction in crime.

"Defund the police"

On May 25, 2020, Minneapolis police officers were called by a grocery store employee who suspected a customer had just pawned a counterfeit bill. They arrived at the scene and attempted to arrest forty-six-year-old George Floyd. Floyd, an on-and-off drug addict, was acting erratically and would not get in the police car. Officer Derek Chauvin ultimately kneeled on the neck of a handcuffed Floyd on the ground for more than nine minutes, even as Floyd protested he could not breathe. Floyd died of cardiopulmonary arrest in that position, for which Chauvin was later charged and convicted of murder.

The death set off an explosion of protests across the country, which the *New York Times* would describe as the largest since the Civil Rights era. Policing and prisons had already been on the nation's mind. Congress by large bipartisan majorities had in 2018 passed its first criminal justice reform in years—the First Step Act—shortening sentences for nonviolent drug offenders. The media and the Black Lives Matter movement had been elevating the use of force by police, spotlighting incidents in which minorities died in shootings or chokeholds. A video of Floyd on the ground—Chauvin's knee on his neck—went viral, and millions took to the streets to protest.

Yet what began as peaceful demonstrations soon boiled into riots, arson, looting, and attacks on police in hundreds of American cities. By June 2020, more than ten thousand people had been arrested, resulting in a whole new round of complaints against law enforcement. Out of the maelstrom came a united progressive call: "defund the police."

The Biden campaign jumped on the Floyd death for its own political benefit, adopting the narrative that most of American society was racist, and that vilifying police forces was a patriotic duty. From his basement in Delaware, the candidate livestreamed his lament that the "original sin of this country still stains our nation today" and contrasted himself with Trump, saying: "This is no time for incendiary tweets . . . this is a national crisis and we need real leadership right now." Days later he meditated on America's problem with "systemic racism" in a speech in Philadelphia. Breezing past the violence and continued attacks on police, Biden again took aim at Trump, comparing him to Bull Connor, the segregationist commissioner of public safety in Birmingham, Alabama, in the early 1960s. When Senate Democrats that June blocked a police reform bill from South Carolina Republican (and African-American) Tim Scott—refusing to even allow it to move to the floor for debate—Biden's soon-to-be running mate, Sen. Kamala Harris, excoriated *Republicans* for playing a "political game" with the issue.

On the direct question of defunding the police, Candidate Biden gave careful answers. He never expressly supported the defund movement. "I don't support defunding the police," he told CBS's Norah O'Donnell. "I support conditioning federal aid to police, based on whether or not they meet certain basic standards of decency and honorableness." At yet other times, Biden suggested he was in favor of giving *more* money to departments, but to be invested in specific areas like training (not necessarily more police officers).

But Biden nonetheless gave comfort to the left's narrative that police abuse was systemic and widespread—rather than limited to discreet actors. He called for a national "police oversight commission," while failing to note that nearly all the police forces accused of brutality or bias were in cities run by progressive Democrats. In his campaign site section on "justice," Biden promised to "root out the racial, gender, and income-based disparities in the system." He promised his Department of Justice would commence "pattern or practice" investigations of police forces nationwide and impose consent decrees on those found guilty of "systemic police misconduct." He disavowed the very crime bill he'd helped pass in the 1990s and instead promised to shift away from "incarceration"—pushing to "eliminate mandatory minimums" for "non-violent crimes," to "end all incarceration for drug use alone" and to "eliminate the death penalty."

Biden continued in his speeches to essentially call the country racist, despite having served as vice president for eight years with the nation's first African-American president, and alongside its first African-American attorney general (Eric Holder). He in August announced Harris as his running mate, a nod to his party's identity politics. After dropping out of the presidential primary, Harris had spent months auditioning for the veep job, in part by leading a Senate Democratic charge to pass "police accountability" legislation. She'd also moved to soothe progressive unease over her time as a California prosecutor by telling readers of the *New York Times* in June 2020 that it was time to "reimagine what public safety looks like." It was "just wrong," she said, to think that "putting more police on the streets creates more safety," and lambasted city police budgets. She argued governments should instead be putting more money into "public schools" and "affordable housing." By the time Biden picked her, the *Times* was describing Harris as "a leading voice on racial justice and inequality."

Biden and Harris kept it up in office. Chauvin was convicted of murder in April 2021. This was accountability, yet the Biden DOJ response was to launch an investigation into the entire Minneapolis Police Department, to keep alive Democrats' narrative of systemic police abuse. Attorney General Merrick Garland issued a moratorium on the federal death penalty, pending a review. Biden stocked his DOJ with prosecutors hostile to police forces. And in May 2022, Biden issued an executive order creating a national database of "police misconduct" and beefing up investigations into police departments.

Local progressive politicians went further. In the weeks and months following Floyd's death, elected officials began announcing their intentions to strip police forces of dollars. The *Guardian* reported in March 2021 that more than twenty major U.S. cities had "reduced their police budgets in some form," collectively cutting $840 million. They included the giants of New York, Los Angeles, Chicago, Philadelphia, Milwaukee, Seattle, Baltimore, and Austin. The Minneapolis City Council even started work to dismantle its police force altogether.

The Waukesha reckoning

But something else was happening in America's cities alongside the defund movement—something that had yet to become a public flash point. Law enforcement had noticed that crime had started to surge even before the 2020 riots. The *New York Times* in July 2020 reported that New York had "surpassed 400 shootings in the first half of the year for the first time since 2016," and that "other cities have seen similar spikes in shootings, most notably Chicago, where the current pace of homicides is poised to near the 778 recorded in 2016—its highest total in roughly 20 years." Some politicians thought the rise might be due to the decision by many states and locales to release criminals from prisons to help stem Covid infections.

The real cause made itself known on a cold November day in 2021, in Waukesha, Wisconsin. Scores of residents had shown up for the annual Christmas parade. As they crowded the streets to watch the floats and entertainment, a red Ford SUV came plowing through the crowds, killing and maiming as it drove in a zigzag pattern to hit as many onlookers as possible. Six people died, including several senior citizens in a local dancing group, as well as an eight-year-old child. Another sixty-two were injured, including seventeen children, many of whom were admitted to the hospital in critical condition.

The perpetrator was Darrell E. Brooks, a thirty-nine-year-old African-American with an extensive criminal record that included charges of battery, sexual abuse, strangulation, resisting arrest, and domestic abuse. Brooks had a long track record of getting booked, getting released for nominal bail, and missing court dates. Only three weeks prior to the attack, he had been arrested for hitting a woman and driving over her leg with the same Ford SUV. He was charged with a second-degree felony—reckless endangerment. Yet he was released on a token $1,000 bail—days before the Waukesha attack.

Waukesha alerted a horrified nation to the left's other assault on law and order: soft-on-crime attorneys. Larry Krasner, elected as district attorney of Philadelphia in 2017, was one of the first lawyers to run as a self-described "progressive prosecutor." But emulators—many of them backed by far-left Democratic donor

George Soros—were soon in charge in nearly every major city in the country: Chesa Boudin in San Francisco; Alvin Bragg in Manhattan; George Gascon in Los Angeles; Rachael Rollins in Boston; Kim Foxx in Chicago. All had come to office pledging to *empty* prisons. They promised bail "reform" and sentencing "reform" and denounced prosecutors who pursued "quality of life" crimes, such as graffiti, farebeating, drug use, or public encampments. Boudin in particular became a progressive celebrity. His swearing-in ceremony in January 2020 even featured a video congratulations from Supreme Court Justice Sonia Sotomayor. Boudin lambasted a U.S. criminal justice system that had "the longest sentences, the largest prison populations, the most bloated law enforcement budgets." He brought the crowd to ecstasy by declaring: "Join us in rejecting the notion that to be free, we must cage others."

The progressive crowd was careful to claim that it intended to focus its efforts on "violent" criminal offenders, and that the public need not fear rising crime. But the stats leading up to May 2020 proved the opposite; criminals at every level were getting a free pass. Police, now getting hit with budget cuts, began speaking out about a revolving door; they'd arrest a bad guy, only to see the same thug back on the street the next day.

That's what happened in Waukesha. An attorney in the office of Milwaukee's progressive prosecutor, John Chisholm, had signed off on Brooks's ridiculously low bail, ignoring the criminal's long rap sheet. Chisholm in a later statement would acknowledge the bail was "inappropriately low" and try to blame the "mistake" on a lack of funding for his overworked office. But this was the same Chisholm who had years earlier bragged about his liberal approach to criminal justice, once saying: "Is there going to be an individual I divert, or I put into a treatment program, who's going to go out and kill somebody? You bet. Guaranteed. It's guaranteed to happen. It does not invalidate the overall approach." Tell that to the families of the six dead in Waukesha.

Reaping the sown

One difference between today's Democratic party and the one in
Carter's day is the modern version's stunning ability to ignore the
possibility that radical action will produce any negative outcomes.
Let's spend $22 trillion! What could possibly go wrong? Let's jack
up taxes on the most productive employers in our country! No
biggie! Oh, and let's empty all the jails *while simultaneously* getting
rid of the police! Surely all of society will operate in peace and
good will!

Wrong. The crime wave of recent years has been epic, shoving the country back toward the 1970s. Cities gave up almost
overnight the decades of progress they'd made with the broken-
window approach, and entire neighborhoods sank back into squa-
lor. Progressive prosecutors' refusal to prosecute "victimless
crimes" turned portions of major cities into homeless encampments, rife with drug use, graffiti, crime, sanitation issues, and
mental-health problems. Urban businesses faced a new onslaught
of brazen thievery and "smash and grab" robberies. The New
York subway system has become a place of terror, with near-daily
accounts of assaults, stabbings, rapes, and the random shoving of
passengers onto tracks.

Progressive mayors like New York's Bill de Blasio encouraged
the mayhem by ending broken-windows policing. Cops were
barred from going after smaller crimes. And in the aftermath of
Floyd they also became more reluctant to confront major criminals, for fear of dismissal or lawsuits. A nonstop flood of viral
videos shows the resulting disorder. Petty criminals brazenly walk
into bodegas and take food. Belligerent gangs of teenagers demand
free goods from scared fast-food employees. Aggressive vagrants
harass people on the street and beat up random passersby.

The nation was outraged by the case of Jose Alba, a sixty-one-
year-old bodega clerk in Harlem who on July 1, 2022, was accosted

by thirty-five-year-old Austin Simon. Simon walked behind the bodega counter, shoved Alba into the wall, and threatened him. When Simon tried to manhandle Alba out from behind the counter, Alba grabbed a knife and stabbed him. Simon died. Shockingly, Manhattan's progressive prosecutor, Alvin Bragg, slapped *Alba* with murder charges. Alba spent nearly a week on Riker's Island with his bail set at a quarter of a million dollars. Public outcry later forced the district attorney's office to drop the charges. New Yorkers were appalled that Bragg brought the hammer down on a man who was simply trying to protect himself from the criminals Bragg routinely let loose on the street.

The United States in 2020 saw its biggest growth in homicides since national records started in 1960—29 percent. The previous largest one-year change was about thirteen percent, according to the *New York Times*. It was worse in certain states and locales. California saw a stunning 31 percent increase in homicides in 2020; New York City an astonishing 45 percent spike. Chicago a more than 50 percent increase. And the nation has only built on that record. CNN reported that more than two-thirds of the nation's forty most populous cities experienced more homicides in 2021 than in 2020, while at least ten registered all-time highs. They included Portland, Philadelphia, Indianapolis, Austin, Columbus, Tucson, and Albuquerque. Chicago racked up 797 murders—the most since 1996. Los Angeles saw a 12 percent rise over 2020.

And it isn't just homicide. The FBI reported a 6 percent increase in 2020 in other incidents defined as violent crime—including aggravated assaults, which soared 12 percent in a year. Cities also witnessed a huge spike in carjackings. It also saw an explosion in theft of *pieces* of cars—with criminals slicing off antipollution devices called catalytic converters to sell the valuable metal components. The National Insurance Crime Bureau reported that thieves stole *twelve times* as many catalytic converters in 2021 as they did in 2019.

One obvious problem: fewer cops to dissuade the criminals. The "defund the police" movement pushed cities into cutting police budgets. Police also began retiring from or quitting major urban forces—sick of ambush attacks, political abuse, and bail reform. The *New York Times* in June 2021 reported that in the twelve-month period ending in April of that year, police retirements nationwide were up 45 percent, and resignations 18 percent.

In some big cities, the hemorrhaging was extraordinary: "In New York, 2,600 officers retired in 2020, according to police statistics, after 1,509 retirements the year before. In Portland, Ore., 69 officers resigned and 75 retired from April 2020 to April 2021, versus 27 and 14 the previous year. In Seattle, resignations increased to 123 from 34 and retirements to 96 from 43," the paper reported. Many officers moved on to forces that still retained the support of local officials and the public.

Another problem: fewer detectives to bring the growing ranks of criminals to justice, leaving them to continue crime sprees. In June 2022, a CBS News investigation found that "across a nation that is already in the grips of a rise in violent crime, murders are going unsolved at a historic pace." Its review of FBI statistics found that the murder clearance rate, or the share of cases in which police arrest a perpetrator or close the case for other reasons, "has fallen to its lowest point in more than half a century." It quoted the head of the Murder Accountability Project, Thomas Hargrove: "It's never been this bad. During the last seven months of 2020, most murders went unsolved. That's never happened before in America."

While carefully avoiding the term "defund the police," the CBS piece acknowledged that low clearance rates came down to a lack of officers and investigators. It gave as one example the city of Jackson, Mississippi, where the police responded to 153 murders in the prior year, but only had eight homicide detectives on staff. It quoted Jackson police chief James Davis: "The whole system is backlogged. I could use more police officers. I could use more homicide detectives." It also noted a "breakdown in trust between their officers and the communities they serve." No kidding.

The investigation also highlighted a tragic aspect of the civil justice movement—one that rarely gets enough attention. The left's brutal war on the police was waged in the name of minorities. But it is African-Americans and Hispanics who most suffer when police numbers fall and crime soars, as the lawbreaking happens more frequently in neighborhoods where they live. Likewise, their killers are less likely to be held to account. "Police are far less likely to solve a murder when the victim is Black or Hispanic," pronounced the CBS investigation, attempting to suggest this proved yet more systemic racism. Actually, it's math. The number of crime victims who are nonwhite is so large as to mathematically produce a lower minority clearance rate. Biden, progressive prosecutors, and the defund movement left the very people they claimed to campaign for more vulnerable than at any time in recent decades, and with fewer resources to make things better.

Rewriting history

It was about midway through 2021—Biden's first year in office— that elected Democrats began to worry they had liability for the rise in crime. The issue hadn't played in the 2020 presidential election as much as Republicans might have hoped. But the GOP continued to elevate the startling statistics, and the party's nominee for the 2021 Virginia gubernatorial election, Glenn Youngkin, was capturing suburban voters' attention by painting his Democratic opponent as soft on crime. "Rising Violent Crime Is Likely To Present A Political Challenge For Democrats In 2022," warned an NPR story in July 2021.

Democrats' first response was to engage in some flagrant revisionist history. Biden's Covid "rescue" plan, passed in March 2021, had shoveled $350 million to states. The *New York Times* explained in a story after passage that this was a blank check to help states, counties, and municipalities with "pandemic-related costs, offsetting lost revenues." The story mentioned some of the spending possibilities: "water, sewer and broadband" projects; retaining government workers; funding for mental-health services. Biden for his part didn't even mention the $350 billion block in his initial statements about the new law, focusing instead on the direct checks it sent to households and its continued enhanced unemployment provisions.

By the summer of 2021, Democrats had a newly invented (a self-serving) reason for the state funds. Biden made a speech in which he called on states and local government to use some of their stash to fight crime. "President Biden said on Wednesday that states could draw from $350 billion in federal stimulus money to shore up police departments," the *New York Times* reported in June. Weeks later, Democratic Congressional Campaign Committee spokesman Chris Taylor bragged in the NPR piece: "House Democrats delivered billions of dollars in the American Rescue Plan that local municipalities are using to fund both police and community-led violence intervention programs."

By 2022, the left had morphed this into the claim that the $350 billion had been provided *expressly* to fight crime. The press happily reported this rewritten history. In a May ABC News story about a Biden meeting with mayors and police chiefs, the news outlet explained, "The Covid-19 relief law included $350 billion for state and local governments to reduce violence." Biden's 2022 State of the Union Address similarly left the impression his party had earmarked the $350 billion for law enforcement: "That's why the American Rescue Plan provided $350 billion that cities, states and counties can use to hire more police and invest in proven strategies like community violence interruption," he lyricized.

Biden was spooked enough by the crime liability that he made a point of using the national address to publicly rebuke the antipolice movement. "We should all agree: The answer is not to defund the police. The answer is to *fund* the police with the resources and training they need to protect our communities." And Democrats made a point to cheer and applaud wildly, the better to suggest they'd been propolice all along. The Democratic National Committee went so far as to claim that Republicans, by voting against the Covid rescue bill, had voted *against* funding the police. It was all wildly false and cynical, but a good measure of how worried Biden and Democrats were about the crime disaster they'd helped create.

The left's other answer to the crime wave was to push another of their favored agendas: gun control. Biden campaigned on banning future sales of so-called assault weapons, and requiring existing owners to either sell them through a "voluntary" buyback program or register them with the federal government. After every unfortunate shooting, he would claim that the real driver of crime was a "gun violence epidemic" and call for his proposals to be made law. Republicans, and even some Democrats, knew this was malarkey. The guns used in most crimes are obtained and held illegally. Punishing law-abiding firearms owners with new restrictions won't make a difference to crime levels, nor will it stop the common denominator in most mass shootings: mentally ill young men. Biden wasn't able to get through any gun restrictions in his first two years, though a bipartisan coalition did pass thoughtful legislation that enhanced background checks for under-21 gun buyers, opening up juvenile records.

The public wasn't buying any of this, as bellwether elections demonstrated. In November 2021, voters not only elected Youngkin in Virginia, they very nearly elected a Republican to run the blue state of New Jersey—after a campaign that also focused on crime. A majority of voters in Minneapolis shot down the ballot initiative to abolish the police. Moderate Democrats who voiced support for rebuilding police beat their progressive rivals for mayor slots in Seattle and New York City. By June 2022, the liberal voters of San Francisco had overwhelmingly voted to recall Chesa Boudin from office, putting an end to his progressive dismantling of law and order in their city.

And in the November 2022 election, Democratic governors and mayors found themselves on defense on crime nationwide. It wasn't just their own handling of the issue that hurt them. Biden, by initially allying with antipolice crusaders, had branded the entire party. A September 2022 poll in three battleground states commissioned by a Biden-friendly SuperPAC found that while approval overall of the president was slightly up, his worst poll numbers were in the areas of crime and public safety (57 percent disapproved) and immigration (60 percent disapproved).

The biggest Democratic defeat was in Nevada, where Clark County sheriff Joe Lombardo pushed out the incumbent governor, Steve Sisolak. But Democrats were also forced to pour money into races in deep blue states and cities as Republicans surged on the crime issue. Most notable was New York State, where Governor Kathy Hochul pulled out a victory against Rep. Lee Zeldin—but only after the left rushed to reinforce her with a final advertising blitz. Meanwhile, Republicans took over the U.S. House in 2022, and primarily because Democrats lost seats in the high-crime states of New York and California.

Political memories are short—or so goes the old saying. But that's not the case when voters face a problem day in and day out, and when it continues to get worse. The electorate has faced a crime outbreak unlike anything in decades, and voters are having no problem recalling who launched it—progressive prosecutors and liberal politicians. And they aren't yet done holding people accountable.

Note the pattern, again. Carter and Biden both made the same mistake—they took on a crime issue that held little for them but downside. But note just how much worse a president Biden has proven to be. Carter inherited a crime wave and failed to fix it. Biden inherited a country that had figured out how to keep crime low, then proceeded to help trash the reforms and progress, plunging the nation back into disorder.

CHAPTER 7

BORDER DISORDER

Every president in modern times has struggled to police the U.S.'s southern border. But only two have made the mistake of inviting a full-blown refugee crisis. Any guesses as to the two?

By the end of April 1980, Carter was reeling. Inflation hit 15 percent that spring; unemployment 7 percent. Oil prices were soaring on the back of Iranian oil supply disruptions. Carter had just suffered the humiliating fiasco of his botched Iranian hostage rescue. Secretary of State Cyrus Vance resigned in protest over the mission. All of this was giving new momentum to Senator Ted Kennedy, by then vigorously challenging Carter for the Democratic presidential nomination.

Into the middle of this maelstrom walked Fidel Castro. The Cuban dictator had doubled down on his economic nationalization program in the 1970s, causing food and housing shortages. The authoritarian had then blocked emigration to prevent a population drain. Desperate Cubans began mobbing the embassies of South American countries, seeking asylum. This culminated in an April 1980 crisis, when some ten thousand Cubans crowded into the Peruvian embassy in Havana. Latin American leaders promised to help resettle some asylum seekers. Carter on April 14, 1980, announced the U.S. would join that effort and accept 3,500, which were supposed to come via Costa Rica.

Castro had taken Carter's measure, wasn't impressed, and fig- ured he could cause some mayhem. (He figured right.) His crafty response to Carter's asylum offer was to announce on April 20 that anyone who wanted to leave Cuba was free to do so, via the Mariel port west of Havana. Cuban-Americans began arranging boats to pick up friends and relatives, and soon a grassroots flo- tilla was ferrying thousands of refugees to Florida. Carter should have made clear the United States would remain in control of both the border and the number of refugees we accepted. He instead gave a speech on May 5 in which he remarked that "we as a nation have always had our arms open" and we "ought to have just as open a heart to receive new refugees." Carter's chief domestic policy adviser, Stuart Eizenstat, would later write: "I cringed when I heard those impromptu if idealistic remarks; they were interpreted by everyone in Cuba—and voters in America—as an invitation to open the floodgates."

The flood soon followed. All told, an estimated 1,700 boats fer- ried some 125,000 Cubans to Florida between April and October. Haitians, suffering under the tyranny of the Jean-Claude Duvalier regime, also started fleeing their country in boats; an estimated 25,000 joined the Cuban exodus to land on Florida shores.

Americans were initially mixed in their views of Carter's effort to rescue some Cubans, especially as it came in the wake of the president's unpopular decision a year earlier to double the number of Indochinese refugees the U.S. had agreed to accept. But Castro wasn't done with his machinations. Seeking to justify the exodus, his government claimed those leaving were scum, "parasites," and threats to the revolution. To back up this assertion, and to cause more trouble, Castro opened his prisons and began the forced deportation of criminals, as well as the mentally ill, prostitutes, and homosexu- als. As headlines about these passengers spread, U.S. opinion turned sharply against the boatlift. Carter deployed the Coast Guard to stop incoming boats, but hundreds continued to slip through.

The sudden swell of immigrants caused chaos in Florida, and

later in other states. Florida governor Bob Graham declared a state of emergency in Monroe and Dade counties at the outset of the boatlift, as the communities of Key West and Miami heaved under the staggering numbers. Authorities initially began processing refugees at local facilities. But as numbers grew and as screening of Castro's criminal deportees became more imperative, the federal government stepped in, and refugees were transferred to makeshift resettlement camps on U.S. military bases: Eglin Air Force Base in Florida; Fort McCoy in Wisconsin; Fort Indiantown Gap in Pennsylvania; and Fort Chaffee, Arkansas.

The latter became the scene of a riot that turned Mariel into an even greater political liability. The federal government used Fort Chaffee in the 1970s to handle Vietnamese refugees. A thirty-three-year-old Arkansas governor by the name of Bill Clinton argued vehemently against now using it for the Cuban arrivals. He wanted the administration to do its first screening on an offshore carrier or at the U.S. base at Guantanamo Bay, so that any criminal elements could be quickly returned to Cuba. The Carter team ignored this request, and by the end of May Fort Chaffee was brimming with twenty thousand Cuban refugees.

The local population was uneasy with the situation, while the refugees grew frustrated with the slow pace of processing. On June 1, 1980, a riot broke out, and one thousand Cubans fled the fort. They were met by angry Arkansans, many wielding firearms. Clinton worried that there'd be a showdown, and the National Guard and state troopers fired warning shots. The Cubans ultimately retreated, but the incident bolstered the narrative that America had become a dumping ground for criminals—even if in reality the vast majority of the Marielitos were anything but.

It was an unforced error by a president whose border security policies overall were far tougher than anything Democrats would contemplate now. Border security was a bipartisan affair in the 1960s and 1970s. Republicans liked it for reasons of law and order. Democrats liked it because it aligned with the wishes of Big Labor, which disliked immigrants willing to work at rates lower than unions demand. It was Democrats who led the charge in the 1960s to get rid of the successful guest-worker mechanism for Mexican workers known as the Bracero Program. And no less than Sen. Ted Kennedy—super liberal—authored legislation in the early 1970s to make it illegal for companies to hire undocumented workers.

Modern readers may be surprised to discover that many 1970s Democrats were for hardening border security, even to the extent of building walls. Growing numbers of undocumented workers and narcotics smuggling had by the late 1970s erupted into a national debate about border security. The Democratic Congress in 1978 even created a Select Commission on Immigration and Refugee Policy, to investigate ways to crack down on illegal migrants.

The Carter administration for its part asked for funding to replace old fencing around ports of entry in El Paso, Texas; San Ysidro, California; and San Luiz, Arizona. The Democratic Congress in 1977 and 1978 happily authorized the money. The furor over that fence project (after a claim the barrier had been designed to "sever" the toes of climbers) became known as the "Tortilla Curtain" incident. In another curious tie between the two presidents, the backlash over that incident launched a border activist movement that continued to grow and today plays a huge role in Biden's own southern chaos. But that was yet to come.

The Mariel boatlift reminded Carter of an important point about U.S. attitudes toward immigration. Americans—then and now—appreciate that we are a nation of immigrants and are sympathetic to the plight of refugees. During the Cold War, Americans were supportive of providing what asylum we could to those fleeing Communist oppression. And the vast majority of Cubans who fled Mariel, and those who followed, became a study in achievement, the realization of the American dream.

Yet Americans—then and now—want to see immigration done in an orderly fashion, in which the government sets the numbers, controls the process, and screens the immigrants. Chaotic border floods offend a U.S. belief in law and order, not to mention a deeply rooted sense of fairness. For every refugee that bum-rushes the border, another would-be immigrant who followed the rules sits in line. Carter's border disorder and subsequent poor handling of screening and resettlement quickly turned Americans against the Cuban boatlift and hurt him politically. It helped to drag out Kennedy's primary challenge and played a role in Carter's presidential defeat. Carter would lose every state in which the Marielitos were processed, and Clinton, running again for governor, would lose the only election of his career. (Clinton apparently *never* forgave Carter for the Fort Chaffee moment.)

Mariel also taught Carter a hard lesson in the realities of border policy: signal, and they will come. American citizenship is a dream for hundreds of millions of struggling people around the world; the only thing that keeps them from decamping their home countries en masse is the knowledge that the United States maintains secure borders and has rules. The day after Carter's promise of "open arms" and "open hearts" for the Marielitos, his press secretary, Jody Powell, labored to insist that his words did not signal a change in overall refugee policy. Nobody believed it, not least the Cubans, who took his words as an invitation to flee in even greater numbers. It would take the Carter administration six months to get Florida's borders back under control, and only then because the U.S. got Castro to agree to help.

The boatlift was a warning to future presidents about the need to constantly project U.S. border strength. Biden once again didn't pay attention.

Obama who?

It was the Democratic Party's right to demagogue Trump's border policies. It was the Democratic Party's folly to allow that rhetoric to spiral into their own refugee catastrophe.

Few things drove the left more crazy than Trump's "zero tolerance" immigration policy. To read the media assaults and Democratic commentary, his administration presided over a whirlwind of forced deportations, evil arrests, and cruel detentions. The right also fed this narrative, bragging about Trump's "wall" and his supposed success at sealing the south.

The reality was far more messy. While Trump succeeded in generating bad headlines, some questionable policies (remember family separations?), and a sharp decrease in legal immigration, his record on apprehensions and deportations was only middling. Trump supporters may be shocked to discover his stats on illegal immigration paled in some ways to those of his predecessor. The Obama administration, for instance, proved more successful at removing illegal migrants. As the Cato Institute noted, in Trump's last year of 2020 the "removal of illegal immigrants from the interior of the United States was the lowest as an absolute number and as a share of the illegal immigration population since [U.S. Immigration and Customs Enforcement] was created in 2003." The outfit noted that this was partly due to growing liberal backlash to *Obama* policies: "Local jurisdictions refused to cooperate with [Trump's] administration, continuing a trend begun during the Obama administration in response to their deportation efforts."

Obama understood all throughout his tenure that lax border security would undercut his argument for comprehensive immigration reform. Democrats chose to forget that wisdom in their desire to turn Trump into a border bogeyman. By the height of the 2020 Democratic primary, every candidate was demagoguing Trump's border enforcement, even though the idea of his policy—a strong border—wasn't much different from that of any past administration. They were also spurred on by the many progressive activist groups and immigrant rights associations that have flowered since Carter's time. At least ten Democratic primary contenders attempted to pander to these groups by embracing fully open borders—calling for *a total decriminalization of illegal border crossings.* They included future vice president Harris, as well as future Biden Transportation chief Buttigieg.

Biden didn't officially join that crowd, but under pressure to appease his left flank he made clear he'd welcome refugees. He sounded like Carter on steroids. He promised to end the president's "detrimental asylum policies." He vowed to safeguard "the dignity of migrants and [uphold] their legal right to seek asylum." He would "welcome immigrants in our communities." His campaign website explained that "Trump has waged an unrelenting assault on our values and our history as a nation of immigrants. It's wrong and it stops when Joe Biden is elected president."

And stop it he did. The new administration was so invested in hating on Trump's stance, it didn't stop to think about the merit of any particular policy or the broader imperative of border security. Biden on his first day pronounced he was ending the construction of the border wall and revoking Trump's presidential order on immigration enforcement. He also sent a sweeping immigration bill to Congress, with a proposal to fast-track citizenship for undocumented immigrants. The message to millions of would-be immigrants could not have been clearer: Get here fast, and you might just qualify for quick citizenship. Even one of Biden's border chiefs, Raul Ortiz, would admit in a deposition in 2022 that his boss's campaign rhetoric had amounted to an invitation.

As Biden flashed a green light to new refugees, his administration meanwhile dismantled the best tools they had for stopping any coming flood. The Centers for Disease Control in March 2020 activated Title 42, a power that lets administrations expel border crossers during a pandemic to safeguard U.S. public health. Covid was still raging, but the Biden administration quickly initiated exemptions to the provision, allowing unaccompanied minors— and in many cases entire families—to remain in the United States.

The administration also quickly moved to suspend Trump's Migrant Protection Protocols, better known as Remain in Mexico. The program required asylum seekers to wait in our southern neighbor while U.S. immigration judges decided whether they qualified for entry. It was designed to force would-be migrants to think hard about whether they had a credible asylum claim, since they wouldn't get an automatic in. And it worked. A 2019 review by the Department of Homeland Security found that total enforcement actions against Central American migrants decreased by 80 percent from May through September of that year. Nearly seventy thousand asylum seekers were sent to Mexico to wait for the courts to rule.

Yet candidate Biden lambasted the program, tweeting in March 2020: "Donald Trump's 'Remain in Mexico' policy is dangerous, inhumane, and goes against everything we stand for as a nation of immigrants. My administration will end it." True to his promise, the administration stopped sending new enrollees into the program, and instead began processing all those waiting in Mexico, waving through even the most ludicrous claims of "persecution." Most were released into the country with the prospect of being allowed to take employment. Because of the extreme backlog in the federal judiciary for immigration cases, it is years before an asylum seeker is summoned to a hearing. Even then, there's no guarantee they'll show up for the tribunal.

The deluge

Even before Biden was elected, migrants began moving toward the border in expectation of more favorable chances of getting into the U.S. His official victory boosted the numbers further, and his first-day actions turned a wash into a deluge. Word spread among migrant communities that the ticket to U.S. entry was traveling with children, and entire families began trekking north from all the usual places—Mexico, Honduras, Guatemala, and El Salvador. But as news of Biden's new border policies got out, these populations were increasingly joined by would-be refugees from Venezuela, Cuba, Haiti, Nicaragua, and Brazil. Border officials were at one point shocked to find thousands of Romanians in the mix.

In April 2021, U.S. Customs and Border Protection reported some 397,000 encounters with migrants in the first five months of the fiscal year, which started in October 2020. It was a real increase over fiscal 2019—which had witnessed its own surge on the back of migrant caravans. And the numbers continued rising exponentially. CBP would soon report 172,000 encounters in March 2021 alone—a 71 percent increase over February.

For all the Democrats' complaining about Trump's "cruel" border policies, they never stopped to consider the greater cruelty of an anarchic border. What began as bad policy quickly escalated into a humanitarian crisis. The long and arduous journey to the U.S. border holds untold numbers of hazards, including scorching heat, desert conditions, and dangerous water. In fiscal 2020 and 2021, record numbers of migrants died trying to enter the United States illegally—some 750 in 2021 alone. Those numbers include children.

The administration proved unable to handle migrants now arriving in droves, and the Biden team in March was forced to send the Federal Emergency Management Agency to the border. FEMA normally responds to natural disasters; this time it was responding to a Biden disaster. Nonprofits and local governments had to go foraging for food, water, Covid tests, and medicines for tens of thousands of migrants jammed into overcrowded, temporary shelters. A beleaguered and undermanned border patrol proved unable to stop the flow.

The worst part was the mass of parentless children. The Title 42 exclusion for kids—allowing them immediate entry—quickly became an article of faith among migrant communities. For every family that made the journey north, another parent chose to send their child over the border alone. By April, CBP was reporting a record 18,890 encounters with unaccompanied minors in

March—doubling the number in February. The Department of Health and Human Services crammed nearly 9,000 in beds in licensed shelters, but thousands more were stuck with CBP or in temporary sites waiting for a slot. The *Washington Post* reported that these temporary facilities were "cramped, austere holding cells with concrete floors and benches. Lights remain on 24 hours a day, agents say, and there are few places to play." When prior surges under Trump produced overcrowding, AOC had lambasted kids in "cages" and "concentration camps." Now the Biden Democrats' own feckless border policy had created a situation of far worse deprivation.

The White House belatedly tried to stuff the genie back in the canteen in late March, dispatching Homeland Security Secretary Alejandro Mayorkas to NBC's "Meet the Press" to declare: "The border is closed." All of America—and the army of tens of thousands marching north—collectively rolled its eyes. Everybody knew the opposite was true, and the numbers continued to grow.

Biden's next trick was to claim the surge wasn't out of the ordinary, just the latest in a cyclical, annual spring uptick: "It happens every year," he insisted. That claim fell apart in October, when CBP announced its end-of-year numbers. The agency in fiscal 2020 had logged 458,000 southwest border encounters. By the end of September 2021 it was reporting *1.73 million* border encounters—a 278 percent increase. The sheer number is as notable as the growth. America had struggled to handle and process Carter's 125,000 Cubans; Biden's policies in his first year led to fourteen times that many people.

Biden was in one area willing to get tough on the border. In July 2021 he decided to crack down on . . . Canada. As migrants flooded the southern line, the administration once again infuriated its northern partner by using the excuse of Covid to delay the reopening of the U.S.-Canada border. Canada had only just announced it would resume allowing Americans free entry; Biden repaid that favor by barring even vaccinated Canadians from touching U.S. soil. The move prompted blowback from Democrats with districts along the northern border, given the revenue hit from lost Canadian business. It was a perfect example of the administration posturing on the pandemic while refusing to handle a full-blown crisis unfolding in Texas, Arizona, and California. Notably, Biden budgets have demanded billions more in social spending, even as they have starved the border budget, leaving agents struggling to keep pace.

Coddling the cartels

The humanitarian catastrophe continued to escalate. One flashpoint came in September 2021, when a throng of Haitians fleeing poverty made it to Mexico and then arrived together in Del Rio, Texas. The administration had been warned of the coming surge but was utterly unprepared. Border agents herded some fifteen thousand Haitians to a temporary shelter under the Del Rio International Bridge. To put that number in perspective, the city of Del Rio itself has a population of thirty-five thousand. The images were shocking: masses of humanity, lacking access to clean water, food or toilets. As the *New York Times* described it, "dense crowds, sleeping on dirt or milling about in triple-digit heat amid conditions of deteriorating sanitation." An understandably angry Texas governor Greg Abbott dispatched state police and National Guard officers to aid the situation, while slamming the administration for being in "complete disarray."

But a porous border brings with it other problems, including crime. Cartels are growing a lucrative business in Biden's border policies. The *New York Times* in July 2022 reported that human smuggling has evolved over a decade from "a scattered network of freelance 'coyotes' into a multi-billion-dollar international business controlled by organized crime, including some of Mexico's most violent drug cartels." These smugglers are now taking full advantage of Biden's border chaos. High-speed chases of smugglers and federal raids of stash houses are now a daily occurrence, and border agents routinely find dozens of migrants who are being held against their will—or worse. In June 2022, authorities discovered the bodies of fifty-three dead migrants in an abandoned tractor-trailer near San Antonio—fifty adults and three children. They'd been left inside with no food or water, and in searing heat.

The cartels are shipping more than humans. Fifteen years ago, hardly anyone in the country had heard of fentanyl, a potent synthetic opioid that can easily lead to accidental overdose. The drug is fifty times more powerful than heroin and as much as a hundred times more potent than morphine. It can be taken on its own, though is increasingly being laced into other street drugs. The United States in 2021 experienced a record 107,000 overdoses, and the majority involved synthetic opioids like fentanyl.

The Mexican border is now the source of nearly all fentanyl entering the U.S. As China started cracking down on fentanyl production, Mexican criminal networks cornered the market. These operations are exploding in scope, as the cartels employ more people to manufacture the cheap, easy-to-produce drug, and as Biden's border policy offers more opportunities for smuggling. In fiscal 2020, CBP seized about 5,000 pounds of fentanyl. It more than doubled that in 2021, seizing 11,000 pounds. It hit 15,000 pounds in 2022. And this is only what the feds seized. State law enforcement also scoops up massive amounts in their own raids.

The media likes to suggest that all these drugs are snuck into the U.S. through official ports of entry, and are therefore unconnected to Biden's border mess. Not true. As former Border Control chief Rodney Scott explained in a September 2021 letter to Congress, the cartels use border chaos to also facilitate smuggling. They "create controllable gaps in border security. These gaps are then exploited to easily smuggle contraband, criminals, or even potential terrorists into the U.S. at will. Even when [Border Patrol] detects the illegal entry, agents are spread so thin that they often lack the capability to make a timely interdiction." Carter's ill-considered policy led to a swell of migrants. Biden's has led to a flood of migrants, drugs, and crime.

Enter the robes

Biden was in such a hurry to reverse all things Trump that his administration meanwhile cut numerous procedural corners in its revised border policy. This invited lawsuits, and the entrance of the federal judiciary into the fray. Just the recipe for even more border anarchy.

Biden suspended Remain in Mexico soon after taking office, and formally terminated the program in June. Yet the administration skipped some usual required steps. The states of Texas and Missouri sued and won an injunction against stopping the program. The administration went through the motions of restarting it, and kept up the fiction that it was operational until the Supreme Court ruled in July 2022 that it could officially shut it down. The Biden team used the program to send all of 4,300 migrants to Mexico from December to June 2022.

That left the Biden team with only Title 42 as a quick means of expulsion. The Trump administration authorized that pandemic-era policy at the beginning of the Covid outbreak and found it an even more efficient way to handle the border than Remain in Mexico. As border management initially spiraled out of control, a panicked Biden team seized on Title 42, and used it aggressively to expel migrants.

The left went into meltdown, and as the pandemic began to wane, it insisted the Biden administration discontinue the program. Bending to progressive pressure, in April 2022, the Biden CDC announced it was terminating Title 42 health powers, saying there was no need for it as the government had the pandemic under control. On the one hand, this was true—the country had largely returned to normal. On the other hand, Title 42 had become the only thing providing any border-crossing deterrence whatsoever. Even moderate Democrats voiced alarm that the program might end.

Biden was saved a month later when a federal judge ordered the administration to continue the policy, ruling that, yet again, the administration had skipped over the necessary steps to halt it. While publicly griping over the ruling and promising to appeal, the Associated Press reported that inside the White House the decision was "greeted with quiet relief." A midterm election was coming in just five months, and for now Biden had been spared the possibility of yet another headline-grabbing border collapse.

That came to an end on November 15, 2022 (a week after the election) when a separate federal judge decreed the administration *must* shut the program down. Biden finally decided he had a problem and needed a new approach. On January 8, 2023, nearly two years after taking office, the president finally sojourned to his chaotic southern border, meeting with border agents and support-service personnel in El Paso. It came on the back of a new enforcement plan, in which he claimed he'd expand restrictions on asylum and require some migrants to apply for refuge from outside the country. Arriving in El Paso, he was hit from all sides—progressives decrying his new policies, Republicans lambasting his negligence. And still, there is no reason to believe the migrant waves will subside.

Poisoning the well

Even as the courts weighed in, one important body did not: Congress. As any number of modern presidents will moan, the legislative branch has for decades been the biggest obstacle to border sanity. Carter had a Congress willing to act, as did Reagan. Since then, Congress has been absent without leave.

The contours of a border compromise have been obvious for years now. Republicans want far greater border security, a demand that is reasonable and clearly necessary. Democrats in return want protections for some classes of immigrants, in particular the "Dreamers"—kids who landed in the U.S. through no fault of their own, many of whom have never known any other home, and yet who still face deportation. Part of any deal needs to be an overhaul of immigration procedures, including a new approach to asylum claims, as well as a smarter program for guest worker visas. Everyone knows this is the potential deal, yet Congress refuses to take on what has become a hot and explosive political topic.

And Biden, more than any recent president, has poisoned the well for a deal. His initial immigration proposal—sent to Congress immediately upon entering office—was more a messaging document than an honest attempt to get something done. It offered little to Republicans by way of security, and instead made sweeping demands for liberalized citizenship. This hardened positions in Congress, making it tougher to find compromise. And the ensuing border chaos then made a deal all but impossible.

Spreading the pain

Carter managed to annoy the citizenry of the four states to which he sent Cubans for processing. Biden managed to annoy citizens everywhere.

By September 2022, more than one million illegal migrants had been allowed to claim asylum in the United States under Biden's tenure. Upon the federal government granting their temporary reprieve, these individuals were cut loose, no assistance provided. Some states and cities—often under Democratic governance—went out of their way to set up aid programs and shelter, at significant cost. Their residents didn't always approve. Far more cities—particularly in border states like Texas and Arizona—simply found themselves on the hook for the enormous expense of integrating masses of new migrants who were unemployed and needed housing, food, and education for their kids.

Southern states remain understandably livid. The federal government has authority over immigration policy—as it likes to remind the states—and is waving through asylum seekers at an unprecedented pace. Yet it refuses to deal with the costs. Despite repeated pleas for more federal help, states have been left to handle the situation on their own. Just one example: The city of Yuma, Arizona, in 2022 found itself trying to handle an influx of 250,000 migrants. It's a city of 100,000 people.

To draw attention to the mess, governors in 2022 began busing or flying batches of immigrants to Democratic "sanctuary" cities—locales that in response to Obama and Trump policies chose to limit their cooperation with federal authorities that were trying to remove illegal migrants. Texas governor Greg Abbott and Arizona governor Doug Ducey began relocating some migrants in the spring of 2022, but doubled down in the summer—busing thousands of migrants to some of the country's biggest cities. Florida governor Ron DeSantis also got in on the act, flying willing Venezuelans in September to the tony enclave of Martha's Vineyard. The left went apoplectic, and California governor Gavin Newsom—always good for some histrionics—suggested DeSantis should be investigated for "kidnapping."

Democratic mayors and governors cried foul, despite an influx that was minimal compared to the number of migrants arriving at border states. New York's Eric Adams claimed his city of 8 million was reaching a "breaking point" with the addition of ten thousand migrants. Illinois governor J. B. Pritzker declared a "state of emergency" after a mere five hundred reached his borders. Washington, DC, mayor Muriel Bowser demanded the Department of Defense send in the National Guard to handle several thousand newly arrived migrants to her city. The federal government refused to intervene, in part, Reuters reported, because to do so would play into the Republican "optics" that there was an immigration "crisis."

The administration's other problem was that it had been shipping migrants around the country long before Republican governors got in on the act—yet had never provided assistance. The administration worried that if it started now, it might be on the hook to deploy resources to pretty much every major city in every state in the country. Critics called the relocations a "stunt," but the buses and flights served their purpose—exposing the magnitude of Biden's border catastrophe.

Even today, the Biden administration continues to maintain the fiction that the border is "closed." And yet the fiscal 2022 year-end statistics exposed that lie. CBP in October 2022 quietly released the grim picture: 2.77 million enforcement actions along the southwest border for the year, more than a million more than in fiscal 2021—the prior annual record. Nearly 20 percent of those apprehended in September 2022 were repeat offenders, meaning the border has become so permeable that migrants are hitting it again and again, despite prior detentions and deportations. They are betting that they will get through at some point.

Biden's border policies are just another example of this president bowing to extreme progressive demands—despite the terrible politics. While Americans might be polarized on the question of citizenship for undocumented aliens, it remains solidly united on the need for border control. A Harvard-Harris poll released in May 2021—as the country watched the initial waves of Biden migrants—found that 80 percent of respondents viewed the situation as a "crisis that needs to be addressed immediately," while 85 percent wanted stronger border controls. That's in line with polls about border security over the decades and explains Biden's terrible poll numbers on his handling of the border.

Carter at least acknowledged he had a problem and ultimately got his Cuban refugee crisis under control. Biden exhibits no interest or will to truly end the growing migrant surges, and no care for the future policy consequences. With every day Biden allows the number of undocumented migrants in the country to swell, he puts an immigration solution that much further out of reach.

CHAPTER 8

A NATION ON FIRE

Jimmy Carter didn't launch America's culture wars, but he stepped up to some modern battle lines. Fifty years later, Biden is now driving the combat into new territory.

America found plenty to argue about prior to Carter. Fights over segregation and discrimination in the Civil Rights era. Campus protests over Vietnam. Disputes over the secularization of school curricula and evolution. The hippie counterculture. The beginning of modern gay rights activism. The Equal Rights Amendment. And let's not forget a Supreme Court decision in 1973 called *Roe v. Wade,* which launched a whole new national abortion divide.

Carter walked into all this in an unusual position. Liberals and activists felt emboldened by victories on race, abortion, gay rights, and the ERA, and they expected the Democratic president to take their causes to new levels. But Carter was a Southern evangelical, whose appeal to traditional American values had helped him into office. He was personally pro-life and pro-family—yet overseeing a party dominated by liberal interest groups. What to do? His answer was to split the difference—turbocharging some liberal causes while ducking others.

Carter's biggest vulnerability was his position on abortion, which became a sudden cultural flashpoint in the wake of *Roe.* To his credit, he never deviated from his own belief in the sanctity of life, and he consistently supported the Hyde Amendment—which bans taxpayer funding of abortions. (Another Democrat who consistently voted for Hyde? Joe Biden.) Carter's positions were met with scathing criticism from activists, including the head of the National Organization for Women, Eleanor Smeal. His response was to dart for the middle ground. He explained that while he was personally opposed to abortion, it was also none of the government's business. He opposed a constitutional amendment to overturn *Roe*.

Identity politics was born in the late 1970s, and Carter played a foundational role. He became the first president, in 1977, to have his staff meet with gay rights activists at the White House. In 1978 he showed up on a campaign stage in San Francisco to support the reelection of Governor Jerry Brown and used the moment to publicly condemn California's Prop. 6, which would have banned gays and lesbians from teaching in classrooms.

He also embraced the nascent world of "affirmative action," putting an unprecedented emphasis on using sex and race to choose his administrative and judicial appointments. He created a National Advisory Committee for Women and gave it the mission of installing more women in government jobs and of finishing the ratification of the ERA. In a 1978 executive order, he directed his commission for judicial nominations to "make special efforts to seek out and identify well-qualified women and members of minority groups" as choices. It was Carter who elevated Ruth Bader Ginsburg to the U.S. Court of Appeals for the District of Columbia—from which Bill Clinton would put her on the Supreme Court.

Newspaper headlines at the time brimmed with "firsts"—the first African-American woman to serve in the cabinet (Patricia Roberts Harris); the first Hispanic to serve as commissioner of Immigration and Naturalization (Leonel J. Castillo). A *Washington Post* story in May 1980 would note that "about a third of the record

260 judges Carter has nominated during his term in office have been blacks, women or Hispanics"—a feat accomplished in part because Congress in 1978 created 152 new judgeships. Yet the practice of so emphasizing diversity injected a new level of animosity into Washington hearings, as was the case in 1980 when the American Bar Association questioned the qualifications of Carter's appointments of the first black federal judges from Alabama. The ABA reports touched off nasty accusations of racism and were a taste of the ugly identity-based confirmation battles that are now routine.

Carter also began the practice of stuffing the court with activist judges. While unwilling to alter his own pro-life views, he bent to demands that he nominate lawyers who were willing and eager to take charge of American social change. His nominations not only landed him in scuffles with conservative members of his own Democrat Senate, they launched the modern judicial wars. To counter Carter's increasingly liberal federal bench, the right mobilized, feeding into the creation of the Federalist Society and today's fight over the soul of the judiciary.

Another legacy: today's raging debate over university admissions. The Supreme Court in 1978 decided *Regents of the University of California v. Bakke,* in which a white applicant who'd been denied admission to medical school sued over the UC's practice of reserving certain slots for minorities. Activists—and many members of his own administration—wanted Carter to support this policy. Yet public opposition was fierce. Once again seeking a middle ground, Carter's Justice Department filed a brief rejecting quotas but suggesting race could and should be a factor in choosing entrants. The high court took this advice, and "racial preferences" were born. The nation is still wrangling with the fallout almost fifty years later.

And Carter takes responsibility for creating the monster that continues to destroy public education today. In the summer of 1976 a previously nonpolitical union decided to endorse its first presidential candidate. The National Education Association started as a conservative outfit and despite its huge membership stayed out of the electoral fray; it didn't think it a good idea to mix politics with the classroom. Oh, for such sanity today!

But Democratic candidates started making teachers offers they couldn't refuse, including the promise of big new federal investments in education. They understood early the electoral benefits of getting millions of teachers' votes. The American Federation of Teachers made its first endorsement of a candidate in 1972, backing George McGovern. Carter wasn't always a favorite of unions. But he nabbed NEA's first endorsement in 1976, along with AFT's. The bait: dollars, and a promise to create a cabinet-level Department of Education.

The pledge came to life in 1979 when Congress created a federal bureaucracy that has ever since excelled in wasting dollars. It also stomps on states' rights by conditioning its funding on obeisance to federal mandates. Carter acknowledged that the "primary responsibility" for education rested with states but insisted the U.S. government had "confused its role as junior partner in American education with silent partner." He claimed his new department was simply designed to let the federal government "meet its responsibilities in education more effectively, more efficiently, and more responsively." This was the president putting lipstick on a pig that had been created purely as a political bribe.

He got his payoff. NEA jumped in early to the 1979 Democratic primary, throwing its weight in September behind Carter. That proved critical for Carter's ultimate victory over Kennedy (backed by ATF). But it was NEA who made out with the most. Not only did the teachers' unions get a new captive creature in a federal Education Department, the union itself became a political juggernaut. As the *Washington Post* reported in July 1980, in four short years, the 1.8-million-member union shop had grown into "far and away the biggest interest-group force in Democratic presidential politics," boasting almost as many delegates to the convention as the giant state of California. Democrats indicated their willing-ness to do anything for the teachers' vote, and Carter, in addi-tion to creating a new cabinet post, ditched his prior support for an innovative new idea known as school vouchers. The teachers' unions have only solidified their iron grip over the party—with horrific consequences for our nation's kids.

Carter's cultural positions in many ways look tame by com-parison to today's radical left. Like many liberals of his genera-tion, he saw affirmative action as a temporary measure, a catchup for a nation that was moving beyond its discriminatory past. He rejected quotas. His policies were generally rooted in belief in the value of work and equal opportunity. He believed in American exceptionalism.

Yet his positions were aggressive for the time and inspired a backlash. Not only did his judicial appointments give rise to a con-servative movement to reclaim the courts, his policies mobilized the evangelical community. Christian voters equated Carter's positions with cultural decay: "secular humanism" in education; the rise of abortion rights; radical feminism; gay rights. Modern historians credit Carter with galvanizing this bloc, creating a reli-gious right that remains a powerful Republican constituency to this day.

Every Democratic president since Carter has leaned more heav-ily into these cultural fault lines—race, identity politics, activist judges, abortion, school indoctrination. Yet most successors still walked a Carter-like line. Clinton embraced identity appoint-ments and affirmative action. Though he also took on welfare reform and had his Sister Souljah moment—condemning the hip hop artist for proposing a "week" to "kill white people." Obama, even as the first African-American president, publicly downplayed race and cultural issues, save the occasional flashpoint that only further sowed division.

But the Biden administration has taken these race and culture wars to new extremes, once again signing up for his party's most radical positions. This is stoking divides in ways unseen since the 1960s and 1970s. Just one example: By 2021, the number of Americans who told Gallup that relations between white and black people were "very" or "somewhat" good were at modern lows—and worse than in the Trump years.

Me-too Joe

Biden never was a cultural radical. Which was precisely why he ended up acting like one.

As the Democratic primary ramped up in 2019, the press simmered with stories about the bad optics of two old white guys at the top of the rankings (Biden and Sanders). Democrats in 2008 nominated their first African-American presidential candidate. In 2016 their first woman. When Pelosi retook the speaker's gavel in early 2019, the press clucked that she was presiding over the most diverse House in history.

All of this was proof positive of the stunning progress America had made in pushing beyond barriers of the past. Yet in a Democratic party and a media obsessed with identity grievances, the storylines were entirely different. The Me-Too Movement. Black Lives Matter. Cultural appropriation. Climate justice. Systemic racism. Mass incarceration. Brown complicity. Trans-exclusionary radical feminism. (Yes, that is a real thing.)

Into this stumbled Ol' Joe, with his fifty-year history of doing whatever his party had been doing at the moment. That included Carter's moment, and decades when the party was far less woke. Biden had long supported the Hyde Amendment. He was an opponent in the 1970s of race-integration busing. He was central to his party's 1994 crime bill, which he'd promised was so strict that "we do everything but hang people for jaywalking." He helped lead the war on drugs and favored the death penalty. He'd bragged that he'd once "voted for 700 miles of fence." He joined legislation prohibiting the federal government from recognizing same-sex marriage. There was also his creepy-crawly track record of touching and kissing women in unwelcome ways. These positions were all toxic in the new progressive movement.

Biden came under fire within weeks of announcing his bid, and by early June had already jettisoned his Hyde support. But it was the second presidential debate, later that month, where his liabilities started flashing bright red. Surrounded by a scrum of hard-left, progressive competitors, Biden was taking a pummeling. Partway through the debate, California Democratic senator Kamala Harris demanded to speak "on the issue of race." She landed a sidewinder, punching Biden over his past opposition to busing and for his previous work with segregationist politicians. The Biden campaign realized it needed a change—and Biden got progressive religion overnight.

The campaign sprinted to the cultural left. It jumped on prison reform, and on vastly expanded asylum rules. Biden banged on about the reauthorization of the Violence Against Women Act and elevated the polarized issue of abortion, promising to codify *Roe v. Wade*. He went to an LGBTQ town hall and claimed that Obama had once kissed him ("I swear to God," he told CNN's moderator, Anderson Cooper). But the shocker came in March 2020, in the heat of his final battle with Sanders, when Biden vowed to pick a woman vice president. No candidate in history had ever made a veep pledge on the basis of identity. Geography? Sure. Experience? Yup. Age? Yes. Reproductive organs? No. It took progressive pandering to a whole new level.

And to a new level still when he chose Harris, who the press rushed to note if elected would be the first of . . . *everything*: first female, first African-American, and first Asian-American vice president. From there it was off to the races. The campaign made "justice" (racial justice, climate justice, energy justice) a top theme, and upon taking office Biden issued an executive order, which his office described as emphasizing "the enormous human costs of systemic racism, persistent poverty, and other disparities, and directed the Federal Government to advance an ambitious whole-of-government equity agenda."

What a difference a few letters can make. Carter Democrats believed in *equality*—an America in which every citizen has equal opportunity. Biden Democrats embrace *"equity"*—the forcible reallocation of resources and benefits, designed to ensure *equal outcomes* between *marginalized communities* and those who have benefited from *discriminatory systems*. An equity agenda by definition segments a country into boxes based on sex, race, gender, income—and then highlights the differences and pits groups against each other. Carter in the 1970s envisioned an America that could move quickly to narrow its divides. Biden adopted an agenda designed to rip the country apart.

How does this work in practice? Corrosively. Consider a program the administration attempted to enact just months after Biden took office. Democrats in their initial Covid "rescue" bill included a nearly $4 billion program to forgive the loans of "socially disadvantaged" farmers. The Biden Agriculture Department later defined this to mean "one or more of the following: Black/African-American, American Indian, Alaskan native, Hispanic/Latino, Asian, or Pacific Islander." Apparently, no white farmer in America has ever had a trouble in the world.

The program was such a blatant violation of the Constitution's equal protection clause that at least three federal courts blocked its implementation within months. Fearing that the Supreme Court might take up the case and use it to dismantle other racial preference programs, the Justice Department declined to appeal the injunctions.

But the administration continued to exploit race for other political purposes. As the nation in the spring of 2021 waited for the jury to pronounce on Derek Chauvin (the George Floyd case),

Biden outrageously interfered in the justice process, publicly saying that he was "praying" for the "right verdict" and that the evidence was "overwhelming." (The nation was lucky this didn't result in a mistrial.) When the jury came back with guilty counts, Biden praised the result but then went further—saying that such convictions were "much too rare" in America, essentially cheering for more police prosecutions. At a time when Americans were struggling to balance justice for Floyd with overall support for law enforcement, comments like these only inflamed divides.

Democrats also exploited race in attempts to pass unrelated legislative priorities. In the wake of the 2020 election mess several GOP states implemented voting reforms. Georgia in March 2021 passed its own modest change, which actually expanded weekend voting, formalized drop boxes, and made it less likely that mail-in votes would get rejected. Yet Biden held a press conference claiming the reform was "un-American" and "sick," equivalent to "Jim Crow" efforts to suppress minority voters. He insisted the only cure was a federal Democratic voting "reform"—a sweeping federal takeover of the voting rules in all fifty states.

Cynicism at its worst. The Democratic bill is hundreds of pages of provisions that the party hopes will help its electoral fortunes. It creates a federal right to mail-in ballots; outlaws voter ID; overrules state laws against ballot harvesting; and enacts same-day voter registration. The left wants this bill for one reason: to ensure Democratic dominance in future elections. And it wants it so badly that nearly all the party now supports eliminating the Senate filibuster's sixty-vote requirement—to ease the path to voting changes and other priorities.

The bill has nothing to do with minority rights, as Biden well knows. Yet he played along with the farce, insisting the takeover was necessary to stop "racist" Republicans from dragging the country back to "Bull Connor" days. He even signed on to the ahistorical claim that the filibuster itself was a legacy of racism and called to eliminate it in the case of the voting bill. This was the same Biden who in 2005 gave a long speech on the Senate floor defending the sixty-vote threshold: "If there is one thing this country stands for it's fair play—not tilting the playing field in favor of one side or the other, not changing the rules unilaterally. We play by the rules, and we win or lose by the rules." No longer.

The "Jim Crow" lies were exposed in 2022, when the Peach State racked up record turnout. Georgia secretary of state Brad Raffensperger would note in December 2022 that Georgia had achieved turnout records for a midterm election. Jim Crow?

* * *

Of all the eerie similarities between the Carter and Biden administrations, one of the strangest is the bookends of the abortion debate. Carter presided in the immediate aftermath of the Supreme Court's controversial *Roe v. Wade* ruling. Biden presided over that opinion's demise.

Few things have roiled America's cultural divide more over the past fifty years than abortion. Sadly, the divide is largely court created. Prior to *Roe,* states were able to craft their abortion laws around the demands of their local citizenry, and more states were moving to legalize it. The high court with *Roe* trod on that power, instead discovering a right to "privacy" in the Constitution that shielded abortion. The decision launched a multidecade, wrenching debate over states' rights and the definition of life. All thanks to one crummy decision. Even liberal scholars acknowledge that Roe and its successor ruling, *Casey,* were extremely poor pieces of jurisprudence.

Sadder yet, the pro- and anti-*Roe* forces spent those years fighting over an issue that America isn't today all that far apart on. Strip away the passion, and polls consistently show the same thing. A small minority of Americans are very pro-choice—advocating abortions up through the third trimester and even to the moment of birth. A small minority of Americans are very pro-life, with some against abortions even in cases of rape or incest. But the vast majority of the country is in the middle, with the view that abortion should be allowed, with restrictions. We might disagree over twelve weeks or fifteen weeks, but the views we share far outweigh our differences.

When Amy Coney Barrett took her seat on the Supreme Court and cemented a conservative majority, states saw their opportunity to put *Roe* to the test. The Supremes agreed to hear in early 2021 a Mississippi law that restricted abortions to the first fifteen weeks of pregnancy, in a case called *Dobbs v. Jackson Women's Health Organization*. The left went nuts, acting as if the United States was on the verge of *The Handmaid's Tale*.

Democrats warned that women everywhere would be stripped of their reproductive rights and thrust into back-alley procedures. This despite every indication that most states would retain abortion protections, and potentially even liberalize current laws. Academics and the left ramped up an intimidation campaign against the conservative justices, lecturing them on precedent and suggesting the court's "credibility" hung in the balance. The media ran hit pieces that all but declared Barrett a member of a religious cult. Democrats began a separate campaign to force Clarence Thomas to resign, based on the political views of his wife.

The hysteria and coercion hit its peak in early May 2022 when a draft opinion was leaked, suggesting a majority did indeed intend to overturn the precedent. Mobs thronged outside the Supreme Court, which had to erect fences. An ad hoc group calling itself "Ruth Sent Us" (a reference to the late Ruth Bader Ginsburg) issued an online invitation for activists to begin harassing the justices and published the locations of their homes. Protesters showed up outside their doors.

This was the moment for Biden—who claimed to want to restore trust in public institutions—to step in and calm the fever, to give a speech on the importance of respecting America's constitutional process. Even the Senate felt compelled in the aftermath of the leak to unanimously pass a bill to provide the justices and their families security equivalent to that of other high-ranking government officers.

Yet the Biden administration refused to condemn the tactics. Asked about the Ruth Sent Us tactics, White House Press Secretary Jen Psaki initially would say nothing more than: "The president's view is that there's a lot of passion, a lot of fear, a lot of sadness from many, many people across this country about what they saw in that leaked document." And Pelosi's House refused to pass the Senate bill, after progressives pettily complained the legislation didn't give equal security to court staff.

It was unsurprising, therefore, when the nation in June was introduced to Nicholas John Roske, the disturbed man who showed up outside the home of Justice Brett Kavanaugh packing among other things a gun, ammunition, a crowbar, a knife, zip ties, and duct tape. His ambition was to assassinate the justice— he felt it "would give his life purpose." He luckily lost his nerve and turned himself in to the police. It nonetheless took a further week for House Democrats to rouse themselves to provide the court more protection. Even then, twenty-seven House Democrats voted no. In doing so, they sent the message that they were perfectly okay with political violence—as long as it was exacted on conservative justices.

Prior to the opinion's official release, activist groups like Jane's Revenge started attacking pregnancy crisis centers across the country and called on comrades to stage a "night of rage" and riots if *Roe* were overturned. Again, this was a moment for Biden to call for calm. Political violence was already on the rise in the United States—the 2017 attack at the Republican congressional baseball practice, the death at the Charlottesville, Virginia, rally, anti-Semitic shootings in synagogues, the George Floyd riots, and the January 6 riots. But the White House sat still, preferring to maintain its narrative that the GOP alone was the party of violence. The weeks following the opinion's release featured more firebombings of clinics, vandalization of churches, and rioting.

Biden greeted the opinion with fury at the court—a terrible show of disrespect for the system, and clearly designed to inspire similar disrespect among his followers. He trashed the decision as "terrible, extreme." And he claimed the justices hadn't produced a "constitutional judgment" but rather had engaged in "an exercise in raw political power." Plenty of presidents have received Supreme Court decisions they don't like, and some outline their legal disagreements. Carter himself disagreed with abortion, yet never spewed vitriol at the high court over its *Roe* decision.

Biden's contempt was worse in that it was nakedly political. Again, American views on abortion have changed over the years; the procedure isn't going away. As predicted, many blue and purple states instantly moved to lock in abortion rights. Judges in some conservative states blocked prior abortion bans, while yet other jurisdictions rushed to stand up ballot initiatives to give voters a say. A few conservative commentators noted that many of the proposed replacement statutes—even in red states—were more liberal than the abortion laws in most European countries. Yet the administration scrambled to make hay with the ruling. Biden announced a flurry of emergency executive orders and actions that he claimed would help women continue to access abortion. All this was in aid of the midterm election and Biden's claim that Republicans existed to strip rights from Americans.

Overall, the left's abortion hysteria was a marginal political winner. Biden continued through the midterms to insist that "ultra-MAGA" Republicans were a national threat, and this claim, as well as the presence of abortion initiatives on ballots, helped Democrats keep the focus on things other than the economy.

But it came at the cost of further escalating the culture wars.

The Supreme Court with *Dobbs* provided the opportunity for the country to remember it can settle its political conflicts democratically. With luck, that may still happen. But the president's demagoguing set the effort back by years. The contrast between Carter's and Biden's handling of this sensitive political topic couldn't be more stark.

Unions v. kids

Carter's decision to pander to a newly powerful education lobby created a toxic alliance that exists to this day. He could claim all he wanted that his federal education takeover was about government "efficiency." It was spin. The president saw an opportunity to capture millions of new teachers' votes, and he sold his party's soul to the union store.

Biden is just the latest Democratic president to take orders from teachers' union bosses. That fealty has most harmed disadvantaged kids, who would benefit from the charter schools and vouchers that unions oppose. Yet it was under Biden that circumstances finally combined to show how utterly destructive the union-Democrat agenda could be for kids everywhere.

Biden spent most of 2020 slamming the Trump administration's handling of the pandemic. It didn't seem to matter that no leader in the world had a grip on Covid, or that Biden wasn't offering change beyond vague promises of better "leadership." The leading left-wing slur was that Republicans weren't "following the science," and they took aim at Republican governors like Florida's DeSantis and Texas's Abbott, both of whom made a priority of reopening and getting kids back to school.

As the nation now knows, the "scientists" and the public-health elite understood the virus about as well as the talking heads, and the country endured years of confusing directives. Yet the liberal establishment managed to divide the country in an entirely new way: "good" blue states that locked down, kept kids out of school and demanded masks vs. "bad" GOP states that opened up and went back to liberty.

This was the state of affairs when Biden took office, and it was the nation's kids who bore the cruel brunt of the politicking. All the science showed that Covid was a minimal risk to children, and the CDC had said in the summer of 2020 that reopening school for in-person learning was a step toward improving overall public health. This was just one of many reasons GOP states had got children back in the classroom.

Yet the teachers' union had fiercely resisted any talk of reopening in 2020 and even into 2021. Members liked their paid vacations. Teachers initially claimed it was too dangerous for them to go back to school, and American Federation of Teachers' president Randi Weingarten in 2020 supported "safety" strikes against reopenings. But as the unions piled on crazy demands, it became clear something else was afoot.

In August 2020 an alliance of progressive groups and teachers' unions held a "national day of resistance" to lay out what they would require before returning to the classroom. They wanted politicians to: cancel "rents and mortgages," "a moratorium on evictions/foreclosures," a "moratorium on new charter or voucher programs and standardized testing," and a "massive infusion of federal money to support the reopening, funded by taxing billionaires and Wall Street." The unions were using their monopoly power to hold kids hostage to unrelated political demands. And they were only too happy to not get what they wanted; they could continue to get paid to do nothing.

As Biden took over, millions of kids were still locked down in big blue cities, their parents desperate for a return to learning. In early February Biden's Centers for Disease Control director Rochelle Walensky made the mistake of speaking truth—and giving them hope. She announced in early February that "there is increasing data to suggest that schools can safely reopen and that safe reopening does not suggest that teachers need to be vaccinated." She added: "Vaccinations of teachers is not a prerequisite for safely reopening schools." The unions lost their minds, and White House Press Secretary Psaki the same day came out to clarify that Walensky was speaking in her "personal capacity" and that this was not "final guidance."

Follow the "science"?

A chastened Walensky later released new "data-driven" recommendations for school reopenings, and they read like a union document. It was one big excuse for continued lockdowns: thirty-eight pages on physical distancing, masking, color-coded zones, new ventilation systems, building cleaning, contact tracing. It also recommended teachers be moved to the front of the vaccine line. In case anyone missed the agency's new direction, Walensky stressed: "CDC is not mandating that schools reopen." No kidding. Good luck to any that tried under that new CDC maze.

Teachers' unions fist-pumped. As well they should have, since, as it turned out, it *was* a union document. In a scandalous May revelation, Freedom of Information documents showed the CDC had closely consulted with AFT in writing its final guidance. The union was allowed to review a draft and make recommendations, and the CDC—that paragon of "science"—adopted at least two of the political body's demands almost verbatim. One was a recommendation that schools make work concessions to any teacher who claimed they or a household member had a "high-risk condition."

The unions had another reason for dragging out reopenings: a payout. So long as schools were closed, the left could claim they needed money to reopen them. That became Democrats' excuse to jam $130 billion for K–12 schools into Biden's March Covid "relief act." But the unions made sure the bill allocated most of the payout in years after 2023, so that it couldn't be used on Covid changes. The goal all along was to give districts federal dollars to hike teacher salaries. Only after this bill was signed did union leaders tentatively suggest that schools might open (as long as they got their other conditions).

This came too late. Parents received confirmation of this in the fall of 2022, with the release of the nation's report card—the National Assessment of Educational Progress. Some kids had been locked out of classrooms for more than a year, and the learning loss was catastrophic. The country managed to erase nearly two decades of progress, as the test recorded a record drop from the last one in 2019. Math scores showed the biggest decline since the testing program began. Reading was little better. Nationwide, NAEP found that only 33 percent of fourth graders and 31 percent of eighth graders were reading at or above grade proficiency. And the loss spanned the gamut—wealthy, low-income, boys, girls, every racial and ethnic group. But hey—at least the teachers got a nice, long holiday.

Critical non-learning theory

The teachers' unions that in the early 1970s remained wary of mixing politics and the classroom have no such inhibitions now. They've become the ideological vanguard of the left's culture shock troops, as parents were about to discover in a whole new way. Lockdowns and "remote learning" were awful, but it did allow something unique; parents got a closer look at what teachers were foisting on their kids. And what they saw was infuriating.

Part and parcel of the Biden administration's new emphasis on "structural racism" was the progressive embrace of its pedagogical counterpart: "critical race theory." It's a neo-Marxist idea that got its founding in higher education in the 1980s, and that holds that American institutions exist to ensure "white supremacy" and elevate the "patriarchy."

An example of this thinking is the *New York Times*'s 1619 Project, directed by journalist Nikole Hannah-Jones. The project seeks to redefine American history, to claim its central and foundational event was not the 1776 signing of the Declaration of Independence, but rather the first importation of slaves to the United States—in 1619. The project has been shellacked by esteemed scholars for its inaccuracies, yet that didn't stop the cultural elite from lauding the project as a new historical basis for education.

CRT is firmly entrenched in colleges, but progressive activists have been working for some time to institutionalize it at the K–12 level. The juggernaut of that change has been the nation's teachers' unions. At the National Education Association's annual meeting in July 2021, the delegates approved a measure calling for "the implementation of culturally responsive education, critical race theory, and ethic (Native people, Asian, Black, Latin(o/a/x), Middle Eastern, North African and Pacific Islander) Studies curriculum in pre- K–12 and higher education." They also demanded "professional development around cultural responsiveness, implicit bias, anti-racism, trauma-informed practices, restorative justice practices and other racial justice trainings" for all school employees. And they asked the union for a study critiquing "empire, white supremacy, anti-Blackness, anti-Indigeneity, racism, patriarchy, cisheteropatriarchy, capitalism, ableism, anthropocentrism, and other forms of power and oppression at the intersections of our society." You don't need a college education—or even an understanding of these ridiculous words—to know they are scary.

Parents already knew. Teachers had been instituting critical race theory and associated curriculum in their classrooms—whether their schools approved of it or not. Moms and dads stuck at home overseeing remote learning were shocked to hear educators indoctrinating even young children in the language of racial distrust and divide. The brainwashing was even more infuriating given teachers refused to return to classrooms and so were failing to educate kids on the basics—math, reading, science. CRT became a flashpoint overnight, as parents began mobbing school board meetings, demanding administrations clarify their positions on racial and racist curriculums. Federal and local politicians joined the fray.

Biden as *president of the United States* might have been expected to reject controversial and revisionist teaching practices, but instead the administration stirred the pot, giving its tacit support to these union demands. When Psaki was asked about the NEA's July resolutions, she refused to condemn them. "The president believes that in our history, there are many dark moments. And there is not just slavery and racism in our history, there is systemic racism that is still impacting society today," she said. "I don't think we would think that educating the youth and next and future leaders of the country on systemic racism is indoctrination. That's actually responsible."

Only months before this press briefing, the Education Department (thank you, Jimmy Carter) published a proposed regulation that laid out the criteria to receive federal grants for history instruction. The rule explained that one of the priorities was "Projects that Incorporate Racially, Ethnically, Culturally and Linguistically Diverse Perspectives into Teaching and Learning." The rule used all the progressive buzzwords, teeing up "systemic racism," "anti-racist practices," the 1619 Project, and Ibram X. Kendi, author of the controversial "woke" bible *How to Be an Antiracist*. The rule was a first step at cementing CRT as basic Education Department policy. Senate Republicans stated their "grave concern" that the department was reorienting classes around "a politicized and divisive agenda," while parents reacted with a blizzard of negative official comments to the rule. Education Secretary Miguel Cardona later in the summer walked back the grant criteria.

The department, after all, had plenty of other controversial diktats to impose on the nation. The Obama administration had kicked off a national fight over transgender rights, an issue that had been bubbling at the state level as schools came under activist pressure to give trans students access to bathrooms of the opposite sex. This is the type of issue that should be settled locally, but the Obama Education Department used its power to impose a national standard. Its Education Department issued Title IX "guidance" asserting that a school must treat a student consistent with the student's gender identity when it came to access to bathrooms—and any school that didn't risked penalties or a loss of federal funding. A federal judge imposed a nationwide junction on the policy, since "guidance" is a sneaky way to end-run official rulemaking. The judge also slapped the Obama team for failing to consider a far less controversial solution: providing trans students with access to private bathrooms. The Trump team later formally rescinded the guidance, returning the fight to the state level, where it boiled and soon also encompassed debates over trans access to locker rooms and sports teams.

The Biden Education Department by June of its first year had jumped back into the fray, again issuing guidance, this time pointing to a 2020 Supreme Court ruling that protected trans rights in employment situations. The administration then doubled down on its campaign to force nationwide transgender acceptance when its Agriculture Department announced in 2022 that it would henceforth hold free school lunches hostage to trans rights: Any facility that didn't abide by the administration's trans demands could lose access to federal nutrition assistance. More than twenty states have sued over both provisions, and at least one court has already stepped in again to pause the rules.

* * *

Carter pandered to school unions because he saw in the NEA and AFT a lot of new votes. The teachers' unions have since grown in size and party influence, making every Democratic president more eager to retain that special interest's campaign money and electoral support.

And Biden has now managed to expose the disaster of that toxic relationship. His over-the-top fealty to the unions—his lockdown and vaccine policies, his antichoice positions, and his radical cultural agenda—finally provoked a rebellion. They fed the mobilization of a far larger constituency: 60 million parents. Those parents marched into the 2021 and 2022 elections loaded for bear and used their voting power to begin a sweeping transformation of school boards across the country (see chapter 10). They are only getting started.

CHAPTER 9

POLITICAL MALPRACTICE

Presidents have two distinct jobs in office. They have to manage policy. And they have to manage *politics*. We know how dismal the record of our two presidents is when it comes to the former. They were also both pretty darn pathetic when it came to the latter.

Carter defenders always feel the need to note that the president's flop of a "malaise" speech never actually used the word "malaise." Carter is lucky this is how history describes the address. What the president *did* say was much worse, and a great example of Carter's poor sense of politics.

Carter's presidency began to unravel in the summer of 1979, as his poll numbers fell to the low thirties. His team proffered sound explanations and suggestions: Carter needed to reconnect with the people; to be clearer on his priorities; to be more engaged on the energy crisis; to push Congress harder to pass his agenda. Carter rejected all these in favor of a theory put forward by a twenty-nine-year-old, Ivy League pollster named Pat Caddell. Caddell in a series of memos claimed that "a crisis of confidence" had seized the nation—that the "stability of the country" was under threat from an American people that were in decline after a generation of psychological trauma. Carter chief domestic policy adviser Stuart Eizenstat wrote in a later book that Caddell felt citizens had become "much more hostile, much more greedy, much more short-term and much more volatile." In short, the problem was America—not Carter.

Members of Carter's inner team objected aggressively to this characterization. Vice President Walter Mondale told Carter that the Caddell prescription was "the craziest goddamn thing I've ever read. There is not a psychiatric problem with America, but real problems with coping economically." Carter nonetheless ran with it, replacing a planned speech on energy with one in which he psychoanalyzed and scolded the country.

On July 15, 1979, the president excoriated his own electorate. He claimed that "in a nation that *was* proud of hard work, strong families, close-knit communities, and our faith in God, too many of us now tend to worship self-indulgence and consumption. Human identity is no longer defined by what one does, but by what one owns." (Italics added.) He complained that people didn't vote; he griped that they weren't as productive; he admonished them for no longer respecting the news media or institutions. Carter then insisted that all would be made right if Americans simply embraced "sacrifice" to solve the energy crisis.

The president made two cardinal political errors with that speech: He'd claimed the country had *lost* its greatness. Then he blamed Americans for it.

Carter had political instincts. You don't go from being an unknown governor of Georgia to the presidency on a fluke. He ran a populist, outsider campaign in 1976, rejected some of his party's more liberal positions, and promised honesty and decency—all of which resonated with a nation weary of scandals and government dysfunction. Yet once in Washington, an outmatched Carter lost the plot. He wrote the book on presidential political errors. It's a book for which Biden is now crafting a second edition.

An inch deep and a mile wide

Carter won the 1976 election—but only barely. As activist Julian Bond would quip: "His support was an inch deep and a mile wide." One of Carter's big mistakes was forgetting that Americans remained wary of him. He overstepped his mandate, governing in a far more liberal fashion than voters expected from a candidate who'd played up his conservative credentials. Consider that one of Carter's very first acts in office was to grant an unconditional pardon to tens of thousands of Vietnam draft dodgers—a move that provoked instant distrust.

He also confused the public with his scattershot approach to policy. Weeks after his inauguration he'd paused his campaign pledge to tackle jobs and inflation. He instead flitted off to embrace the energy crisis. Yet energy remained low on the electorate's priority list. It soon lost track of the administration's themes as Carter—determined to fix *all* of government—flooded the zone with so many policy initiatives that even Congress didn't know where to start. Voters weren't interested in his grand plans to turn Alaska into one big national monument, or his creation of judicial nominating commissions. They wanted someone to fix the high prices that were sapping their bank accounts and the high unemployment that was undermining families. Those issues just kept getting worse.

Another mistake: buck passing and blame casting. Carter in some ways was one of the weirdest personalities to ever hold the presidency—a combination of Christian humility and stubborn arrogance. The "malaise" speech was a perfect example of this bizarre nature. While few remember it now, the entire opening of that 1979 speech was Carter's acknowledgment of his own mistakes. This sort of self-reflection was quite common inside the Carter White House.

Yet that very piety turned Carter into moralizer in chief. He believed in self-reflection, but also always believed that his introspection made him the smartest and most virtuous person in the room, and it drove him nuts that others didn't subscribe to his ideals. He was forever bashing on Congress as lazy, trashing on corporations as greedy, and scoring Americans for their self-indulgence. This self-righteousness left the impression that Carter blamed everything that went wrong on someone or something else.

Even Carter's clothing equaled a finger wag. Just a few weeks into his presidency, he addressed the nation in a "fireside chat" that would set the tone for his entire, sermonizing presidency. Wearing a cardigan sweater to make his point about conservation, Carter lectured: "I realize that many of you have not believed that we really have an energy problem . . . but we have to act." He implored Americans to keep their thermostats at 65 during the day and 55 at night. Carter would go on wearing his cardigans—a constant reminder to his citizens that they needed to sacrifice, sacrifice, sacrifice. Unlike Biden, Carter did try to unify the country. Though his rallying cry of "eat your spinach" mostly served to unify the country against him.

That tone was a mistake, and it played a part in the president's undoing. Former Carter speechwriter Hendrick Hertzberg would explain that his boss was a "Low Church Protestant, where it's a sin not to have a hard wooden bench to sit on in church." Americans thought they were electing a regular guy—a farmer with Main Street values who promised honesty. What they got was a Sunday school teacher who told them to take their seat on that hard plank and to like it. They didn't.

Which leads to Carter's greatest political failing: his lack of an optimistic vision. Midway through Carter's presidency, the Brookings Institute's Stephen Hess wrote an early eulogy: "Let us assume that Jimmy Carter is an intelligent, decent, hardworking man," the essay began. "How, then, can a president . . . with many advisers of high caliber, produce such an undistinguished presidency?" The answer, explained Hess, was that "Jimmy Carter is the first Process President in American history," a man who "believes that if the process is good the product will be good." Yet Hess noted that "process is only a tool for getting from here to there—it is not a substitute for substance."

Carter knew what he *didn't* want government to be—complex, bloated, corrupt. But he had no overriding vision for the country. He moved from here to there, reacting to specific problems or interest groups, shifting from one crisis to the next. The notion that Carter wasn't in control became a theme. In the summer of 1979 (just prior to the "malaise" speech) the *New York Post* ran a blistering editorial, noting: "The United States is now a victim of a loss of nerve and will, wracked by indecision and groping for a glimpse of inspirational and innovative leadership."

One consequence of this failure of vision was that none of Carter's resets made a difference. Give the guy credit—he was willing to change course (something Biden refuses to do). Carter initially ignored military budgets, but later ramped up to confront the Soviet threat. He replaced Miller at the Federal Reserve with the inflation-fighting Volcker. He at one point fired half his cabinet. But absent a vision, these steps were reactionary and usually came too late. Carter's policies were bad, his politics equally so.

Biden's long straw

Biden managed to alienate the public almost from the get-go and has been mired underwater since midway through his first year. The numbers aren't just a rejection of Biden's radical policies. His *political* instincts are abysmal.

Biden has always been a subpar politician, making it all the more mind-boggling that he landed in the White House. He's mostly been lucky. Don't expect the press to recall it now, but prior to Obama's choice of him as vice president, Biden had been a middling senator and a bit of a punchline. His 2019 announcement was his *third* run for the presidency. He'd flamed out in 1988, after newspapers published numerous examples of his plagiarism, and after Biden exaggerated his academic credentials. He flamed out again twenty years later, coming in as an afterthought in 2008 to Obama and Hillary Clinton.

But Biden pulled the long straw. Obama chose him as a running mate in hopes he'd lend some experience to the ticket, especially given Biden's credentials as a member of the Senate Foreign Relations Committee. It was risky, since even by then Biden had a reputation as a loose (and loquacious) cannon. "I think I have a much higher IQ than you do, I suspect," Biden grumped at a New Hampshire voter in 1987. He said in 2006 that you "cannot go to a 7-Eleven or a Dunkin' Donuts unless you have a slight Indian accent." He in 2007 dropped jaws when he described opponent Obama this way: "I mean, you got the first mainstream African-American who is articulate and bright and clean and a nice-looking guy." Biden had shown in the Senate that he could clamber onto his party's top priorities (crime) and beat up Republican nominees (Robert Bork, Clarence Thomas), but as primary voters in 2008 agreed, he was hardly a leader or presidential material.

Biden's luck held in 2019 when he drew a field of strongly progressive primary competitors. He moved left, but not far enough to blow his "moderate" credentials. As the press fretted that a Sanders-like radical would lose to Trump, Democratic primary voters pushed Biden over the finish line. The nominee then studiously promoted his twin themes of Covid management and national unity.

Biden won, but—like Carter—only barely. And, like Carter, he misread his mandate. America expected a grandfatherly figure— the one who'd called on the country to "turn the page, to unite, to heal." It wanted him to shepherd them through Covid and calm political tempers. Biden instead rolled over to the demands of his progressive left and within months proposed to fundamentally restructure American life, to transform the nation into a European-style social-welfare state.

This agenda was exceptionally wild in light of his congressional majority. Carter at least had solid Democratic majorities in his House and Senate. Biden barely *had* control. Republicans lost the White House in 2020, but voters also punished House Democrats, reducing the party to its narrowest majority in modern history. And the electorate sent up a fifty-fifty Senate, giving Democrats control by virtue only of Vice President Harris's tie-breaking vote. This was not a mandate for change.

Yet Biden polarized the country by pushing his party to jam through his priorities by means of legislative trickery. Democrats seized on the budget reconciliation process as a way to avoid the filibuster and imposed the $1.9 trillion Covid "rescue" bill. Biden's approval rating started slipping almost at exactly that point. Ignoring the political warning signs, he pressed on.

While Candidate Biden broke with progressive calls to pack the Supreme Court, President Biden created a commission to study the idea. Biden was likewise initially reluctant to join calls to end the Senate filibuster and turn Congress into a version of the British parliament. He pushed back initially, arguing that the filibuster's demise would "throw the entire Congress into chaos." But as his progressive wing pushed him, he did an about-face and made an exception. In January 2022 he said he supported breaking the filibuster in the case of the left's giant federal voting takeover. And one exception led to another. By June 2022 he supported also killing the filibuster for any abortion rights legislation.

He also did a poor job overseeing his own party. As Democrats in mid-2021 descended into squabbling over the Build Back Better agenda, Biden sat idly by. Democrats fought over tax changes, the scope of Medicare additions, the length of entitlements. Biden could have stepped in at any moment to outline the White House's preference and get people on the same page. Instead, the president let the warring factions war—for months. House progressives at one point in the fall of 2021 took the president's own infrastructure bill hostage to their demands. He did nothing. Activists started waging vicious pressure campaigns on holdouts—protests outside Manchin's houseboat, activists trailing Sinema into bathrooms shouting demands. Biden didn't say a peep about this harassment. Whatever you think of Carter, he was deeply involved in every congressional fight. Biden's recalcitrance produced a year of ugly headlines about a divided party and a flailing agenda.

When Manchin finally agreed in the summer to a limited modified hangout version of BBB, the press celebrated this as proof of Biden's legislative mojo and later suggested it was the reason Democrats did better in the 2022 midterm elections. But that was fiction, in aid of a floundering president. Biden did little to make any of it happen politically. If Democrats stanched the bleeding in 2022, it was because in the final stretch they rallied (again) around the issue that had worked for them in 2020: fearmongering over Trump and issues like abortion. This isn't a plan for the long-term. It didn't alter the hard facts that exit polls showed a country deeply dissatisfied with the economy and with Biden as president.

Exhauster in chief

If Carter played national schoolmarm, Biden has played national dean of detention. What's the only thing worse than a president who nags you to do what he wants? One who *makes* you do what he wants.

Biden, like Carter, proved he could moralize with the best of them. As Covid continued in the winter of 2020-21, the new (and self-righteous) Biden administration decided to turn public-health etiquette into a national badge of honor. Disdainful of states that loosened lockdowns and social distancing, the president began lecturing citizens to wear their masks. In his own version of the

Carter cardigan, Biden made a point of wearing two masks at the same time—even when he was standing outside or entirely by himself. On a visit to the National Institutes of Health in February 2021, he informed the country that it should continue to wear masks at least until 2022 (despite having no knowledge of the virus's trajectory), and that it was a "patriotic responsibility." "We're in the middle of a war with this virus," he hounded.

The CDC would later acknowledge that cloth masks were largely ineffective. But all that mattered to Democrats was the science of control.

And for those who didn't want to wear one? He'd make them. Immediately upon taking office, Biden imposed mask mandates on every inch of land over which the federal government could plausibly claim some control—federal buildings, airlines, airports, interstate travel on buses and trains, even in the middle of national parks. This executive order inspired most blue states and localities to keep their mask mandates in place—to the growing fury of many Americans. The administration kept extending this mandate, well after most jurisdictions were open and functioning normally.

Travelers suffered under the travel mask mandate all the way until April 2022, when a federal judge struck it down as an abuse of federal health powers. The ruling left it up to airlines to decide what to do, and it says something that most major carriers dropped the mandate by the end of that very day. The media, backing Biden, howled in protest and ran polls suggesting Americans really did love their face muggings. Really! But these clearly weren't polls of actual travelers. While walking through a crowded Denver airport days after the ruling, I did my own informal survey. Maybe one in ten travelers had a mask on. The rest looked relieved beyond description.

Biden similarly hounded the nation on Covid vaccines, and then boosters, and then more boosters. In a 2021 address he complained of the small minority of unvaccinated: "What more is there to wait for? What more do you need to see? We've made vaccinations free, safe and convenient... We've been patient, but our patience is wearing thin. And your refusal has cost all of us." Wow. How so? This was an exercise in dramatics, not science. Even by this time the CDC had been forced to acknowledge that vaccination did not prevent Covid transmission. Holdouts were not putting anyone other than themselves at risk. There was also at this point no hospital crisis.

But they would be compelled. The administration in September 2021 announced sweeping vaccine mandates for federal workers, larger companies, and health care staff. While the Supreme Court blocked the corporate mandate, it allowed the White House to require vaccines as a condition of employment for any person who worked in a medical facility that received Medicare or Medicaid funds. Thousands of medical workers lost their jobs. These front-line workers had put themselves at risk to save lives at the height of the pandemic, and Biden rewarded them by stripping them of their jobs. The military similarly discharged thousands more service members—people who risk their lives to protect the country—for failing to get the Biden jab. In neither of these scenarios was the administration willing to take into consideration the people who had already caught Covid and had natural immunity or the people who had other legitimate objections to the vaccine.

And Biden wondered why his popularity kept dropping. He was acting like the moralizing Carter.

Biden's moralizing has come back to bite him. His Department of Justice in August 2022 took the unprecedented step of raiding a former president's home. The FBI descended on Donald Trump's Mar-a-Lago estate as part of a dispute over classified documents, and Attorney General Merrick Garland appointed a special counsel to look into whether Trump's possession or handling of the material amounted to criminal activity. Biden in a September interview slammed Trump, wondering how "that could possibly happen" and calling his predecessor "totally irresponsible."

This was all a bit humiliating when in January 2023 it came out that Biden attorneys had discovered classified material in an office Biden used at the University of Pennsylvania. Moreover, they'd found that material in early November, but kept it quiet for months. Further searches by Biden attorneys and the FBI turned up yet more classified documents in the garage and other rooms of Biden's Delaware home, including material both from his time in the Senate and as vice president. The Justice Department had been so aggressive in its approach to Trump, that Garland felt he had no choice but to assign a separate special counsel to investigate the self-righteous Biden. House Republicans found themselves with an entirely new line of Biden investigation—namely, whether the president's possession of classified material created national security risks.

Especially given accusations that Biden's family members have engaged in influence peddling with U.S. adversaries. Just prior to the 2020 election, the New York Post published emails it said came from the laptop of Hunter Biden—the president's son. Those emails showed Hunter had cashed in on the Biden family name in lucrative dealings in China and elsewhere and raised questions about how much Joe Biden knew about the transactions. Candidate Biden joined Democrats and the media in declaring the laptop Russian "disinformation." Yet media investigations would later confirm the laptop was real, as would Hunter himself in several 2023 letters to government officials.

This raised huge new questions about Joe Biden's truthfulness, as well as the risks associated with his mishandled classified documents. The Biden family grifting and document scandal—and all their parallels to Trump—meanwhile amounted to a huge embarrassment for a man who smugly presented himself as the moral opposite of his predecessor. Biden threw stones and they came back to shatter his own glass house.

One of Biden's worst habits is to equate the failure to support his agenda with a lack of decency. According to the president,

Americans who don't get behind his federal voting takeover are "racist." Those who support returning abortion decisions to state legislatures are antiwomen. People who disagree with his spending "threaten" our basic "economic rights." He at one point compared Republican ideology to "semifascism." Most leaders upon becoming president recognize that they now serve and represent all Americans and try to speak in inclusive tones—Carter certainly did. Biden's divisive language—in which he casts every GOP voter as dangerous—has hardened half the country against him, which accounts for his stuck poll numbers.

Listening to him is also just exhausting.

The buck stops there

Carter's self-righteous language left the impression he was blaming problems on everyone but himself. Biden doesn't leave an impression. He *outright* blames problems on everyone else. It's fair to say that not once in office has Biden taken responsibility for any mistake—not even ones that were flamingly obvious (like his horrific Afghanistan withdrawal). He either denies a problem exists entirely or faults others. The excuses have started to make voters question his leadership.

Energy prices? Biden essentially shut down any new oil or gas production, blocked pipelines, and strangled producers with regulation and red tape. As prices crept up (starting the minute he took office) he blamed pandemic supply chain problems. Then—in no particular order—oil and gas companies, refineries, retailers, OPEC, and Putin.

Inflation? The administration blamed it on the pandemic, and insisted it would prove "temporary," "limited," "passing," or "transitory." When that wore thin, Biden turned to "Putin's price hike." He also tried to cast it off on the Federal Reserve. While economists might argue over the degree to which Biden's massive spending played a role in higher prices, even the left-leaning Associated Press's fact-checkers acknowledge it is a "clear factor" and that Biden "pumped more money into the economy than it could handle." But Biden continued to dispute the laws of gravity. "I'm sick of this stuff," railed the president in March 2022. "We have to talk about it because the American people think the reason for inflation is the government is spending more money. Simply not true." The administration even continues to claim spending *reduces* prices. To this day, Biden insists inflation is the work of some magic, hidden gremlins.

Rising crime? Biden blamed it on *Republicans*, bizarrely linking it to the "political violence" that he claims the GOP supports. And his finger-pointing goes on. He blamed industry leaders for not telling him sooner that there was a crisis in the supply of baby food. In a surreal statement, his administration blamed the border fiasco on Trump, claiming it inherited "a broken and dismantled immigration system." He also blamed Afghanistan on Trump, though it was Biden and Biden alone who made the call on when to withdraw. He blamed rising Covid cases on social media.

This arrogance—the inability to acknowledge fault—explains why Biden has never helped himself by pivoting, firing staff, or opting for a reset. His administration has had plenty of moments where it might have won some respect from the public by demonstrating political accountability. It could have taken a few of the military scalps responsible for the botched Afghanistan withdrawal. As the border disintegrated, it might have asked for the resignation of DHS chief Mayorkas. As inflation spiraled, it could have brought in a new economic team. But that would be to admit there was a problem, and this administration is congenitally unable to admit anything. Harry Truman's desk sign read: "The buck stops here." Biden's reads: "The buck stops there." (With an arrow pointing out of the Oval Office.)

Another Biden trick that makes the public wary is claiming the opposite of reality. His administration has repeatedly insisted the border is secure. Biden continues to call his Afghanistan withdrawal a brilliant move. As inflation soared, the president kept insisting that his economic plan was working and things were getting better. Yet Americans watched their inflation-beset dollars go up in smoke.

When caught out, the administration changes the definition of words. In April 2021, the *Washington Post* wrote that the administration was debating passing its "infrastructure plan on the votes of Democrats alone" yet calling it "a bipartisan victory." How so? According to senior Biden adviser Anita Dunn, "If you looked up 'bipartisan' in the dictionary, I think it would say support from Republicans and Democrats. It doesn't say the Republicans have to be in Congress." Put another way, if a couple of faceless conservatives out in America supported the bill, Biden would call it "bipartisan"—even if not a single Republican voted for it.

It's unclear how much of this is spin, and how much is the latest in Biden's long history of just . . . making things up. Over his time in public office the president has claimed: that he finished in the top half of his class in law school; that he was appointed to the Naval Academy; that he "had a house burn down" (and that his wife barely escaped); that he was arrested protesting for Civil Rights; that he was arrested in South Africa; that he was arrested trying to sneak into an all-woman dorm room; that he "used to drive an 18-wheeler" and a "tractor-trailer"; that he traveled "seventeen thousand miles" with Chinese president Xi Jinping.

Media fact checkers have found these to be untrue or exaggerations. Jimmy Carter promised never to lie to Americans, and (the usual political spin aside) he held true to that vow. Biden by contrast has created for himself a reputation that rarely sits well with the public—that of a lying politician. His promises don't matter. And his explanation of the current facts doesn't correspond with reality. That's never good politics.

Who's in charge?

Carter lacked a vision—and that helped account for his poor leadership. Biden presents a vision. The problem is that Americans no longer trust it is his own.

Rumors have plagued the Biden administration from early days that the president isn't actually in charge. At nearly every event I attend, one of the first questions from the audience is: "Who's running things?" Good question. Part of the concern stems from Biden's decision to adopt such a far-left agenda—which is out of keeping with most of his career. Part of it is this administration's centralized makeup. Trump's team recruited highly capable cabinet secretaries, and largely left them free to work their reforms. The Biden White House is top-down. Orders come from a cloistered group of Biden advisers and czars, who filter every decision through the administration's "whole of government" initiatives on climate, race, and equity.

But most of it comes from Biden's age and his growing appearance of confusion, uncertainty, weakness, and decline. For a sense of how bad it is, take a few minutes off this book and look up some clips of Biden during his vice presidential debate with Paul Ryan in 2012. Yes, Biden rudely interrupted. But there was no question the vice president was sharp, fiery, and knew his talking points.

Today's Biden has trouble getting out full sentences. He can't figure out how to exit stages. His gait is stiff. His off-teleprompter comments are cringeworthy. There is nothing energetic or inspiring about the Biden presidency. And his mistakes have grown more alarming. In 2021, he proved unable to remember the name of the Australian prime minister, with whom he was doing a joint press conference. At an event in September 2022, he called to a congresswoman: "Jackie, are you here? Where's Jackie?" Jackie Walorski and two aides had died in a high-profile car accident in August. In November 2022 he claimed to have spoken to the inventor of insulin; a man who died prior to Biden's birth.

None of this is meant to be mean; age affects us all. Even Carter threw a red flag. Just shy of his ninety-fifth birthday, Carter was asked at an event in 2019 if he had ever considered running again. "I hope there's an age limit," he laughed, then added more seriously that he didn't believe he'd have been able to perform the duties necessary of a president at age eighty. At that very moment, Biden was asking to be put into the presidency at the age of seventy-eight.

Americans want to feel confident that their commander in chief is in charge, yet few in America now trust this one. Democrats and media understand the problem—even if they weren't willing to call it out when it mattered, before the 2020 election. They waited until Biden was ensconced in office, his poll numbers in the tank, to pull out the long knives. In a particularly brutal piece, the *New York Times* finally tackled the subject in June 2022, in a piece quoting "dozens of frustrated Democratic officials, members of Congress and voters" expressing "doubts" about Biden's "abilities." They followed it up in July with the headline: "At 79, Biden Is Testing the Boundaries of Age and the Presidency."

Now they tell us.

By the fall of 2022, Biden had become so toxic—his approval ratings so poor—that Democratic candidates actively shunned his presence on the midterm trail. In one notable episode, Biden took a day to help reelect Georgia senator Raphael Warnock. He did it from a phone bank in Massachusetts.

At a time of economic disruption, voters want a president who has a policy plan—but also one with the ability to demonstrate energy and determination. That's called *politics*. Such leadership matters even more in today's environment. Entire generations of Americans have never experienced high inflation; this is a first. A 2022 Gallup poll showed Americans have the lowest optimism at any time in three decades about the younger generation's chance at success. Surveys consistently show Americans are dissatisfied with the national situation.

The country risks slipping back into that "crisis of confidence" that Carter warned about so many years ago. That's an opportunity for the GOP to present the optimistic contrast. Much like a fella did in 1979, by the name of Ronald Reagan.

CHAPTER 10

MORNING IN AMERICA

Not to take anything away from one of America's greatest presidents, but Ronald Reagan's formula for defeating Jimmy Carter in 1980 was pretty straightforward: He was the anti-Carter.

That strategy produced one of the biggest landslide victories in the history of presidential elections. Reagan captured 489 of 538 electoral votes, the most ever won by a non-incumbent presidential candidate. He won nearly 51 percent of the popular vote, and it would have been higher had not Republican representative John Anderson run as an independent and siphoned some 6.6 percent of voters. Carter took just six states, including his home turf of Georgia and Mondale's Minnesota. Riding on Reagan's coattails, Republicans retook the Senate for the first time in twenty-five years, while the House GOP gained a net of thirty-five seats.

But the election marked something even more lasting: It cemented a political realignment that started in 1964 with Barry Goldwater and became the Reagan Era. Carter's epic mishandling of government—his embrace of liberal policies and big government—lost Democrats far more than an election. He lost the party a generation. A traumatized nation in 1980 turned again to hope and freedom. The Reagan Era's ideas and policies would dominate for decades.

(L)MAGA

As straightforward as Reagan's election strategy was, don't under-
estimate the intellectual strength and courage—or the sheer
amount of time—it took for him to arrive as that anti-Carter.
Ronald Wilson Reagan began in Hollywood as a Democrat and
didn't even register as a Republican until he was in his fifties.

His national political debut in 1964—in a speech supporting
Goldwater for president, entitled "A Time for Choosing"—put
him at odds with the GOP's then-dominant moderate and liberal wings. His political evolution continued through his time as
California governor (1967–74) and through his failed 1968 and
1976 presidential bids. It included embracing philosophies and
policies that were still far from mainstream in the Republican
Party. No less than George H. W. Bush in the 1980 GOP primaries slammed Reagan's embrace of supply-side philosophy as
"voodoo economics."

Yet the Reagan who went into the 1980 general campaign knew
what he was about, and the contrast with Carter couldn't have
been starker. Americans had lost faith in one Carter policy after
another. Reagan proposed in each of these areas to do the opposite, and to do so with refreshing new approaches to governance.

Carter, the technocratic tinkerer, flooded Washington with
proposals that put government at the center of problem-solving.
Reagan argued the federal government had overspent, overstimu-
lated, and overregulated. Carter Democrats called for tax hikes;
Reagan called for tax cuts. Carter stood up huge new federal
bureaucracies; Reagan wanted to slash the size of government.
Carter put the federal government in the lead; Reagan wanted a
return to states' rights.

The contrasts continued in discreet policy areas. Carter
preached energy sacrifice, solar panels and synthetic fuels; Reagan reminded voters that the United States was an "energy-rich"

nation, but saddled with Washington regulation. Carter laid out federal spending programs designed to help the inner cities and reverse crime; Reagan proposed economic development zones to free local areas to grow their own prosperity. Carter erected a new federal education bureaucracy; Reagan called to dismantle the Department of Education and supported tuition tax credits for private school students. For the record, the newly powerful NEA *hated* Reagan.

Reagan didn't lead with cultural issues, but here too he presented a contrast. He called for a constitutional amendment to reverse *Roe v. Wade*, and he took aim at Carter's judiciary, promising that his jurors would stick to the Constitution. In his only debate with Reagan, Carter talked about his affirmative action policies and his record of bringing more minorities into public service. Reagan in the same debate said that he'd use the presidential bully pulpit to work for a day when "things will be done neither because of nor in spite of any of the differences between us—ethnic differences or racial differences, whatever they may be—that we will have total equal opportunity for all people."

Carter embraced détente and arms reductions, and only at the end reversed himself to call for defense investments to counter the Soviet threat. Reagan wanted a substantial military buildup. As the election raged, Carter was still mishandling the Iranian hostage crisis. Reagan hit the president for not being more forceful.

But Reagan's greatest contrast was his tone—his unrelenting optimism in the future of the country. He had over his years ditched the pessimism that haunted conservative intellectual thought, its perpetual, hand-wringing belief that it was already too late. While millions of red-ball-capped Americans might not know it, Donald Trump didn't come up with MAGA—he just made it shorthand. It was Reagan's 1980 campaign that coined the slogan: "Let's Make America Great Again."

Reagan's sunny belief in the American people was summed up most eloquently in his closing address to the nation, the night before the 1980 election. He took a swipe at Carter's blame of America, saying: "I find no national malaise, I find nothing wrong with the American people. Oh, they are frustrated, even angry at what has been done to this blessed land. But more than anything they are sturdy and robust as they have always been." He said it was Americans who had been "burdened, stifled and sometimes even oppressed" by government and vowed "an era of national renewal. An era that will reorder the relationship between citi-zen and government, that will make government again responsive to the people." He recalled, as he often did, the words of John Winthrop, a founding figure of the Massachusetts Bay Colony, describing the United States as a shining "city on the hill." And he asked the nation to choose between two "visions of the future."

The nation chose Reagan's, and decisively. In doing so, it helped change the trajectory of political thought and power for decades to come.

The Republican Party was itself transformed. Reagan's election hastened the decline of the moderate-liberal wing of the GOP—Thomas Dewey, Dwight Eisenhower, Nelson Rockefeller—that had defined post–World War II conservatism. Out was their big spend-ing, their cultural liberalism, their support for labor unions, and their belief that government programs would work if just managed more efficiently. The new Reagan coalition of fiscal libertarians, social conservatives, and defense hawks now defined policy.

It transformed the Democratic Party, left reeling by the popu-larity of what began to look like an enduring conservative major-ity. The left's loss of a third consecutive presidential election in 1988 forced the party to reevaulate its positions and paved the path for "New Democrat" Bill Clinton, who claimed to walk a line between competitive markets and government programs. This was the Democrat who proclaimed (if only so!) that "the era of big government is over." Democratic liberals were put on the defense, and only in more recent years have progressives reasserted their power over the party.

Mostly, it realigned the electorate. People flocked to the Republican Party. By December 1984 (just a month after Reagan won a landslide reelection), a Gallup poll showed that the percentage of Americans who described themselves as Democrats had fallen to the lowest level since the end of World War II. Those who called themselves Republicans had grown to 31 percent of the electorate, up from 21 percent in 1977. A *Washington Post*/ABC poll found that some 20 percent of the electorate (35 million voters) had switched party affiliation over the previous five years, with a net gain of 14 million for Republicans. Of first-time voters in 1984, nearly 40 percent called themselves Republicans, compared to 34 percent for Democrats.

Reagan would in 1980 rack up forty-nine states. In that contest, men voted for Reagan by 62 percent, women by 58 percent. He won every single income bracket save the very lowest rung (which nonetheless voted for him by 46 percent). And he won every single age bracket. Astonishingly, especially in light of today's voting public, Reagan attracted a booming youth movement. Those under the age of twenty-five supported Reagan by 61 percent. While Reagan overall lost the Hispanic vote, Cuban Americans in 1984 gave him the vast majority their support.

Reagan also attracted new voters, since a huge source of his strength was his ability to convert. Following the 1984 reelection, pollster Stanley Greenberg conducted focus groups of "Reagan Democrats." He did a particular study of Macomb County, Michigan, which voted 63 percent for John F. Kennedy in 1960, but in 1984 went 66 percent for Reagan. Greenberg attributed the enormous shift to Democrats' loss of the working class. Huge swaths of voters no longer felt Democrats cared about economic aspiration or opportunity, but existed to transfer wealth to the poor, the unemployed, and disadvantaged groups.

These voters benefited from Reagan's economic policies—for the first time in a long time. They enthusiastically applauded his views on strong national defense. They appreciated his rejection of the Democratic Party's loosening cultural mores on pornography, crime, and abortion. And they loved his belief in the American Dream. These Reagan Democrats exist even today. Only—as conservative commentator George Will noted—we don't call them that anymore. Today, they are the Republican base.

The fortieth president of the United States didn't accomplish all this through magic. Voters in 1980 were attracted to his vision but would've happily chucked him if he'd proven a continuation of the Carter mess. His success was rooted in results. With Volcker by his side, Reagan tamed inflation. His tax reforms and deregulation led to extraordinary economic growth, what my first editorial-page boss, Robert Bartley, described in his book *The Seven Fat Years*. The president stared down air-traffic controllers at home and the Soviet Union abroad. People prospered and felt safe, and once again began to fulfill the promise of the shining "city on the hill."

A few other things that Reagan had are important to note as this book moves to today's politics. One of Reagan's strengths was his willingness to embrace innovative policies. He had an enormous amount of help, in that the 1980s marked the flowering of the conservative think tank movement. This was the era of the Heritage Foundation, the American Enterprise Institute, the Cato Institute, the Hoover Institution, and the Center for Strategic and International Studies. Many of these had been around for a long time and had started exerting their influence in the 1970s. But Reagan's presidency gave them the opportunity to inject their policy proposals into Washington, as well as into states that were increasingly liberated from DC and able to act as laboratories of democracy. The Republican Party became the party of ideas—the party that wanted to think, innovate, advance.

Reagan also had fellow Republicans. He carried throughout his political career a sharp memory of the way liberal Republicans had chewed up Goldwater. He developed his eleventh commandment, which he honored the rest of his life: "Thou shalt not speak ill of another Republican." He was a leader, and his insistence that his party refrain from tearing each other to pieces was a key aspect of the Reagan revolution. It didn't shut down debate. It didn't foreclose argument. But it did ensure that the GOP was in it together for a bigger purpose: setting the country on a new path.

The last Reagan attributes? Words and wit. No one doubted he was a fighter—just ask the air traffic controllers he fired, or Mikhail Gorbachev for that matter. But he didn't do it with insults, barbs, and scare tactics. The "Great Communicator" did it with ideas, explanations, gentle barbs, outright humor, and lots of smiles. And that drew people in.

See no evil, hear no evil

The Biden White House did something odd in the wake of the 2022 elections: It claimed victory.

Biden senior adviser Mike Donilon in mid-December 2022 penned an internal memo, promptly leaked to the press. As Biden's second year came to a close, Donilon claimed that all signs showed it'd been a smashing success. "We see the President's approval rating on the upswing, a resilient economic climate, and strong support for the President's agenda," he brayed. He gave a passing nod to the possibility that the Supreme Court's *Dobbs* decision, and Democratic fearmongering over Republican "extremism," might have given the party a midterm leg up. But he insisted that what "hasn't been fully reported on—or fully understood—is how important a role the achievements and the agenda of the President and the Democrats played in the midterms."

Right.

White House staffers exist partly to make the boss look good, and it's possible Donilon penned the memo entirely to prod the press to adopt this narrative. But if the memo is the type of smoke Biden's advisers are blowing at him in the Oval Office, a whole lot of folks deserve to be canned. Biden's polls remain dismal, the economy is struggling, and the American people continue to strongly reject the president's agenda. The midterms were no victory for the White House.

What Biden *has* earned with his radical policies is the same potential for a dramatic political shift as befell Democrats in 1980. As then, Americans are struggling with high inflation, the threat of recession, layoffs, the loss of stock market wealth, international threats, a porous border, rising crime, and cultural upheaval. It's been decades since the country has witnessed the toxic combination of all these calamities, and many Americans had grown complacent. Yet older voters are now remembering the ugly Carter years. And many younger voters are confronting for the first time the shock of living with inflation. It's a wake-up call and it has created an electorate that is newly aware of the consequences of poor government.

Adding to the left's problem is that voting demographics are simultaneously shifting, as blue-collar workers and minorities once again question the Democratic Party's commitment to them, and as more Americans migrate to red states. The country is changing. On one side a cloistered coastal elite. On the other, average Americans who see little in a Biden agenda and who worry that inflation, taxes, and regulation are crushing their ambitions.

As in 1980, the conditions are ripe for a political sea change. The question: Which party will figure that out first?

Midterm truths

Midterms are meant to be a judgment on a presidency—and to listen to the White House and most of the press corps, the 2022 judgment was favorable. Wrong. In a curious twist, those midterms became a judgment on *Republicans*, and there were two conflicting sets of results.

One set showed smashing GOP successes, as voters rose up to

reward Republican governors and legislators who'd demonstrated leadership and competence. The shining example was Florida, where Governor Ron DeSantis and his GOP legislature shunned Covid lockdowns, grew the economy, expanded school choice, fought for parents' rights, and stared down woke corporations.

DeSantis stormed to reelection, whupping former Democratic governor Charlie Crist by nearly twenty points. Four years earlier, DeSantis won his first bid for the governorship by a mere 32,000 votes. In 2022 he won by *1.5 million*. Exit polls showed he swept nearly every demographic: Hispanics, women, white men, older voters, independents, married voters. He won the rural vote (69 percent), the suburban vote (58 percent) and, astonishingly, the *urban* vote (55 percent). It was an unadulterated triumph—a Democratic trouncing—and in a place the press still calls a "swing state."

His success buoyed GOP politicians up and down the ballot. Florida Republicans obtained supermajorities in both the Florida Senate and Florida House. Republicans swept all statewide offices, locking Democrats out of government. Senator Marco Rubio won his own reelection by more than sixteen points, destroying Rep. Val Demings—despite her outspending him. And the GOP picked up four U.S. House seats, leaving Democrats with just eight of twenty-eight districts. That's what you call a good night.

But Florida wasn't an island. The same phenomenon played out across the country. In Ohio, Governor Mike DeWine enacted tax cuts, balanced budgets, brought in new business, and invested more money in crime fighting. He won reelection by twenty-five points. Republicans retained every statewide office and increased their majorities in both of Ohio's legislative chambers.

In Iowa, Governor Kim Reynolds implemented a flat tax, attracted private investment to the state, and deeply invested herself in school choice. When members of her own party in the state House strangled her bill to create up to ten thousand scholarships a year for education expenses—including private school tuition—she jumped into GOP primaries and helped oust nearly every opponent. The electorate rewarded her. She won reelection by nineteen points, and her GOP emerged from the midterms holding every statewide office, a state Senate supermajority, and an expanded majority in the state House.

Texas governor Greg Abbott, like DeSantis, bucked Covid lockdowns and grew his economy, but also threw resources at Biden's lawless border. He beat Democratic darling Beto O'Rourke by 11 points. In New Hampshire—a blue state—Governor Chris Sununu cruised to reelection by 16 points. In Vermont—an even bluer state—Governor Phil Scott beat his Democratic opponent by an eye-watering 47 points.

Or consider Georgia. Governor Brian Kemp became the center of a firestorm in the wake of the 2020 election, as he and Republican secretary of state Brad Raffensperger refused to bend to Trump's demands that they disavow Biden's victory. Trump vowed to get Kemp kicked out of office and recruited former senator David Perdue to mount a primary challenge.

But Kemp had done a bang-up job as governor. He pushed through Georgia's electoral integrity reform; was one of the first governors to loosen Covid restrictions; signed bills expanding school choice and allowing Georgians to carry firearms without permits; pushed broadband into rural areas; and continued to oversee a strong economy. Those accomplishments ended up mattering far more to Georgia voters than Trump's grievances.

Kemp trounced Perdue in a May 2022 primary, beating him by fifty-two points. He then went on to crush Democrat Stacey Abrams by eight points in the general election.

These victories were a repeat of what Republicans had seen a year earlier, in Virginia's 2021 state elections. GOP businessman Glenn Youngkin entered the governor's race the distinct underdog, running against former Virginia governor Terry McAuliffe and with the knowledge that the GOP hadn't won a statewide election in Virginia in more than a decade. Yet even by this time

Biden's inflation was starting to bite, and Youngkin ran a campaign focused on quality-of-life issues: the cost of living, education, crime, and a promise to kick-start the state economy. He beat McAuliffe by two points—a twelve-point swing from Biden's 2020 results. GOP candidates also won their races for lieutenant governor and attorney general—and won back Virginia's House of Delegates.

And yet the 2022 midterm also held a very different set of Republican results—those for the U.S. Congress, and certain marquee state races. Even here, there were GOP bright spots. Republicans retook the House from Nancy Pelosi for the first time in four years. It was a close-run affair, and the party won its majority with only a handful of seats to spare—despite predictions it would do far better. Still, a win is a win, and the victory provided a definitive end to the worst of Biden's legislative proposals.

Republicans also won solid victories in some Senate seats that Democrats spent a fortune to try to capture. Senator Ron Johnson—considered the most vulnerable GOP incumbent of the cycle—beat the progressive Mandela Barnes. Rep. Ted Budd comfortably won North Carolina's open Senate seat. State attorney general Eric Schmitt even more comfortably took Missouri's Senate slot. Senator Chuck Grassley—who the media suggested was in trouble—won reelection by twelve points.

Elsewhere? The GOP bombed—despite spending its own fortune. Republicans hoped to recapture a fifty-fifty Senate but ended up going backward. The party's challengers to Democratic incumbents flamed out in New Hampshire, Arizona, Georgia, and Nevada—all seats the GOP should have won easily. Republicans also lost retiring senator Pat Toomey's seat in Pennsylvania, handing Chuck Schumer an outright Senate majority.

The defeats were even more humiliating in state gubernatorial races. Candidates frittered away GOP-held governorships in Arizona, Maryland, and Massachusetts. And they failed in their effort to knock off weakened Democratic gubernatorial holds in Michigan, Minnesota, Wisconsin, New Mexico, New York, Pennsylvania, and Oregon.

What accounts for such starkly different results? Especially given the mixed outcomes sometimes showed up in the same state? In Georgia, Kemp won his reelection by eight points, yet GOP Senate candidate Herschel Walker lost his runoff by three. By the White House's logic, Warnock's victory proved Georgia voters want a Biden agenda. But that's crazy, given they voted for Kemp's agenda by far larger margins—an agenda diametrically opposed to everything Democrats stand for.

The answer is simple—even as it also holds invaluable warnings for both parties. Voters don't approve of the Biden agenda. They just happened in many important races in 2022 to dislike the Republican candidate more than they disliked the Democrat.

And it turns out most of those disfavored Republicans had something in common: strong ties to Trump.

Senate Republican leader Mitch McConnell took a shedload of flak in August 2022, when he expressed doubts about a Republican Senate takeover, noting that "candidate quality has a lot to do with the outcome." He was criticized for dunking on the GOP's Senate slate, but he was right. In any number of crucial primaries, Trump waded in to push his preferred winner over the line. Yet he based his endorsements on whether a candidate subscribed to his 2020 election claims, not on whether they were viable general election winners.

They weren't. Trump jumped in early in the Pennsylvania primary to back TV doctor Mehmet Oz for the Senate, though Oz had only recently moved to the state and had never held elected office. Trump also helped secure the gubernatorial nomination for Doug Mastriano, a little-known state senator who in 2020 attempted to overturn Biden's Pennsylvania victory. Oz struggled to raise money, was accused of carpetbagging, continued to alter his positions, and ultimately lost the seat to John Fetterman—a radical progressive who barely campaigned given he was recovering from a stroke. Oz's fail handed Democrats their outright majority in the Senate. Mastriano's loss was even more embarrassing; he was routed by fifteen points by Democratic attorney general Josh Shapiro.

The exact same script ran in state after state. Trump helped venture capitalist Blake Masters emerge as victor in a bloody GOP primary for the Arizona Senate seat, despite Masters's history of provocative statements that put him at odds with conservative voters. The former president backed Herschel Walker in Georgia, even though the former NFL star was dogged by claims of violence. He helped secure the GOP Wisconsin gubernatorial nomination for businessman Tim Michels, who wrapped himself in knots in the general election over his position on abortion.

Having secured their nominations, most Trump-backed candidates ditched their 2020 election talking points and campaigned on conservative issues. But they were already on the record. And Democrats masterfully did to these candidates exactly what they'd done to candidates in 2020—they tied them to Trump and fearmongered. Biden crisscrossed the country recalling the January 6 riot and insisting "democracy" was on the ballot. Democrats ran ads warning about radical "ultra-MAGA" candidates. Trump over the course of his four years in office made himself unpopular with moderate and suburban voters—particularly women. The left's scare tactics worked again, souring swing voters on 2022 candidates who were tied to Trump.

The one exception to this general rule was J. D. Vance, author of *Hillbilly Elegy*, who Trump helped secure the GOP nomination for the Ohio Senate seat. Vance pulled it out, despite running a shambolic campaign, beating Democratic representative Tim Ryan by a surprising six points. Yet the victory came only after Republican groups bombed the state with outside money. And Vance's victory owed a great deal to DeWine's twenty-five-point gubernatorial reelection, which helped pull other candidates over the line.

Trump continues to say that most of the people he endorsed in 2022 won their elections. But many of those endorsements were in solidly red seats, and many in down-ballot positions. In the races where it mattered most—control of the Senate and of gubernatorial mansions—Trump's record was one of defeat.

Democrats had another unusual advantage: abortion. For all the party decried the Supreme Court's *Dobbs* decision, the issue helped the left immensely in swing states. And activists played it beautifully. The left understood the possibility the Court could overturn *Roe v. Wade* even as the justices heard oral arguments in December 2021. And it got an early confirmation of the likely result when Alito's draft decision leaked seven weeks prior to the actual release. When the *Dobbs* decision finally hit, activists were primed in key states to get abortion initiatives on the ballot, helping to drive up turnout and bolster the narrative of "extremist" Republicans.

The GOP should have recognized the peril, especially after Kansas held an early referendum in August 2022, and 59 percent of voters in that bright-red state rejected an amendment that would have let state legislators impose new abortion restrictions. The message: The country had changed since *Roe v. Wade*, and most Americans want abortion to be accessible, though with reasonable limits. This premise was proven easily in states like Florida, where Republican leaders clearly set out their position in early 2022 by adopted a law allowing abortions up to fifteen weeks. Republicans made the case for it and didn't suffer in the midterm results. But too many Republicans in 2022 failed to clearly enunciate their positions—allowing Democrats to define them as a threat to abortion rights.

That proved politically deadly in swing states like Michigan. Even after *Roe*, the state retained on its books a 1931 law broadly banning abortions save in cases of the life of the mother. Almost immediately upon the high court overturning *Roe*, Michigan courts blocked the 1931 law from kicking back in. It was highly unlikely the law would ever have been enforced. Yet liberal activists rushed to get an initiative on the ballot to expand and enshrine abortion rights in the state constitution.

Democratic governor Gretchen Whitmer infuriated her state with excessive Covid lockdown rules, and alienated parents with school closures. She was eminently beatable. But she seized on the abortion initiative, suggesting that without her at the helm, abortions would become history: "The only reason Michigan continues to be a pro-life state," she warned in September 2022, "is because of my veto and my lawsuit [to keep the 1931 law at bay]."

Her opponent, Trump-backed TV personality Tudor Dixon, allowed herself to be painted as a zealot. The media ran story after story quoting women in Michigan who were longtime Republicans, but who were conflicted about giving Dixon their vote. They spoke in the election: Whitmer won by ten points, and 57 percent of the state voted to enshrine sweeping new abortion rights in the constitution. Faced with a law that went beyond their comfort zone on abortion rights—or a Republican candidate whom they didn't trust with the issue—Michiganders chose the former.

Biden proved again that Democrats are good at using bogeymen to distract voters ("democracy," Trump, reproductive rights) to distract from day-to-day concerns—especially when Republicans let them. But the GOP may not make the same mistake twice, and Trump won't always be around to pound as an "ultra MAGA" threat to "democracy."

And that's the warning part for Democrats.

"El sueño americano"

Along the border at the bottom tip of Texas sit three U.S. House districts—the Twenty-Eighth, the Fifteenth, and the Thirty-Fourth. They are longtime Democratic strongholds, and the Thirty-Fourth had been in that party's hands for 150 years. It's a district that is 84 percent Hispanic and voted for Hillary Clinton by more than twenty-one points in the 2016 election.

Then came June 2022. In a special election to fill the open seat, Mayra Flores became the first Mexican-born woman to be elected to the U.S. Congress. As a *Republican*. A mother of four and married to a Border Patrol agent, she ran as an out-and-out conservative. "Washington liberals are killing the American dream, attacking oil-and-gas jobs and causing prices to skyrocket," explained one of her ads. "We must secure our borders and keep our families safe." She is pro-life and promised to defend religious liberty. Flores told her audiences her story of leaving Mexico at age six, picking cotton with her parents in Texas to make ends meet on her way to citizenship at fourteen. She introduced herself with: "Soy el sueño americano" (I am the American dream). Hispanic voters liked what they heard—and turned their backs on their longtime Democratic patrons.

Flores served only a handful of months. She was edged out in the regular election in November, after new maps shaped the district to more heavily favor Democrats. Yet even as she lost, Monica De La Cruz picked up the neighboring Fifteenth—becoming the first Republican in history to represent *that* 80 percent Hispanic district. De La Cruz's opponent, Michelle Vallejo, ran as an unrepentant, big-government progressive. It all proved too radical for a south Texas Hispanic community that is largely blue-collar, religious, pro-family, and aspirational.

The Texas results are part of a change rippling through the electorate. British pollster Michael Ashcroft (Lord Ashcroft) presented an interesting analysis of U.S. voters in the wake of the 2022 election, based on a sweeping survey of twenty thousand Americans and focus groups in swing states. The data confirmed a couple of points.

Over the past forty years, the Democratic Party has more and more come to represent higher-educated, wealthier, urban voters. The more financially secure a Democratic voter, the more they support welfare benefits, government spending, and higher minimum wages, and the more they believe the nation is racist and that government needs to police speech. Over the past forty years, the Republican Party has more and more come to represent working class and rural voters. Intriguingly, it is these less educated and less financially secure voters who most question big government and transfer payments (though they might be the group most likely to benefit from them), and who most think America is full of opportunity and that government should stand up for free speech. Swing voters remain in the center of all these positions. Think suburbanites.

Ashcroft obviously isn't the first person to make these observations—it's grown evident as elections have rolled on. But his analysis helped confirm the degree to which the parties have traded places, and how big a problem this is becoming for Democrats. To put the risk simply: There are a hell of a lot more working-class and middle-class individuals in the country than there are wealthier ones. And the Democratic Party is starting to hemorrhage portions of these longtime constituencies.

Democrats began to fret about this in the wake of Trump's election, though they (typically) chose to look at it through the lens of race. They questioned why they'd lost so many white, blue-collar workers in key states like Pennsylvania and Wisconsin. And they (typically) decided to ignore the problem. The party has long placed its bet on the theory that simple demographic changes will cement its power: White working-class voters (who typically vote Republican) are declining, while minority voters (who typically vote Democrat) are on the rise.

Stanley Greenberg—the same pollster who analyzed Reagan Democrats—attempted to set them straight in a 2017 essay. He explained: "Democrats don't have a '*white* working-class problem.' They have a '*working-class* problem,' which progressives have been reluctant to address honestly or boldly. The fact is that Democrats have lost support with *all* working-class voters across the electorate, including the Rising American Electorate of minorities, unmarried women and millennials."

Hispanics are a case in point. Democrats have long taken them for granted. But the further Biden marches to the left, the harder a time Hispanics have recognizing the party they first joined. They remain largely Catholic and pro-family, yet progressives want zero restrictions on abortion. Hispanics are primarily working-class, yet progressives want to shut down their oil, gas, and coal jobs. Hispanics are proud of their efforts to obtain citizenship and embrace law and order, yet progressives want an open border. The left no longer believes in the value of work or family and characterizes America as systemically racist and a threat to the globe. This is out of step with first- and second-generation immigrants who, like Flores, still believe in "el sueño Americano."

One-time Democratic presidential candidate Julian Castro predicted in 2018 that the rising Hispanic vote would by 2024 deliver Democrats Florida, Texas, and Arizona—"a big blue wall of seventy-eight electoral votes." He was correct that Hispanic voters—the largest minority group in the country—are becoming an ever more consequential piece of the electorate. Only they are fleeing the Democratic Party.

The first rumbling of this appeared in the 2020 election, when Biden saw his winning margin among Hispanics drop by sixteen points compared to what Clinton obtained in 2016. That's huge. As left-leaning political scientist Ruy Teixeira explained in the *WSJ* in 2020, the desertion of the Democratic Party spanned the gamut of the Hispanic vote: "The slippage happened all over the country in 2020 and among all the different ethnicities lumped under the Hispanic label. The Democratic advantage among Hispanic voters in the presidential election declined 28 points in Florida, 18 points in Texas and Wisconsin, 16 points in Nevada, 12 points in Pennsylvania and 10 points in Arizona. Nationwide, the Democratic margin was down 26 points among Cubans, 18 points among Puerto Ricans, 16 points among Dominicans, 12 points among Mexicans, and 18 points among other Hispanic ethnicities. Data sources agree that these shifts were primarily driven by working-class voters without a college degree, who make up the overwhelming majority of the Hispanic population."

The shift in some jurisdictions was eye-popping—both for its scale and rapidity. In Texas's Rio Grande Valley, Zapata County (nearly 95 percent Hispanic) voted for Clinton in 2016 by a thirty-three-point margin. Four years later, Trump won it by five points. In nearby Starr County, Clinton won by fifty-eight points. Biden won by just five.

Republicans built on these gains in the 2022 election. Compared to the 2018 midterms, Hispanics support overall for the GOP jumped about ten points, according to a *Politico* story about exit polls conducted by the major news networks and Edison Research. But the shift was even more monumental in states like Florida, where Hispanics became the foundation of the GOP's big night, turning out to elect DeSantis and Rubio. Both men won outright majorities of the Hispanic vote—Rubio got 56 percent and DeSantis 58 percent. And both flipped the urban, Hispanic stronghold of Miami-Dade County, which no Republican had won in 20 years.

Yet it isn't just Hispanics moving right. While the 2022 election didn't deliver a red wave nationwide, Democrats lost support from nearly every category of voter compared to the 2018 midterms. Republicans grew their support among men by 10 points. Democrats lost their support among women by 11. Democrats lost support among every age group—including the 18–29 youth vote. Asian support for GOP candidates spiked 17 points. African-American women support for Democrats dropped by 7 points, and by 11 points among African-American men. Democrats lost urban voters, while Republicans gained rural and suburban support. Republicans did better at every education level.

Houston, Democrats have a problem

Part of the shift is a newly proactive Republican Party, wise to the opportunity of inroads. The GOP jawboned for decades about its need to more actively recruit and court disaffected minority voters. But it's only been in the past five years that the party has fully embraced that mission. The Republican National Convention in 2020 featured an unprecedented lineup of nonwhite and nonmale speakers—each one describing what had drawn them to conservative principles, and each sending the message that it is okay to be a Republican. The Republican National Committee started investing millions to set up community centers in Hispanic, Jewish, Native American, Asian, and African-American population areas. In the 2022 midterms, the party held more than five thousand events at these thirty-eight voter outreach centers, placed across nineteen states.

Just as important, Republicans started recruiting minority candidates to represent the party. The GOP fielded an historic number of minority candidates in House races in 2022. These new politicians are giving millions of voters a reason to take a closer look at the party. There is little question that DeSantis's victory in Florida was in part due to his running mate—Lieutenant Governor Jeanette Nuñez, a Cuban-American from Miami.

All this helps explain why Donilon's post-midterm memo about "support" for Biden's agenda was such a crock. Democrats held down their midterm losses by scaring moderate voters in swing states with wild claims about Trump-tied candidates and abortion. But that pyrrhic victory is papering over voter alignment shifts and a public that is deeply skeptical of radical, progressive policies. It's overall unhappy with Biden's performance. Biden's polling numbers remained largely unchanged after the election, and far from healthy. An Associated Press poll in December 2022 determined that only one-quarter of adults said economic conditions were good; three-quarters described them as bad.

And here's the final, important point: All signs point to a Democratic Party that will move even further left. Polls suggest that the portion of the Democratic electorate least enthused with Biden is the progressive movement. For all the president's radicalism, this faction is still dismissive of his efforts and hostile to a renomination. "He's deeply unpopular. He's old as shit. He's largely been ineffective," Corbin Trent, a cofounder of the progressive No Excuses PAC and a former communications director for Alexandria Ocasio-Cortez, told *Politico* in early 2022.

As of the writing of this book, Biden had not yet decided whether to run for reelection. But even if he does, the potential remains for a liberal primary challenge—a repeat of 1980. Massachusetts senator Ted Kennedy, frustrated that Carter hadn't adopted even more of his agenda, decided to challenge the president. He ultimately failed, but his bid roiled the party and pushed Carter further left, putting the president in an even weaker position in the general election. Any man or woman who seeks to become the Democratic Party's next nominee will feel enormous pressure to cave to today's ascendant progressive base. Whether the nominee is Biden or a replacement there is little to indicate the Democratic Party will embark upon an ideological course correction.

Like Carter in 1980, Biden has created the conditions for a lasting shift among the electorate. But Republicans risk throwing it all away. The 2022 midterms proved that it isn't enough for Republicans to just bash on Biden policies. If the economy is bad in 2024, they might eke out another win. But such a small victory will hardly equal a mandate for real change.

If Republicans want to take full advantage of today's economic and political situation—if they want to step toward another Reagan era—they are going to have to embrace an overhaul. The movement needs to recommit itself to a principled, conservative agenda. It needs to become again the party of ideas, optimism, and outreach.

CHAPTER 11

BOUNCING BACK

In September 2022, Republican leader Kevin McCarthy unveiled his "Commitment to America," the House GOP's midterm agenda. Republicans had spent the previous nineteen months lambasting the Biden administration and Democrats overall for their spending and for their use of arcane procedures to jam through huge and unvetted bills. House Republicans now laid out what they proposed to do about it. The Commitment began with the GOP's promise that it would "curb wasteful government spending." And it ended with vows to hold "Washington accountable" and "end special treatment for Members of Congress."

Three months later, Senate Republicans let the country know just how much they cared about those promises. With the clock ticking toward a government shutdown, McConnell locked arms with Schumer to announce a $1.8 trillion "omnibus" spending bill. The monstrosity had been crafted in backrooms, teemed with tens of billions in additional domestic spending, and was stuffed full of thousands of earmarks that funneled taxpayer dollars back to member districts. The 4,155-page bill also became a vehicle for dozens of separate yet consequential pieces of legislation that lawmakers hadn't bothered to pass earlier in the year. Appropriators unveiled the bill in the dead of a Monday night, and the eyesore had already passed the Senate by Thursday—with no opportunity for members to read its contents or debate its provisions. Your government at work.

And Republicans wonder why voters didn't trust them more in the midterms?

The gospel of Milton Friedman

For a party to get it right, it first must figure out what it's getting wrong. One of the biggest mistakes the GOP has made in recent years was misreading Trump's 2016 victory, taking his narrow victory as some sort of huge political realignment. That read—which is wrong, wrong, wrong—is encouraging the party to step away from too many of its core principles.

The conventional wisdom—now rife in newspapers and academic publications—is that Trump rode to office on a new wave of "populism." Populism can mean a lot of things, but it generally refers to politicians who appeal to "the people" against an established "elite." Populists can be found across the political spectrum and can encompass everything from left-wing socialists to right-wing nativists. Whatever the ideology, populist leaders generally succeed by favoring policies that claim to benefit "the people." Those can include good ideas, though just as often populist policies lack principle or do damage to the economy or to institutions. Think Hugo Chavez, who rallied Venezuela's poor against its wealthy to seize power, then dismantled the country's constitutional checks and imposed a devastating Marxist agenda.

Trump absolutely *employs* populist rhetoric—he loves to bash on the GOP "establishment." And he absolutely used his candidacy to highlight two areas of GOP policy that had grown "unpopular" with the base—immigration and trade. His promise to build a wall tapped into a long (bipartisan) unhappiness with illegal immigration, and its effect on welfare, health care, and education. His opposition to sweeping multilateral trade agreements struck a chord with workers who feel these pacts hurt U.S. jobs. Trump's critics, including the press, obsessed on these two aspects of his presidency—since it best allowed them to present Trump as xenophobic, authoritarian, and reckless. Trump helped by highlighting these policies far more than his others.

And yet these were but a small piece of the Trump policy agenda. Everything else about Trump (even if he rarely credited the source) was straight out of the Reagan policy playbook. And *that playbook* was the basis of his success in the presidency. He ran on promises to cut taxes, replace ObamaCare with a market-based alternative, get rid of regulations, unleash the energy sector, rebuild the military, and nominate originalists to the federal judiciary. Trump could have run as a "populist" independent, but he chose to compete in (Reagan's) Republican Party. He could have chosen anyone as his running mate—including an actual "populist." He instead chose Mike Pence—a movement conservative with long and deep ties to the Reagan policy establishment.

Pence headed up the presidential transition team, and he used his connections to recruit the most Reagan-like administration since Reagan himself. Conservative reformers who'd spent decades chomping at the bit flocked to DC on the promise they'd be allowed to enact bold change. And they did. Trump is no policy guy, but he was wise enough to let these people get on with it, largely free of micromanagement.

While the press ignored (or complained about) most of this agenda, the results were remarkable. Trump Republicans in 2017 enacted a substantive tax reform, cutting individual and corporate rates and closing loopholes. The administration withdrew from the Paris Climate Accord. It dismantled entire programs in Obama's administrative state. His cabinet officials slashed regulations. A year into Trump's tenure, the *Federal Register* (the compilation of all the national government's rules and regulation) sat at 61,308 pages—the lowest count since 1993, Bill Clinton's first year in office. His departments handed power back to the states, imposed new rules to police bureaucrats, fought for free speech on campuses, brought more financial transparency to unions, and opened up new tracts of federal land for energy exploration. The Pentagon took the first steps toward restoring its might.

These actions produced the economic strength that preceded Covid lockdowns—and set Trump up for reelection. Jobs and pay grew at every level of the economy. Unemployment hit record lows. U.S. businesses—no longer penalized by an unfair corporate tax system—brought investment back home. Home ownership increased. Millions of Americans got off the welfare rolls. Trump might occasionally sound populist, but 90 percent of his agenda was straight up, free market religion, direct from the gospel of Milton Friedman. This earned Trump an appreciative public. As the economy hummed, his approval ratings hit highs in early 2020. Had the pandemic not hit, that Reagan agenda likely would have returned Trump to office.

Yet too many Republicans have fallen for the view that Trump's secret sauce is rabble-rousing and catering to the masses. This is convenient for liberals and the media, who hate the proven success of Reagan policies and would like nothing more than for the GOP to ditch them in favor of a more "populist" agenda. Especially because some Republicans have now decided that the way to be "populist" is to look like Democrats.

This "New Right"—which favors something amorphous called "national conservatism"—claims that Reaganism is old, fuddy-duddy, and dead. The biggest threat to the nation, they argue, is cultural decay, and on that we must fight, fight, fight, and remain in a state of perpetual outrage. The right, they say, needs to embrace government and use it to *conservative* ends—to hand out giant subsidies to encourage people to have more babies, and promote policies that require cultural norms. It must protect Americans—especially working-class Americans—from the evils of big business and the free market, with new levels of protectionism, regulation, antitrust, and centralized industrial policy.

Lincoln was dedicated to the proposition that all men are created equal—but only in their God-given rights, not in their makeup or talents. NatCons reject this. They, like the left, want to rig the system in favor of some.

All this was neatly laid out in a document in early January 2023 from Florida senator Marco Rubio—who intends to take another run at the presidency, and now thinks his ticket is a NatCon agenda. In his "Plan for American Renewal," Rubio describes the country in doomsday terminology—America is on the "brink," its communities "hollowed out, institutions torn down, faith marginalized, and the common good ignored." (Talk about a "malaise" speech.) The answer is to put "Wall Street in its place," by giving the federal government control over the direction of investment. The country, says Rubio, needs much more legislation like the semiconductor giveaway, with Washington directing more sectors of the economy. In a naked play for the blue-collar vote, Rubio calls on Republicans to wrap their arms around unions and to "knock down the traditional four-year college model." He also wants more federal involvement in K–12 education (Carter would love that), a crackdown on Big Tech, and huge new tax credits and spending for parents with children.

One thing NatCons have in common: Few give any indication they've ever *met* one of the blue-collar workers they claim to speak for. I grew up in a blue-collar household. My father was an auto mechanic who ran his own small repair shop. We lived a modest, working-class life. Dad wasn't resentful of the wealthy; he'd have liked nothing more than to join their ranks. He didn't hate Wall Street or big business; he understood that they, like he, provided jobs. He disliked unions, given seniority rules that put time-served ahead of hard work. He was proud to be blue-collar and felt dignity in his profession; yet he didn't resent college graduates and was also proud when all four of his girls received some form of postsecondary education. As a small-business owner dogged by taxes, OSHA rules, and environmental regs, he generally subscribed to Reagan's belief that the nine most terrifying words in the English language are: "I'm from the government, and I'm here to help." He'd have snorted at Rubio's claim that more government is the answer to today's mess.

Also bizarre is that these national conservatives appear to be using Trump as the motivation for their new approach—even though it bears little relation to how Trump won office or governed. Trump is a businessman; he *didn't* run against corporate America. His administration spent its time in office lowering taxes and removing barriers so that more businesses would invest in the U.S. He *didn't* run against wealth. The very idea is hilarious; there's few things Trump loves talking about more, especially his own. Yes, he finally made the federal government pay some overdue attention to career and technical school. But he wasn't hostile to university education. Trump also didn't use a "people's" mandate to grow government power. Quite the opposite. His administration focused almost entirely on *rolling back* the size and scope of the federal bureaucracy.

The biggest problem with the NatCons is that not a thing they offer is new. Americans who want bigger government and class warfare already have a party: Democrats. As conservative David Harsanyi wrote in November 2022 in an amusing essay in the *Federalist* entitled "National Conservatism Is a Dead End": "Young NatCons, many of whom I know and like, seem to be under the impressions that they've stumbled upon some fresh, electrifying governing philosophy. Really, they're peddling ideas that already failed to take hold 30 years ago when the environment was far more socially conservative and there were far more working-class voters to draw on. If Americans want class-obsessed statists doling out family-busting welfare checks and whining about Wall Street hedge funds, there is already a party willing to scratch that itch. We don't need two."

He added that the New Righters who mock "zombie Reaganism" might remember that the "'80s fusionist coalition, which stressed upward meritocratic mobility, free markets, federalism, patriotism, and autonomy from the soul-crushing federal bureaucracy, was by all historical measures more successful than the Buchananism that followed or Rockefellerism that preceded. Zombie Reaganism was a dramatic success not only in 1980 but also in 1994 and again in 2010 and 2014. The 'shining city on a hill' might sound like corny boomerism, but it's still infinitely more enticing than the bleak apocalypticism of Flight 93."

Spending like sailors

The good news is that the New Righters remain a minority in the party. The bad news is that some of their ideas are beginning to filter into GOP positions, diluting the party's principles.

McCarthy's "Commitment to America" highlights a bit of this tension. It contained more than thirty different proposals, cobbled together from every corner of today's conservative moment— free marketers, culture warriors, NatCons, protectionists, you name it. That's why the promises were at times in conflict. The Commitment promised "pro-growth tax and deregulatory policies," which is fab. But how does that gel with the promise to have Washington rein in "Big Tech" and micromanage "supply chains"? It promised to restore freedom—which traditionally means limiting the scope of the federal government. Yet it also promised to institute national policies to "ensure only women can compete in women's sports" and to "support 200,000 more police through recruiting bonuses." Both are noble goals, but both are jobs for state legislatures.

The bigger problem with the Commitment was that too few voters believed it. "Curb wasteful government spending"? Since when?

Spending isn't a new problem for the party. Republicans always campaign on spending curbs but also lose all impulse control when they get in power. George W. Bush promised spending discipline, but when 9/11 resulted in the U.S. invasion of both Afghanistan and Iraq, he was unwilling to choose between guns and butter. Spending went up for both.

The Tea Party Republicans won the 2010 election on a mandate to cut spending and did briefly fulfill that promise—at least while opposing Obama. Total fiscal outlays starting in 2012 fell two years in a row—from $3.6 trillion in 2011 to $3.45 trillion in 2013. That kind of spending restraint is all too rare and prior to the Tea Party years had happened only under the Reagan presidency and the beginning of the Gingrich Congress.

But it didn't last. Spending started creeping up again in the latter Obama years, and Republican discipline disappeared entirely with Trump in the Oval Office. The GOP passed its tax reform, which was great for the economy. But Republicans who pass tax cuts have an obligation to keep spending in check—not just to align outlays with tax receipts, but to deny the left the claim that tax cuts amount to deficit spending. Trump occasionally vowed to get serious about cutting federal dollars but never did, and without presidential leadership Republicans all but abandoned the fight. The Trump years set the stage for Congress's now-annual "omnibus" blowouts, in which both Republicans and Democrats feed at the trough.

The problem has only grown worse as Republicans have turned ever more (as NatCons propose) to the Democratic strategy of *buying* votes. If it felt like there was a notable absence of Washington voices calling for calm during the 2020 pandemic, it was because both sides were too busy falling all over themselves to take credit for the $1,200 household checks and enhanced unemployment insurance they jointly air-dropped over America as part of their five Covid bills. If it felt as if there was no appreciable difference on spending between the parties the first two years of Biden's tenure, it's because so many Republicans wanted to use

the infrastructure bill and the semiconductor subsidy extrava-
ganza to claim credit for redirecting money to their home states
and districts.

Spending is corrosive in its own right—but also serves as a
gateway to further unprincipled behavior. So strong has been the
GOP lust for dollars in the Biden era, it was willing to abandon
other policy fights. Take infrastructure. There is a conservative
argument to be made for investing infrastructure dollars in federal projects—national highways, federal airports, sea harbors.
And in the past, the Republican price for a bipartisan deal would
have been some red lines and required reforms. A principled GOP
deal would have demanded that any deal restrict funding to *federal* infrastructure—rather than asking federal taxpayers to float
state projects. It would have demanded permanent changes to the
National Environmental Policy Act and othered federal red tape
that add years to the permitting process. It would have drawn a
line at money that intruded in private markets.

What happened in the 2021 infrastructure deal? Democrats
got everything their hearts desired—hundreds of billions in additional federal spending, a binge of green subsidies, and new federal dominance in private markets like broadband. Republicans
got nothing in return—save spending. So eager were they to funnel money home they missed what might have been the best shot
in decades to institute some reform.

Or take that semiconductor blowout. The Republican excuse
for deciding to engage in this legislation was a semiconductor chip
shortage exacerbated by Covid supply chain problems. GOP pro-
ponents argued the United States needed to be more competitive
in the manufacture of advanced chips (including those used in U.S.
military weapons), given the risk that China could invade Taiwan,
which currently has a near monopoly on their production.

Yet what began as a modest exercise in incentivizing more U.S.
chip production soon turned into a subsidy orgy of corporate

welfare and federal research dollars. Democrats received a huge new boost to the size of government, and new rules on union and prevailing wages in the manufacture of new chip plants. Republicans? They got a reputation for indulging in corporate handouts, as well as for acting like Chinese central planners. All so that they could spread some bucks back home.

Pretty much everything you need to know about Republican spending attitudes was highlighted in March 2021, when the House GOP caucus voted to bring back earmarks—102–84. Republicans had sworn off this gateway to spending a decade earlier—when it still had fiscal religion. But when the Democratic House announced it would restore the practice, Republicans clambered on board.

GOP spenders over the years have invented all kinds of arguments for why earmarks are . . . good! A favorite is to drape this spending in the cloak of "constitutional duty"—claiming earmarking is a way for legislators to assert "authority" over dollars, rather than ceding decisions to the Biden administration. This might wash if the GOP didn't routinely vote for bills that cede hundreds of billions of dollars of spending decisions to the administration—with never any requirements for accountability. GOP porksters simply like stealing taxpayers' hard-earned money and giving it to their pet projects. The new House Republican majority voted in 2022 to again embrace earmarks—this time by even greater margins, 158–52. The final 2022 omnibus contained thousands of earmarks—worth billions—and nearly half of them went to Republicans.

Spending isn't the only challenge. The GOP is increasingly calling for punitive measures on business, playing off American economic struggles and frustration with censorship and wokeism. I'm all for some legitimate corporate bashing; companies often deserve more than they get. Big Tech's censorship of free speech is appalling, and an area for policy discussion. Corporate America remains in hock to progressive cultural demands, and CEOs have no business wading into debates over Georgia's electoral reforms. The Chamber of Commerce undermined the economy when in the 2020 election it tried to curry favor with the left by juking its scorecard to justify its endorsement of antibusiness House Democrats. Woke financiers like BlackRock's Larry Fink are pushing the left's radical climate agenda via their insistence on ESG policies across Wall Street.

Yet the Republican rush to capitalize on public fury—to compete with Democrats as anticorporate and antiwealth—has led to kneejerk proposals to regulate, tax, and punish companies in ways that would have harmful consequences for prosperity. Do Republicans really believe they can do a better job of managing markets than the market itself? Have they forgotten that companies pass higher taxes on to consumers? Oh, and by the way: How does any of this mesh with the simultaneous NatCon calls to manage the economy by showering corporate welfare on specific industries?

Speaking of outrage, the GOP also needs to rethink its embrace of Trumpian tariffs. This was an area where Trump really was a populist. The former president channeled American anger and imposed tariffs of up to 25 percent on Chinese goods. It was meant to punish China for unfair trade practices, but it ended up punishing U.S. concerns. China is the main supplier of many supplies and goods for our manufacturers, and taxes on imports are passed along to American companies. China of course retaliated with its own tariffs, wracking huge harm on American farmers and small businesses. The Trump administration ended up writing billions in checks to prop up farmers hurt by its own trade policies. And while Trump claimed to believe wholeheartedly in "better" trade deals—bilateral agreements that emphasized the "free" part of trade—he never got around to getting one done. The party has continued to drift on this vital issue.

Brain drain

If only the GOP spent as much time working on policy ideas as it did laughable earmark justifications. Americans at this point know very well what Republicans are against—Biden, and everything Biden stands for. But what do Republicans want? The GOP needs to recommit to the job of understanding, adopting, and explaining free market innovations to their audiences.

Republicans took from Trump the lesson that the party needs to fight. It was an important message. What they forgot is that it's as important to fight *for* something as it is to fight against. That was easy to lose sight of during the Trump presidency. The former president was very good at pummeling opponents and bragging about successes. But he didn't care much for policy and bounced from issue to issue, and so struggled to articulate a steady, coherent vision.

It didn't help that Congressional Republicans also lost some of their most articulate policy leaders. Whatever your view of Paul Ryan's speakership, he was an expert on budgets and taxes, and that made all the difference in the Obama years and during the Trump tax reform. The late and inspiring Oklahoma senator Tom Coburn—who came to Congress after a career as an obstetrician—made it his mission to educate his party on health care and remains the reason the GOP was once able to put forward a comprehensive, market-based reform. But policy evangelists like these remain too far and few between. Too many Republicans find it easier to complain on cable TV than to learn the minutiae of Medicare reimbursements or the ethanol program—and figure out a way to fix things.

This isn't lawmakers' fault alone. Washington has no lack of think tanks and policy scholars. Unfortunately, too few consider their main duty to be the education of policy makers. Starting even in the George W. Bush years, some of the biggest conservative think tanks decided they'd be more influential if they became more political. They started training activists, putting out scorecards, serving as waiting posts for politicians in between administrations, and even erecting campaign arms. Research and ideas fell by the wayside.

This has robbed legislators of an invaluable resource. In 2012, former Bush administration official Tevi Troy explained in *National Affairs* what an organization like the Heritage Foundation meant in the Reagan years: "When Ronald Reagan won the presidency in 1980, Heritage spotted its chance to influence policy more directly, and worked to compile a comprehensive conservative policy agenda for the new administration. Titled *Mandate for Leadership*, the publication contained more than 2,000 specific policy recommendations, from ways to pursue a more assertive approach toward the Soviet Union to minute alterations of environmental regulations. By the end of Reagan's second term, more than 60% of these proposals had been adopted by the administration." Commentators would later call that Heritage document "the bible of the Reagan Revolution."

What is the bible today? Where are the Republicans who are campaigning on consumer-choice health care or free market environmentalism? And where are the big ideas, and the courage? When was the last time a leader of the GOP warned about the (still) coming meltdown in Social Security finances?

To be fair, this wilderness wandering is partly a function of being out of power. With Democrats in the White House, mixed views on Trump, and an unknown GOP presidential field, it's unclear who the party's leader is or will be. At the same time, Republicans don't have the luxury of spinning their wheels. The Biden Democrats have created an economic mess and a disaffected public. If conservatives hope to capitalize on this for the long run, they need to start making compelling arguments now.

The GOP doesn't have time to indulge in an existential crisis as to what they should look like in a post-Biden world. They need party leaders, think tanks, and presidential candidates who recommit to getting back the Reagan mojo.

* * *

And it's not that hard.

When McCarthy unveiled his Commitment, he helpfully supplied his members with "pocket cards" that listed all the policy proposals—the better to remember them at stump speeches. I remember thinking: *Hmmm.*

Reagan didn't need a pocket card. He was a details guy, sure, and in his 1980 and 1984 campaigns he had an answer at the ready for any specific policy question. But his success was in connecting with Americans on a few compelling and straightforward themes. They were promises that people could relate to, especially in the wreckage of the Carter years. And they are promises that are just as potent now given Biden's overreach. They essentially come down to three big vows: limited government, competent government, and a strong America.

Limited government

Reagan began his 1980 election eve address by noting that American skepticism of big government is woven into its soul, going back to its founding: "Americans today, just as they did 200 years ago, feel burdened, stifled and sometimes even oppressed by government that has grown too large, too bureaucratic, too wasteful, too unresponsive, too uncaring about people and their problems."

Does anyone really feel much different now? The liberal media will attempt to convince with polls or anecdotes that the country wants a welfare state. But the recent economic success of the Trump years proves the opposite. Given the opportunity to work and achieve, that is what many chose to do. Millions of

Americans left behind food stamps and other welfare programs. And Americans—left, right, or center—remain hostile to government that seeks to tell them what they can drive or eat, or what is acceptable to say, or what their kids must learn in school. They have seen again the extraordinary power government has to make the economy worse, not better.

Limited government comes down to the following:

Fiscal sanity

Republicans first and foremost must remember that the basic rule of limited government is fiscal restraint. Every dollar provided to the federal bureaucracy is a dollar bureaucrats will use to intrude in American lives. And in ways our Founders never envisioned.

Republicans need to stop talking about merely "cutting spending." The new goal needs to be a complete overhaul of the federal budget, in line with federalist principles. As Friedman once noted, up until 1930, Americans viewed the federal government as a "keeper of the peace and an umpire." Federal spending was usually less than 5 percent of national income, while state and local government usually spent several times that amount. This was rooted in the sound belief that government closest to the people knows best its needs. Spending at all levels of government combined rarely rose above 15 percent of national income.

By contrast, in fiscal 2021, federal spending alone hit 30 percent of GDP. Friedman warned even in the 1970s that we had come to view the feds as "responsible for treating every social and personal ill," and Democrats have worked hard to cement that view by giving the federal government ever more power. It's time to reverse the roles. Especially because the federal government is the *least* capable of managing most tasks. As Friedman famously wrote: "If you put the federal government in charge of the Sahara Desert, in five years there'd be a shortage of sand."

The current U.S. domestic discretionary budget is an embarrassing spectacle of duplicative programs, wasteful agendas, and entire workforces that exist solely to intrude on states' rights. Most of this funding can and should go away.

The question should be: What jobs can *only* the federal government perform? Only the federal government can maintain federal infrastructure. But it's time to get rid of the huge surface transportation programs that transfer federal tax dollars around from "giver" to "taker" states. Only the federal government will engage in certain types of basic scientific research. Yet that definition has narrowed over the years as private industry becomes more competitive in technology, space exploration, and biotech. The federal government requires dollars to maintain the judiciary, and a stable currency, and a diplomatic corps and certain offices. But arts funding, educational grants, mental health counseling, midnight basketball—it all needs to go. And earmarks need to become a thing of distant memory.

It's time to reconsider getting rid of entire pieces of government. There is no more rationale today for the Department of Education than there was in Carter's day. It exists to dictate testing standards and to grant or withhold money on the basis of woke ideology. Someone please justify the existence of the Agricultural Department's Rural Housing Service. The United States Geological Survey was— as its name makes clear—set up in 1879 to catalog the nation's geology and mineral resources. That mission was accomplished eons ago, which is why the outfit now explains it has "evolved" and exists to "provide science about the natural hazards that threaten lives."

If Congress lacks the courage to get rid of other useless departments, it should at least have the backbone to get rid of their more wasteful or intrusive programs. Axe the Department of Energy's Weatherization Assistance Program and its Advanced Technology Vehicle Manufacturing Program. (Tesla has that covered.) Kill the Department of Agriculture's McGovern-Dole International Food for Education Program and its Water and Wastewater Loan and

Grant Program. Why is the federal government in the business of funding rural water projects?

Why do we have an Appalachian Regional Commission—a byproduct of Lyndon Johnson's era? The U.S. still funds an Institute of Peace, an Endocrine Disruption Screening Program, and the Inter-American Foundation. The National Endowment for the Arts and Humanities receives *more than a hundred million* dollars a year. Trump proposed eliminating more than sixty-two agencies and programs in his budget, but Democrats balked and Republicans lacked the will for a fight. Yet Republicans would only win plaudits from zeroing them out altogether.

The country by significant majorities *does* want the federal government to continue providing a basic social safety net. That's understandable. This nation is hardworking and enterprising, but also generous. It knows that people occasionally fall on hard times and need a helping hand. It also understands the importance of government retirement programs and that our older generations spent a life paying payroll and other taxes, in return for a promise of Social Security and Medicare.

Yet it's time to reevaluate those programs through those lenses. Democrats continue to plus-up welfare programs and eliminate incentives to get people back to work. Their ambition is to transform them from temporary programs for the needy into permanent middle-class entitlements. Republicans are going to have to start digging out.

A thriving economy is always the best way to move people off the rolls. But it's also time for root-and-branch reform. Especially in the wake of the generous government pandemic benefits that inspired millions of Americans to stop work altogether, feeding today's labor shortage. A GOP government needs to reimpose sensible work requirements for welfare—and double down on programs that help people back to gainful employment. It's time to simplify and pare back the Earned Income Tax Credit, which is rife with abuse. It needs to take a hard look at alternatives to

Head Start—a program that has never worked since its creation in 1964. And let's have the federal government *exit entirely* the student loan business. Obama promised the federalization of that market would save taxpayers money. It is instead costing hundreds of billions.

This needn't be an exercise in scrooge-ism. Former Speaker Paul Ryan in 2016 chose to get serious about poverty, as part of House Republicans' "Better Way" initiative. This dovetailed with South Carolina senator Tim Scott's "Opportunity Agenda." Both offer real, considered solutions to chronic welfare—tax-advantaged zones in distressed communities, targeted intervention programs. More important, the approaches emphasize the *benefits* of opportunity and upward mobility. Republicans have for too long allowed Democrats to paint them as heartless or ignorant of the struggles of jobless Americans. This is a chance for Republicans to turn the tables—to note that Democratic programs that keep people locked in a cycle of dependency and despair are dehumanizing to millions of Americans who want a better life.

It's also past time for the GOP to fulfill its promise to overhaul health care—to repeal ObamaCare and to move millions of Americans off Medicaid and the Children's Health Insurance Program. Americans deserve free market programs that will provide better benefits, more mobility, and lower costs. Trump Republicans nearly accomplished some of this in 2017 until sabotaged by a few recalcitrant Republican senators. But the party has at the ready the policy framework for a transformation to a patient-centered system that prioritizes choices, competition, and flexibility. There is no time to waste as Democrats double down on their push to turn today's government-run health programs into Medicare for All.

And while Republicans will wince, they must seize the third rail of Social Security and Medicare—and hold tight. GOP promises of fiscal discipline will fall flat so long as the party closes its eyes to these two main drivers of costs—both of which in their current forms are financially unsustainable. Social Security and Medicare alone account for more than one-third of all federal spending. Add in Medicaid and ObamaCare, and those four programs equal half. Social Security trustees estimate the program will be able to continue paying full benefits only until 2035 and is on track for insolvency. Spending on Medicare continues to explode and will continue to eat up a bigger portion of the federal pie—crowding out other priorities.

No one thinks the U.S. government should renege on its promises to pay out to hardworking Americans who paid in. Yet even as Social Security disintegrates, entire generations of younger people have grown comfortable with 401(k)s and investing, and more interested in controlling their retirement futures. Even twenty years ago, George W. Bush was able to build support for the partial privatization of Social Security, and today's political grounds are more fertile. Likewise, there are no lack of proposals for a redesign of Medicare for future generations, to create a program that is more market-based and provides better care to an aging population. These topics may be scary for some politicians. But America is aching for fresh ideas. And anything is better than today's autopilot status quo.

Regulation

The Biden Democrats are using regulation to encroach on every aspect of American life. The federal government now dictates what cars we can buy, and what washing machines, and what types of windows. It decrees what ingredients can go in our food, and what labels go on packages, and where we can build homes. It pronounces on what schools must teach, how doctors practice medicine, and the process by which real estate agents are allowed to obtain appraisals. It decrees how businesses go about hiring, and what loans banks can offer, and which credit cards we can have. It's ludicrous.

Trump upon taking office immediately signed a brilliant executive order, requiring agencies to revoke two regulations for any new one they issued. This groundbreaking approach resulted in one of the first serious examinations of stupid rules in decades and is what resulted in that dramatic decrease in the number of pages in the *Federal Register*. Yet Biden has worked hard to restore those rules that were cut, plus many more.

Republicans can double down on the Trump deregulatory approach. This will prove easier if they first go through that process of cutting entire programs from the executive remit—that alone would take a lot of regulations off the books. Then subject each rule to the same question: Is this the federal government's job? The feds have some role in maintaining environmental and safety standards—even Reagan believed in those goals. But most regulations are federal overreach. They are also an insult—treating Americans as if they aren't smart enough to make their own decisions about how they travel, what they eat, or how they use their money. The GOP will be tempted to regulate some disfavored industries, like Big Tech. But it would be wiser to see if market forces correct the overreach. Give Elon Musk a chance.

Taxes

Ask any American this: If it came down to it, would they rather give their tax dollars to the state and local governments that educate their kids, collect their garbage, run their local clinics, and provide tangible services? Or would they rather give it to a federal government that sinks it into programs that many American never see? That's an easy one. If we want to get back to that system—where state governments are again preeminent—we must tame the federal beast. And the way to do it is to starve it. Lawmakers will have more reason to chop and cut programs if the spigot gets turned off.

The 2017 Republican tax reform was a good beginning—but only a beginning. It's ridiculous that some Americans are asked to pay a top income tax rate of 37 percent to the federal government—and in addition to 7.65 percent in FICA taxes, as well as Medicare surcharges. It's equally absurd that corporations continue to pay 21 percent in taxes—given that tax is passed on to others. And it's dumb that the United States continues to levy capital gains and dividend taxes given their distortionary effects on investment. Estate taxes are both unjust and immoral—the government cravenly taxing a life of work and saving, and for a second time given the assets were taxed at the time of earning.

Republicans have an opportunity to thrill American taxpayers (and hugely disappoint the accounting profession) with an overdue leap to a flat tax. This would simplify the tax code, which is alone an excellent reason to do it. It would encourage savings, investment, and growth. It gets rid of political favoritism, denying well-heeled lobbyists the ability to wangle tax breaks. And it would make taxes more fair. Republicans have an equally exciting chance to implement business tax reforms that will zero out punishing taxes on capital and the make the United States the investment envy of the world.

Cultural modesty

Reagan did address cultural and moral issues, usually by reinforcing traditional values. A vital part of his coalition was the social conservative movement. Yet Reagan's promise to that group was very different from what is today being touted by some in the GOP.

Reagan understood that a big-tent Republican party would disagree on many cultural questions—abortion, gay marriage, school prayer. What he also knew is that all the elements under that canvas nonetheless had something in common: a deep skepticism of a federal government that seeks to impose liberal values on the country. Americans for Tax Reform president Grover Norquist famously described the Reagan coalition in these wonderfully accurate words: the Leave Us Alone Coalition.

That's vastly preferable to the New Right's approach, one that advocates for the federal government to impose moral and cultural values on the nation from on high. They studiously ignore the backlash that such policies always and inevitably inspire. (For proof, look at the tens of millions of Americans furious over the Obama-Biden attempts to foist transgender policies on the country.)

They ignore that such an approach narrows the attractiveness of the conservative movement—alienating anyone who does not subscribe to proscribed cultural positions. Mostly, they forget that it isn't the federal government's job to legislate morality. One of the country's biggest problems is *too much government*—government that crowds out churches, charities, and social groups. As Reagan correctly noted, these "private and independent social institutions . . . not government, are the real sources of our economic and social progress as a people." Want to revitalize them? Limit government.

All this counsels a modest GOP approach—in both rhetoric and legislation. The country has changed a lot since the 1980s and views have moderated on issues like gay marriage and abortion. Millions of moderates, minorities, and even younger voters are frustrated by Biden policies and would be open to a new approach. But the GOP won't make any gains if its cultural platform immediately repels these Americans. The 2022 midterms—and Democrats' effective use of abortion—show the risks. The GOP ticket is to campaign for positions that unite the country, while avoiding the temptation to legislate values—whether that be with spendy child-tax credits, or federal rules on behavior.

The GOP might remember one other Reagan lesson—forgotten amid the brutal punch-ups of the Trump years. Politicians have an enormous ability to influence the culture simply by acting as role models. Reagan's geniality, his humor, and his tolerance reminded Americans that not everything has to be a cage fight. If politicians want to see a change in the culture, they could start by acting like grown-ups.

Competent government

Americans are generally disgusted by DC, and with good reason. Nothing works—and that's a national scandal. Lincoln noted that the men who died at Gettysburg had done so in the noble cause of preserving a "government of the people, by the people, and for the people." Today's government is a hot mess of arrogant and inept bureaucracies, failed programs, and a dysfunctional Congress. Every institution seems to have forgotten that it's supposed to be working *for* the American people.

Reagan promised Americans that he'd cut government, but that he'd also work to ensure that what remained operated competently. The challenge is bigger now. The civil bureaucracy—what we call "the swamp"—operates with impunity, writing rules and regulations that Congress never authorized. Changes in attitudes toward government employment have also changed the makeup of that bureaucracy. It is almost universally left-wing and hostile to any conservative administration. Reagan had another advantage over today's GOP: a functioning Congress, one in which both sides believed in committees, debates, and problem-solving—rather than partisan slugfests.

Republicans could endear themselves to the public with a vow to heal DC—to make it work again. And the simple answer is a return to the separation of powers. Congress must reembrace its job of legislating—of producing detailed bills that make clear what is and isn't allowed. And the next Republican president must make a priority of reining in the "fourth branch of government"—of putting strict limits on a federal bureaucracy. And now is the time to do it, given the backing such changes would get from today's conservative Supreme Court.

Regular order

Congress hasn't operated the way it was meant to operate in more than a decade now—and longer than that in certain functions. Process arguments can be boring, but things in Washington have grown so dire that a process fix is now paramount. It's time for a GOP Congress to commit to "regular order."

Regular order is the way democratic institutions are meant to get things done. In the U.S. Congress it looks like this: Elected members are seated on committees of jurisdiction, with powers over their specific areas of government. Those committees draw up bills, which are then "marked up" via amendments from all sides and voted to the floor. The full chamber then debates the legislation—again, with amendments—and holds a vote for passage. In cases where the Senate and House pass bills on a similar subject, negotiators from both chambers meet in conference to work out differences. The final product is sent back to the House and Senate for final votes. There once was a time when every American schoolkid understood how this worked thanks to watching that famous *Schoolhouse Rock* video.

Unfortunately, most of today's Congress missed "I'm Just a Bill." It fights and investigates, but little else. Leaders—unwilling to cede control to committees—retreat to backrooms and draw up their own legislation in secret. They deny members the ability to see it, read it, debate it, or amend it. They drop it on their chamber at deadline and hold a take-it-or-leave-it vote. One chamber goes first; the other rubber-stamps the product.

This controlled chaos has become too common, even when it comes to Congress's most basic duties—funding government. By law, each chamber is supposed to pass twelve separate appropriations bills each year by the end of September. Congress instead ignores its job, passes "continuing resolutions" to give itself more time, then ignores its job some more, and finally ends up producing thousand-page omnibuses, on deadline, which pass before anyone has time to read them. The U.S. Congress has not successfully complied with its budget process in twenty-five years.

The dysfunction helps explain the rapid rise in government spending. There is no transparency and no accountability. But it also explains Washington's increasingly hostile partisanship. Bodies that short-circuit due process deny their members the opportunity to work together and create buy-in. It particularly infuriates the minority party, as they are shut out completely of legislating. The whole mess is undemocratic. It amounts to a handful of powerful legislators deciding the direction of the entire country. In some places, they'd call that authoritarian.

The only upside to this smoking mess is that it has become so egregious that members are now fighting back. McCarthy only obtained his votes for House Speaker in early 2023 after agreeing to substantive process reform. But Republicans in both chambers need to be passionate about returning to regular order.

Article I

The Constitution explains that the legislative branch exists to pass laws. Again, tell that to Congress. It has become profoundly lazy. This explains the rise of the administrative state.

A lot of this is purposeful. Democrats figured out long ago that the federal bureaucracy is on its side and hardwired to expand government. By deliberately writing vague statutes, Democrats give government workers the opportunity to fill in the blanks. The swamp has pushed this to the limit, helped by Supreme Court precedents that say judges must give deference to regulators. The High Court is now trying to rein some of this in, but the "fourth branch" is still firmly in charge.

This Democratic strategy is helped by the previously described congressional dysfunction. Legislation that goes through committees— that is subject to debate and amendments—receives scrutiny. Legislation that is drawn up in staff rooms is hurried, sloppy, and unvetted. The more the GOP uses regular order to write bills that are tight, detailed, and prescriptive, the less opportunity the administrative state has for mischief, or for future Democratic administrations to "find" new powers in loosely written law.

Congress has also over the years ceded too much of its authority to the executive branch. An excellent example is its decision in 1976 to give sweeping powers to presidents to declare national emergencies, which when activated give them extraordinary powers. Trump pushed the boundaries of this when he declared a national emergency at the southern border. The precedent is concerning as Democrats now call on Biden to declare national emergencies over climate change, gun crime, and poverty.

One of the great benefits of the Supreme Court's 2022 session were its series of decisions that tried to put entities back in their lanes. With *Dobbs*, it returned the question of abortion to the states. With *West Virgina v. EPA*, it told bureaucrats not to meddle in authorities reserved to Congress. With its religious liberty cases and its firearm ruling, it warned the states off intruding in constitutionally protected rights. The GOP needs to embrace this project itself and revive a legislative branch that is failing in its only purpose—legislating.

The power of the purse

Again, laziness. Republicans talk often of exerting their power over the purse, but rarely do so in a way that matters. But a GOP legislative branch's control over money remains its most powerful means of directing government. They'd impress Americans by using it to its max.

Take the example of grants. The same day that the GOP in 2022 voted to embrace earmarks—claiming it had a "constitutional duty" to decide where money went—a significant chunk of the House GOP voted with Democrats to give the Justice Department $50 million to hand out in grants for re-entry programs for former prisoners. That money would become the sole discretion of Biden Attorney General Merrick Garland. DOJ decides which communities and which (liberal) nonprofits get checks.

Congress now routinely hands out these types of lump sums to the executive branch. California Republican Rep. Tom McClintock in a floor speech in 2022 noted that grant making has become the "third-biggest expenditure of the federal government, behind only Social Security and national defense." It costs some half a trillion dollars a year, or approximately $4,000 in an average family's taxes.

Republicans need to put an end to it. They can either direct the funds themselves or insist that executive branches allocate dollars via competitive bidding. The GOP can also start conditioning future dollars on the performance of past ones. And it needs to exercise its ability to zero out budgets completely, denying dollars to departments that aren't meeting standards or complying with congressional demands. All of this will admittedly take a great deal of work and make some departments unhappy. But fixing Washington's broken bureaucracy will require breaking a bit of china.

Civil service reform

The swamp is out of control, and it doesn't stop with excessive rulemaking. Washington's two million civil "servants" now ally with just one political party, and actively work to undermine Republican administrations. These are the likes of Lois Lerner, the former administrator whose IRS department targeted conservative nonprofits. Or the "anonymous" bureaucrats who every day of the Trump administration leaked documents designed to damage their political bosses. Or the EPA's "scientific integrity official," who took it upon herself to investigate whether Trump's Senate-confirmed head to that agency was fit to serve in his job. The arrogance is jaw-dropping.

The GOP could do itself and the country a favor by making reform a top priority. A 2011 American Enterprise Study found that government workers receive wages that are about 14 percent higher than what similar workers in the private sector earn. When you factor in benefits the compensation mismatch grows to some 60 percent. It is no surprise that a number of America's wealthiest counties surround Washington DC. The payouts are the result of automatic increases, bonuses, and seniority systems. And most of the federal workforce is shielded by rules that make it practically impossible to fire or discipline bad employees or to reassign duties.

It's been forty years since the last real civil service overhaul, so the time is ripe. The GOP needs to overhaul the current merit system (which insulates civil servants from accountability), reevaluate federal union privileges, and create more political positions to manage the rabble. Former Wisconsin governor Scott Walker's own public-sector union overhaul proved both popular and effective at diminishing the power of the bureaucracy to dictate outcomes. Trump had the opportunity to run on civil service reform in both 2018 and 2020 but ignored it. The GOP shouldn't make that mistake again.

But it can double down on the Trump-era effort to move pieces of the federal bureaucracy to other parts of the country. The model here is former Agriculture secretary Sonny Perdue's decision in 2019 to move a bit of his department to Kansas City. Federal bureaucrats freaked out and hundreds quit. But the decision was wise on every level.

Perdue's decision moved employees closer to the people they regulate. The relocation was also to a part of the country that was more affordable and saved taxpayer money. And the new digs opened the possibility of recruiting local employees who weren't genetically hostile to conservative governance. Republicans can't go on forever with a federal bureaucracy that works to undermine it. Relocations are an opportunity to rebalance the workforce.

Besides, why should all taxpayer dollars from every state go to an elite few who live only in Fairfax and Montgomery Counties? As the left might say, let's spread the wealth around.

There is sense in leaving the Departments of Defense, Treasury, and State in Washington. But why is the Interior Department thousands of miles away from most of the land it governs? How about moving entire sections of the Department of Housing and Urban Development nearer to the inner cities it claims to exist to help? If we are going to continue to have a Department of Energy, let it sit where we produce some energy.

Washington is in a slump—and has been for decades. The GOP has a chance to sell the country on dynamic reform—to reimagine a government that is smaller, more responsive, more competent.

A strong America

As Americans in 1980 readied to go to the polls, Reagan asked them to think through several questions as they made their choice. On the issue of national security, he posed: "Is our nation stronger and more capable of leading the world toward peace and freedom or is it weaker? Is there more stability in the world or less? Are you convinced that we have earned the respect of the world and our allies, or has America's position across the globe diminished?"

As in 1980, America is processing the U.S. withdrawal from overseas conflicts. A certain faction of Republicans are using this moment as a "populist" opportunity to rile up the country, to critique the wars in Iraq and Afghanistan, to complain about U.S. aid to Ukraine, and to argue that Washington has an obligation to focus on its own people. They want the U.S. to turn inward.

"Peace through strength" is as powerful a philosophy today as it was in the 1980s, and Reagan's aspirations are still what most citizens hope from national security. They want a strong America that has the respect of the globe and is a stabilizing influence.

Biden's abysmal handling of border security, his humiliating withdrawal from Afghanistan, his failure to maintain the military, and his lack of a China policy means Republicans have a great deal of fixing to do.

Yet they can reassure Americans of their safety—and of our nation's role in the world—with a few straightforward promises and policies:

Our fighting forces

For more than a decade, Democrats have successfully demanded "parity" in discretionary spending: equal annual percentage increases for both domestic pork and our military. This has put Republicans in the terrible position of either allowing domestic budgets to balloon or robbing the military of crucial investments. American hard power is declining rapidly, even as we face huge new threats from China and Russia.

A 2022 report from the Heritage Foundation measured the U.S. military's ability to handle two major regional conflicts at once—say, one in the Middle East and one on the Korean peninsula. Disturbingly, it found the United States possibly unable to handle even a single conflict. Trump did manage to give a one-time boost to military spending. But Biden has ignored it, and military budgets are being hit even harder by Biden inflation. Chapter 5 detailed the sorry shape of the equipment and numbers of our Navy, Air Force, Army, and Marines.

Republicans can promise that they will give our fighting men and women the equipment they deserve and need to protect America, and adequately compensate them for the sacrifices they make. The GOP can vow to end parity and to move money they cut from bloated domestic budgets to security investments. They also need to reassure Americans that they will double down on oversight—there are still too many stories of Pentagon waste. Yet huge sums of money could be saved simply by giving the military the security of a budget designed for long-term planning—allowing them to lock in more cost-effective contracts.

And Republicans can promise an emphasis on the newest battlefield: cyberwarfare. The country is at growing risk that America's enemies will use hacking or a virus or other advanced technology to paralyze basic infrastructure. And that's not taking into account cyberattacks on major companies or foreign meddling in elections. The United States so far has taken a haphazard approach to combating cyberthreats; it needs a prioritized focus.

Leadership

Biden's reckless withdrawal from Afghanistan embarrassed our allies, abandoned Afghanis, and made the U.S. look weak. While he has managed to keep an alliance united behind Ukraine, his general approach is to cede diplomacy to multilateral institutions like the United Nations. That's no way for America to lead.

No one wants America diving into conflicts. But the best way to keep conflict from breaking out is for America to send the message that it will not sit idly by as dictators sow discord or threaten peace. Republican leaders can make clear that America will lead a willing coalition to punish those who threaten the world with nuclear weapons, terrorism, or territorial land grabs—and leave open the possibility that punishment will go beyond financial sanctions.

Republicans meanwhile can promise to perform a long-overdue analysis of its membership in some of these global institutions, whether it be the World Health Organization or the International Energy Agency or U.N. agencies. Is the United States' membership and funding worth it, or are we simply giving cover to rogue regimes and liberal agendas?

A secure border

Biden's border mismanagement has in some ways made this a simpler promise for Republicans in the short-term. Americans would at the moment be grateful to any party that presented a plan for stopping the unchecked flow of migrants, criminals, smugglers, and drug runners across the southern border.

Republicans will have to offer more than a wall. They can promise to shift money they cut from domestic spending to finally standing up an effective border patrol and security. Similarly, they can shift funds to help the judiciary get a handle on the obscene backlog of asylum claims. They can vow to use congressional and presidential power to change current asylum laws, toughening standards or requiring those seeking refuge to apply for it at designated processing centers outside the country. Or they can work again with Mexico to restart programs that require asylum seekers to wait outside the United States for approval.

In the medium-term Republicans will need their own plan for immigration overhaul. Trump made a dirty word of "amnesty," but something must be done about millions of illegal immigrants— especially the many Dreamers who were brought here as children. Republicans also need to recognize that the more the U.S. cracks down on legal immigration, the greater the pressure will grow at the border.

They might remember that with American birth rates declining, this country of immigrants will continue to need new workers (look at our current labor shortage). They might even acknowledge that many of these newcomers remain the embodiment of the American dream—and are increasingly open to the Republican message of work, family values, and free markets. The trick is proposing a merit-based immigration system that attracts the best to our shores, alongside a guest-worker program that allows foreigners to come to earn and leave when work is done.

Energy independence

Energy is the lifeblood of every economy, and central to U.S. national security. Carter found that out when OPEC sent the country into a tailspin. The United States under Trump was the closest it had ever been to the dream of "energy independence." But Biden's climate policies have put us back in the position of begging the Saudis.

Republicans must promise an aggressive energy agenda. They can call it "all of the above," but it should mostly focus on what we have most readily available—fossil fuels. The U.S. has vast stores of energy offshore and on its federal lands, and technology that allows us to tap it with minimal disturbance and the highest environmental standards. The GOP needs to remind the country that any transition to renewables is still many decades away. Rushing that transition will spike energy prices and risk other vital national security infrastructure, like the electrical grid. And putting ourselves in hock to global energy disturbances will result in repeats of the swooning gas prices and heating bills of recent years.

Republicans also need to vow to overhaul the current five-year U.S. leasing system, which is too short-term. Fossil fuel companies need to be able to plan for the long run rather than be held hostage to every climate alarmist who makes it to office. And while the GOP is at it, it needs to set up a new mechanism to open federal lands to mining. The pandemic highlighted how dangerously dependent the U.S. is on places like China for the vital rare earth elements necessary for modern technology. The U.S. has many of its own minerals, including on national lands.

Republicans can promise to return our public lands to their original multiuse function. On Roosevelt Arch, in Yellowstone Park, the inscription reads: "For the Benefit and the Enjoyment of the People." The benefit part was pure Gifford Pinchot, the first chief of the U.S. Forest Service, who believed in market forces. It's only in recent times that the environmentalists have taken over, squeezing out businesses, hunters, fishermen, and snow machiners. Let's have American lands benefiting us again.

* * *

This doesn't cover every issue, obviously. The GOP needs a big, rollicking debate on Big Tech, crypto currencies, and how to craft new free trade agreements. Let's be honest: America looks a lot different than it did in Reagan's day, with new challenges and new threats. But the fundamentals haven't changed—not at all. The message of limited government, competent government, and a strong America is a winner—especially as Americans recover from the Biden wreckage.

So long as there's someone skillful enough to deliver it.

CHAPTER 12

IT TAKES A REAGAN

There would never have been a Reagan revolution without . . . Reagan.

Reagan's philosophy of government was powerful. His policies were a compelling antidote to the Carter years. But what propelled the Reagan revolution was Reagan himself: his ability to explain that agenda, to connect with voters, to give people optimism, to invite them to buy in to a better future for the country.

Today's Republicans can have all the best ideas in the world, but without a competent spokesperson they will never capitalize on the opportunity Biden Democrats have provided. The candidates in the upcoming GOP primary will be tempted to campaign in Trump's image—to show they have fight, to call names, to cast blame, to describe the nation in apocalyptic terms. But for a candidate to alter today's political dynamic—to create a bigger and lasting coalition—they will need to change the tone and move beyond sound bites. It's totally possible to be both tough and principled—yet to also be inviting. That was Reagan's genius.

The elephant in the room

I spent the Christmas of 2015 with my parents in Oregon. We didn't know it then, but it would be my last with my dad, who was even then struggling with cancer and who wouldn't make it through the following year.

Dad loved politics. He felt it was his civic duty to be informed—and to make sure everybody else was, too. His little automotive repair shop never had more than one or two employees at a time, but everyone who worked there had to listen to talk radio—first Rush Limbaugh, and then whatever liberal commentator followed. I helped out at the shop after school, and this became the basis of my own political education. Some of my best childhood memories involve having political talks with my dad (that, and watching my mom melt down over Jimmy Carter).

And Dad knew a lot. He understood monetary policy, and the ups and downs of trade deals, and the ins and outs of tax policy. In all my years of political commentary, I have yet to meet a person as astute as my father on the topic of politics. So it surprised the hell out of me that Christmas of 2015, when out of the blue he announced: "You do know that Donald Trump is going to be our next president, right?" As I started to laugh, he surprised me even more by saying there was no one else he would vote for.

At the time, Trump was viewed as a long shot. I didn't buy Dad's prediction. But he was on the vanguard of an American frustration. Tens of millions of voters felt the Republican Party—and politics as a whole—needed a kick in the butt. Trump's brash style and business background appealed to a broad swath of the country who felt the conservative moment had lost its way and its punch. And Dad—as with most things he ever told me—was right.

The editorial page of the *WSJ* certainly had some doubts about Trump. Yet he was elected by the country; we respected that decision and chose to evaluate him in the same ways we have every other president—through the lens of our philosophy of free markets and free people. We didn't deny his legitimacy or his mandate. We praised him for the good work his administration did on taxes, regulation, and the general cause of conservative government. We defended him against the unfounded accusations of Russian collusion and helped unwind the scandalous FBI actions that led to them. We also criticized him at those times when he exceeded his authority, or promoted bad policy, or in general acted in ways unpresidential.

The conservative electorate now must do the same thing. As of the writing of this book, Trump was already a declared candidate for the 2024 GOP primary. He jumped in nearly two years before Election Day—an unprecedented move—making him the literal elephant in the room. Not since Herbert Hoover (1940) has a former president mounted an overt bid to return to the Oval Office. And that makes it fair for Republican voters to feel conflicted over how to handle the moment. Is he still the leader of the party? Do they have an obligation to support a former president?

I'd argue the obligation is something else. For the good of the country, and the good of Washington, and the good of the cause of freedom, they need to look at Trump with a dispassionate eye, to take it all in—the good, the bad, the ugly.

That starts with giving Trump his due. The man gave GOP leaders the wake-up call they needed, reminding them of the importance of battle, and highlighting issues where they'd grown out of touch with their base. He delivered a solidly conservative agenda, doing more to limit government and implement free market policy than any Republican since Reagan. He survived an extraordinary assault on his presidency—from the FBI, federal bureaucrats, state attorneys general, and a Democratic Congress. Most of those attacks were unhinged and unfair. One of Trump's best attributes was his refusal to bow to liberal and media pressure, a quality that also allowed him to tackle policies that spooked other conservative leaders. Having met Trump, I can also attest he has an abiding belief in America and in American exceptionalism.

The problem is that Trump has an even "huger" and more abiding belief in Trump and in Trump exceptionalism. And that always takes precedence. Psychologists might struggle to put a precise definition on Trump's personality—but a label is certainly warranted. Egomaniac? Bully? Narcissist? Anger management issues? I have a home in a blue-collar community in Alaska, which is full of Trump voters. Even they acknowledge they've grown tired of the drama and antics and unpredictability. Many of my neighbors had doubts and concerns about the 2020 election. But they were deeply disturbed by Trump's attempts to disrupt the normal handover of power, and his failure to intervene sooner to stop what happened on January 6. Can the country risk another moment like that?

An additional question is whether Trump is the man for this moment. There is his age—he'll be seventy-eight years old as he seeks the Republican nomination in 2024. It's true that age is just a number, and Trump remains lucid and energetic. If he won again, he'd also be limited to just one term. The Twenty-Second Amendment is clear that "no person shall be elected to the office of the President more than twice." He'd nonetheless be eighty-two his last year in office.

That's older than Biden is now, and the speed with which Biden has declined—both mentally and physically—has made the country think twice about the wisdom of electing older commanders in chief. A Suffolk University/*USA Today* poll in December 2022 found that the vast majority of registered voters want the next president to be *much younger*. Fifty percent of registered voters said their "ideal president" would be between fifty-one and sixty-five. Another 25 percent wanted the next president to be no older than fifty. Only 0.4 percent want a president older than eighty.

These views are a reaction to Biden, but also to a general feeling that Washington has too long been captive to an octogenarian set that refuses to cede power to a younger generation. When Nancy Pelosi finally stepped aside as House Democratic leader in 2022, she was eighty-two years old and had run her party for twenty years. Her deputy, Steny Hoyer, was eighty-three; party whip

James Clyburn was eighty-two. Senate Republican leader Mitch McConnell in that same year was eighty.

Age aside, the bigger question is whether Trump can be that spokesman for this unique moment. If Republicans want to create a movement, they need someone who captures the public imagination with an uplifting articulation of smaller, better, stronger government. Trump is many things, but "great communicator" is not one of them. He's blunt and brash, prone to hurling demeaning nicknames ("Lyin' Ted," "the Flake," "Joe Munchkin") and lashing out at even his allies. While his most ardent supporters love this style, it is offensive and off-putting to millions of voters who would like a bit more civility in politics. He will alienate millions of potential votes off the bat.

Trump also isn't an ideas guy. His instincts led him to the Republican Party, but he has little interest in studying or explaining its philosophy or ideals. His passion is the political fight. As anyone who has ever watched him at a podium knows, he has great difficulty staying on topic. Can anyone imagine Trump making an impassioned, motivational case for limited government or for freedom abroad? It's just not his jam.

Add in Trump's baggage, which would inevitably swamp a second term. Credit him for the real estate empire he created. But that business provided Democrats fertile ground for attacks and nonstop claims that Trump was taking actions solely to benefit his businesses or his children. These attacks were largely without merit, and unfortunate. We should want Americans with experience in real life to lend their time to public service. But the situation was what it was, and Trump's refusal to release his taxes or let go any of his business enterprises only gave Democrats fodder.

Even if Republicans took over both houses of Congress, it would be no guard against endless investigations. State attorneys general would again go on the hunt; "independent" ethics officials would swarm; and there would be ceaseless calls for attorneys in his own Justice Department to investigate this or that accusation. As Trump in 2022 put his name in the presidential hat, he hadn't even cleared the legal troubles from his last time in office—DOJ investigations, a grand jury in the state of Georgia, a probe in New York.

There is a reason House Democrats dragged out their January 6 Committee hearings and reports right up to the midterms. They wanted Trump front and center. They know how politically polarizing Trump is, and he became their foil on the campaign trail. It helped them keep the Senate and several state governorships and denied McCarthy a more workable House majority. They'd love nothing more than to have Trump on the ballot again. Especially because they are pretty confident they can beat him. They did it already.

Finally, there is the fact that Trump would be limited to just one term. He might accomplish some things, but the achievements would all be at risk if another chaotic term soured the country and put Democrats back in the Oval Office—again. The alternative is for Republicans to nominate a younger Republican who captures the public imagination and has eight full years to cement an agenda.

The conservative electorate—and the American electorate—will ultimately make its choice. Some Republicans will feel they owe a debt to Trump. The question is whether the debt is worth another four years of pandemonium.

Crowd the field

One of Trump's motivations for jumping into the 2024 race so early was a desire to clear the field. It was meant to be a show of strength, to deter other Republicans from getting in the race. Yet his initial campaign fell flat, coming as it did in the immediate wake of the GOP's failure to win back the Senate in the midterms—in no small part because of Trump's Senate endorsees.

If anything, the low-energy launch made Trump look weak. Potential rivals almost immediately began visiting Iowa, recruiting campaign staff and talking to donors. Ron DeSantis's second inaugural address, in January 2023, sounded far more like a national campaign launch than it did the swearing in of a state governor. He compared Florida's successes to Washington's failures, and outlined his vision for lower taxes, smaller government, education reform, law enforcement, and an end to judicial activism.

Even Republicans who supported Trump in office now view his attempts to regain the presidency with alarm. Many immediately started worrying about the risk of a crowded GOP field. They remembered 2016. Trump never commanded more than about 35 percent of the primary vote, but the rest was split between many other candidates—a number of whom refused to drop out until late in the game. The opponents divided the field, allowing Trump to come out on top.

A day after the 2022 midterm elections—and about a week before Trump announced—a Republican Washington aide circulated a memo. It argued that GOP politicians should follow the lead of Sen. Tom Cotton—who had just announced he would not run for the presidency. The memo exhorted Republicans to "clear the field for DeSantis." Trump, it argued, could not win the presidency again and would also harm GOP efforts to capture Congress. Yet "the more candidates in the race, the harder it is for DeSantis and the easier it is for Trump." It called on aspiring politicians to refrain from the old game of entering the race solely to get noticed for future cabinet positions. And it called on donors to unify behind DeSantis.

This pressure will continue for Republican leaders to bow out and to anoint one opponent to Trump. But that would be unfortunate, and a disservice to voters. DeSantis is a talented and accomplished politician. His extraordinary reelection and ability to convert more than a million new voters already has some in the press talking about "DeSantis Democrats." But there are dozens of other talented people in a new generation of Republican leaders. Primary voters deserve to compare their agendas, their demeanors, and their records.

Primaries are meant to be grueling tests that demonstrate a candidate has the ability to spar within a party and operate under fire. It's also meant to be a form of on-the job training, one that hones the ultimate victor into a better nominee and prepares them for the rigors of a general campaign and possibly the White House. Anyone who wants to be president should have to work for it.

This is too big a moment for Republicans to simply crown an heir apparent.

A "choice" candidate

Let's imagine that scenario, one in which the GOP gets a big, loud contest. There's no lack of contenders. DeSantis. Mike Pompeo. Nikki Haley. Tim Scott. Mike Pence. Rick Scott. Chris Sununu. Glenn Youngkin. Josh Hawley. Ted Cruz. Marco Rubio. Kristi Noem. John Bolton. Larry Hogan. Greg Abbott. The field is potentially huge. What should conservative voters look for?

The first attribute will have to be the willingness to fight. Whatever one's views of Trump, the conservative base isn't going to return to politicians who roll over for a liberal agenda. The next Republican leader will have to demonstrate their willingness to go toe-to-toe on even the most controversial subjects. Democrats have for decades rallied their friends in the media and prominent outside institutions to project Republicans as anti-environment, anti-poor, anti-tolerance, anti-grandma, blah, blah. Prior GOP candidates danced around these issues, and that often got in the way of a bold agenda. Trump changed the formula, and conservative voters will continue to demand leaders who take on tough subjects, and who will confront media and liberal biases and lies.

But that doesn't mean the next Republican leader has to act and punch like Trump. It's one thing to stand for principles, another to belittle your opponents, write in all caps, or call a woman "horse-face" on Twitter. Just look at Reagan. He was tough, but he rarely used harsh rhetoric. He called on humor or gentle jibes, and when he did attack it was in professional, not personal, terms. One of Reagan's signature lines in his 1980 campaign was: "A recession is when your neighbor loses his job. A depression is when you lose yours. And a recovery is when Jimmy Carter loses his."

Or consider how Reagan confronted the withering attacks on his age as he ran for reelection in 1984 (when he was all of seventy-three years old—a youngster by comparison to Biden). The hammering had come from Democrats and the media, but also from his opponent, Walter Mondale, who searingly accused the president of "leadership by amnesia."

The issue was raised directly by journalist Henry Trewhitt in the final Reagan-Mondale debate in October 1984. "You already are the oldest president in history," said Trewhitt, noting that presidents sometimes go for days without sleep. "Is there any doubt in your mind that you would be able to function in such circumstances?" Reagan responded: "Not at all, Mr. Trewhitt. And I want you to know that also I will not make age an issue in this campaign. I am not going to exploit, for political purposes, my opponent's youth and inexperience." It was a drop-the-mike moment. The audience exploded—even Mondale laughed. It neutralized an issue and revived Reagan's campaign, putting him on track for the biggest victory in modern election history. All with one humorous line.

The next Republican nominee needs to be someone who can invite everyone in. Yes, there is a hungry working-class electorate that deserves to be recognized and has needs. But the GOP would be foolhardy to narrow its ambitions to a single demographic of the country. As the Lord Ashcroft analysis highlighted, there are tens of millions of Americans who fall in the middle right now on the nexus of fiscal and social issues. They are unhappy with the economy, inflation, their schools, and crime. There are also tens of millions of minorities who feel taken for granted by the Democratic Party. There is a younger generation that is currently a solid Democratic voting block but also the most entrepreneurial and anti-establishment generation yet. They all want to be invited in. But they will feel alienated by a GOP nominee who claims their views on cultural issues are heresy, or that the only way is the "Republican" way and that every idea outside that orthodoxy is evil.

I'd bring in here Mitch Daniels, who worked for George W. Bush and later served two successful terms as the governor of Indiana. Daniels made a point of not dividing his constituents up between Republicans and Democrats. He talked to "Hoosiers"— and he made clear he represented them all. Reagan had the same philosophy. Read through that election eve address, or so many of his other political speeches. He didn't harp on the word "Republican." He spoke to Americans, and that made Americans (even Democrats and independents) feel they could join his cause.

Look for a candidate who can make this a "choice" election. The press these days likes to categorize every presidential election as either a "referendum" on an incumbent, or a "choice" for the future. Races aren't usually that simple, but there's some merit to the distinction. Whoever the 2024 Democratic nominee, it will be tempting for a Republican opponent to simply ask voters to render judgment on Biden's governance, to throw the bums out because of inflation, or global insecurity, or crime. But Americans are tired of all-negative campaigns. They want something more. They know what's gone wrong. They are hungry for a vision for how to make it right.

That involves ideas, and conservatives should want a candidate who thrills to policy reforms—and isn't afraid to embrace new approaches. The conservative movement has continued to generate edgy new policy proposals over the years, many at the state level. Educational choice. Changes to occupational licensing. Legal reform. Innovative tax and market policies. In plenty of areas, the oldies are still goldies—lower taxes, less regulation, strong defense. But society continues to throw up new challenges for which conservatives need to work out some answers: the rules surrounding crowd-sourcing apps, how to handle Big Tech censorship, privacy in a digital world, cross-state tax regimes in today's online marketplace, new forms of free market environmentalism.

The need for a Republican leader to have an idea-centric, coherent philosophy is even more important given the left's growing insistence that the free market has failed, and that it's time to embrace a radical approach. Their own ideas are a combination of old and crazy—modern monetary theory, the end of private property, guaranteed income. History has repeatedly shown these lead to poverty and ruin. Yet if a Republican leader is unable to point out these failures and explain a better alternative, those socialist views could continue to gain traction.

Finally, look for a record of accomplishments. This is usually an easier thing for governors, given they've already run an executive branch and had a chance to implement an agenda. But there will likely be administrators and senators in the race, too, and not all these folks are created equal. Have they done anything in Congress other than give speeches? Have they passed legislation, shown leadership on specific issues, proved they can run something? Plenty of politicians talk a good game, but they should have to demonstrate they've produced more than jabber. Running the federal government is no small thing, and Biden has shown the risks of terrible management.

* * *

How good does the next GOP nominee need to be? Good enough to keep their own party.

This book has laid out Biden's extraordinary failures, and the equally extraordinary opening the GOP has to change the political dynamic. But Republicans are divided in a post-Trump presidency, and the risk is that the crack grows wider.

Trump likely has a real primary fight on his hands, and it is far from guaranteed he'll come out on top. But what happens if he loses? Little in Trump's history or character suggests he will accept defeat gracefully. He might continue to rail against the GOP nominee and encourage his followers to sit out an election. He might launch an independent presidential bid and threaten to take his most loyal supporters with him. The only chance of victory in these scenarios is for a GOP candidate who is so good as to form a coalition commanding enough to overcome the loss of a bit of the traditional base.

Does the GOP have a new Reagan? That needs to be the question that guides voters through all the coming turbulent months. Jimmy Carter went down in history as the man who lost the Democratic Party the country. Joe Biden's governance has been far worse, and the conditions exist for yet another revolution. But Republicans may have only one shot at reclaiming that shining city on the hill. It is, once again, as Reagan said, "a time for choosing."

Choose wisely.

ACKNOWLEDGMENTS

The publishing world can be a scary place, and I remain forever astonished and grateful that I was so lucky to immediately land with the best of the best. This is my third book with the inestimable Twelve Books, where the team made this one every bit as rewarding as the past adventures. I do not know where publisher Sean Desmond gets his preternatural calm—or his ability to inspire—but I do know how lost I'd be without his helmsmanship. My thanks as well to the rock-star publicity and marketing team of Megan Perritt-Jacobson and Estafania Acquaviva; to Jim Datz for the captivating cover; to Bob Castillo for overlooking my continued failure to absorb the *Chicago Manual of Style*; and to Zohal Karimy for keeping the ship afloat.

Best of the best is also the only term for Jay Mandel, of William Morris Endeavor—as well as the ever-reliable Jessica Spitz—who are always looking out for me. Again, I am so fortunate to have landed in such capable hands.

I'm blessed to work every day with the smartest people in the editorial business. My colleagues at the *Wall Street Journal* are unparalleled and a constant source of renewal. So many of the subjects, controversies, and ideas in this book came first from conversations in our weekly meetings, or from the pages of the *WSJ* itself. I am still amazed that I get paid to spend time in the company of such gifted editors and writers, including my longtime (long-suffering?) boss and motivating force, *WSJ* editorial page editor Paul Gigot.

Thank you to my mother, Ann Strassel. As noted at the beginning of this book, Mom first introduced me to the name Jimmy Carter. She also spent a stretch with us in Alaska during book-writing time, doing piles of laundry and kindly overlooking the fact that I was ignoring her while holed up in my office. Moms are the best! (Especially at rolling with ungrateful children.) A shout-out to the Strassel girls, Kandis and Tish, for always taking care of things on the Oregon home front. Hugs to Nick and Sharrie, who made their own trek up and who separately helped ensure the moose freezer got restocked. (*Mmmm.* Moose tacos!)

Also, thanks to my bestie, Collin Levy, whose regular updates on moving, kids, office permits, horses, school schedules, recipes, and sport courts kept me grounded—even if she didn't know it. And my thanks to Dan Berg, who is always there backing us up in everything we do.

As always, my most heartfelt gratitude to my husband, Nicholas Van Dyke. Nick *loves* talking politics. The way his eyes light up in our discussions—and his astute observations and insights—are a constant source of inspiration. I'm grateful to him for the beautiful office he built for me. (Work is work, but it's better with a view of a library.) Whenever I start a book project, Nick doubles down on household management, which means he's the only reason those projects get done. The children are already a bit sad this one is at an end—since Nick is by far the better cook. And since he likes steak.

As for those kiddos: Book-writing is time consuming, and my children are always remarkably gracious and grown-up about sharing me with my computer. But I owe them special thanks this time around, as this project took place amid some important moments in their own lives. Frankie: Starting middle school is a big deal, and you are rocking it like AJR. Your pizza dough is unparalleled, and I am so proud in so many ways. Stella: Nordic ski goddess. Thanks for giving me such a fabulous reason to escape the office and scream you on in the snowy mountains. BTW, I retain ultimate belief in your growth plates. Oliver: Congrats on those college applications. I'm not sure which of us was sweating more over our words. But it was an honor sharing with you a joint-deadline moment. Isn't writing fun?

INDEX

Index

ABOUT THE AUTHOR

Kimberley Strassel is a member of the *Wall Street Journal* editorial board. She writes a weekly column, "Potomac Watch," which appears on Fridays. She is the bestselling author of *Resistance (At All Costs)* and *The Intimidation Game*.